The Ruin of a Christian

The Ruin of a Christian

By
John R. Rice

Founder The Sword of the Lord. *Author*
Prayer—Asking and Receiving; The Home:
Courtship, Marriage and Children; Revival
Appeals; When Skeletons Come Out of
Their Closets; Twelve Tremendous
Themes; The Coming Kingdom of Christ;
What Is Wrong With the Movies; etc., etc.

With Introduction By
Evangelist Hyman J. Appelman, D.D.

THE SWORD OF THE LORD
Murfreesboro, Tennessee

ISBN 0-87398-710-1

PRINTED IN UNITED STATES OF AMERICA

*T*HE BURDEN, the passion of the author's heart is evangelism. Keeping people out of an eternal Hell by getting them to repent of their sins and trust Jesus Christ for salvation is the all-consuming desire of my heart. I am an evangelist by God's call, by heart's choice, and, I trust, by His anointing.

But evangelists are given, says Ephesians 4:11, 12, "For the perfecting of the saints . . . for the edifying of the body of Christ." Evangelists have a definite ministry to the saints of God. The Holy Spirit through Paul commanded Timothy to "do the work of an evangelist" (II Tim. 4:5); but in the verses immediately preceding, Timothy was reminded that all Scripture is profitable "for reproof, for correction, for instruction in righteousness" (II Tim. 3:16). And Timothy was commanded to "preach the word . . . reprove, rebuke, exhort with all longsuffering and doctrine" (II Tim. 4:2). Doing the work of an evangelist, Timothy was to reprove Christians, rebuke Christians, and exhort them. He was to do it with long-suffering patience and tenderness and to do it with doctrine, that is, with Bible teaching. But such Bible teaching is no dry, abstract thing. This is doctrine applied to Christian living. This is the Bible on how to live, not on what to believe.

Revivals depend on God's people. Lost people cannot start a revival and they cannot stop one. Rather, God says, "If my people, which are called by my name" shall meet God's requirements, then God will hear and forgive and heal and bless (II Chron. 7:14).

The way to have a revival, the way to get many lost sinners saved, is to reprove and rebuke and exhort God's people, according to the Scripture, until their sins are felt and ab-horred, confessed and forsaken.

So we send forth these Bible messages with the fervent prayer that God may use them to revive His people and that when God's people are led to turn from their sins, their lights will shine brightly, their testimony will be with power and that they will be able to win multitudes of sinners to Christ.

The preaching may be ordinary, but the themes in this book are not ordinary themes. They are great themes; pungent, arresting, convicting themes, reiterated throughout God's Word. God has graciously seen fit to bless the preaching of many of these messages in cities throughout America to bring revival. If preachers are by this book encouraged to preach on the great texts, themes and Scriptures here expounded, I shall feel very grateful to God. God's people need Bible reproof, Bible rebuke and Bible exhortation to make them fruitful and bring revival.

These chapters were first published in the weekly paper, *The Sword of the Lord*, published at Murfreesboro, Tennessee, of which I am editor. Hundreds of letters from readers tell how many hearts have been blessed by them, many homes transformed, many ministers stirred and heartened by them. Thus I am encouraged to send them forth in book form.

Oh, for the breath of God, the moving of the Holy Spirit upon every person who reads this book! Reader, will you join me in prayer that God will mercifully bless these messages to the hearts and lives of thousands to turn God's people from sin and to bring revival to many?

In the language of I Peter 5:1, "The ministers which are among you I exhort, who am also a minister," that you keep Paul's inspired command for ministers to "reprove, rebuke, exhort with all longsuffering and doctrine" (II Timothy 4:2).

John R. Rice

TABLE OF CONTENTS

INTRODUCTION

By Evangelist Hyman J. Appelman, D.D.

*J*OHN RICE'S book on Prayer is one of the mightiest appeals, explanations, challenges that has been written in a long while. This book is equally as good. It is desperately needed. The message of it is mostly to Christians, but there is enough gospel in it, enough passionate proclamation of the plan of salvation to lead any sinner to Christ. The great value of the volume lies in the fact that there are so many backslidden, drifting, hesitant, "at ease in Zion" church members, saved and unsaved, who need this constraining presentation of their duties, their obligations, their privileges.

I read the book through in one sitting. It searched my soul, my life, my motives. The careful, prayerful reading of it is sure to lead to a rededication of all life to the Lord Jesus Christ. We preachers should delve into it first. We should then move heaven and earth to pass it around among all of our people.

Everything John Rice writes is readable. This book is unusually so. Every chapter is eminently worthwhile. My own heart was especially stirred by the chapters on *Lukewarmness,* on *The Curse of Hidden Sins,* on *Break Up Your Fallow Ground.*

Indeed and indeed I am grateful to the Lord for both author and book. Without any reservation, I recommend it unhesitatingly to everyone everywhere.

HYMAN J. APPELMAN

Chapter 1

THE RUIN OF A CHRISTIAN

*T*HE DOWNFALL of Lot, the ruin of his family, and the utter destruction of his city and of the surrounding population is a sad, sad story, one from which all of us need to learn. It will pay you to read attentively the Bible story which is given in Genesis, chapters 13 and 19.

The Bible Story

"And Lot also, which went with Abram, had flocks, and herds, and tents. And the land was not able to bear them, that they might dwell together: for their substance was great, so that they could not dwell together. And there was a strife between the herdmen of Abram's cattle and the herdmen of Lot's cattle: and the Canaanite and the Perizzite dwelled then in the land. And Abram said unto Lot, Let there be no strife, I pray thee, between me and thee, and between my herdmen and thy herdmen; for we be brethren. Is not the whole land before thee? separate thyself, I pray thee, from me: if thou wilt take the left hand, then I will go to the right; or if thou depart to the right hand, then I will go to the left. And Lot lifted up his eyes, and beheld all the plain of Jordan, that it was well watered every where, before the Lord destroyed Sodom and Gomorrah, even as the garden of the Lord, like the land of Egypt, as thou comest into Zoar. Then Lot chose him all the plain of Jordan; and Lot journeyed east: and they separated themselves the one from the other. Abram dwelled in the land of Canaan, and Lot dwelled in the

cities of the plain, and pitched his tent toward Sodom. But the men of Sodom were wicked and sinners before the Lord exceedingly." —Gen. 13:5–13.

Now in chapter 19 we read:

"And there came two angels to Sodom at even; and Lot sat in the gate of Sodom: and Lot seeing them rose up to meet them; and he bowed himself with his face toward the ground; And he said, Behold now, my lords, turn in, I pray you, into your servant's house, and tarry all night, and wash your feet, and ye shall rise up early, and go on your ways. And they said, Nay; but we will abide in the street all night. And he pressed upon them greatly; and they turned in unto him, and entered into his house; and he made them a feast, and did bake unleavened bread, and they did eat. But before they lay down, the men of the city, even the men of Sodom, compassed the house round, both old and young, all the people from every quarter: And they called unto Lot, and said unto him, Where are the men which came in to thee this night? bring them out unto us, that we may know them. And Lot went out at the door unto them, and shut the door after him, And said, I pray you, brethren, do not so wickedly. Behold now, I have two daughters which have not known man; let me, I pray you, bring them out unto you, and do ye to them as is good in your eyes: only unto these men do nothing, for therefore came they under the shadow of my roof. And they said, Stand back. And they said again, This one fellow came in to sojourn, and he will needs be a judge: now will we deal worse with thee, than with them. And they pressed sore upon the man, even Lot, and came near to break the door. But the men put forth their hand, and pulled Lot into the house to them, and shut to the door. And they smote the men that were at the door of the house with blindness, both small and great: so that they wearied themselves to find the door. And the men said unto Lot, Hast thou here any besides? son in law, and thy sons, and thy daughters, and whatsoever thou hast in the

*city, bring them out of this place: For we will destroy this
place, because the cry of them is waxen great before the face
of the Lord; and the Lord hath sent us to destroy it. And Lot
went out, and spake unto his sons in law, which married his
daughters, and said, Up, get you out of this place: for the
Lord will destroy this city. But he seemed as one that mocked
unto his sons in law. And when the morning arose, then the
angels hastened Lot, saying, Arise, take thy wife, and thy two
daughters, which are here; lest thou be consumed in the iniquity of the city. And while he lingered, the men laid hold
upon his hand, and upon the hand of his wife, and upon the
hand of his two daughters; the Lord being merciful unto
him: and they brought him forth, and set him without the
city. And it came to pass, when they had brought them forth
abroad, that he said, Escape for thy life; look not behind thee,
neither stay thou in all the plain; escape to the mountain, lest
thou be consumed.*

.   .   .   .

*"Then the Lord rained upon Sodom and upon Gomorrah
brimstone and fire from the Lord out of heaven; And he over-
threw those cities, and all the plain, and all the inhabitants of
the cities, and that which grew upon the ground. But his wife
looked back from behind him, and she became a pillar of
salt.*

.   .   .   .   .   .

*"And Lot went up out of Zoar, and dwelt in the mountain,
and his two daughters with him; for he feared to dwell in
Zoar: and he dwelt in a cave, he and his two daughters. And
the firstborn said unto the younger, Our father is old, and
there is not a man in the earth to come in unto us after the
manner of all the earth: Come, let us make our father drink
wine, and we will lie with him, that we may preserve seed of
of our father. And they made their father drink wine that
night: and the firstborn went in, and lay with her father; and
he perceived not when she lay down, nor when she arose.*

*And it came to pass on the morrow, that the firstborn said
unto the younger, Behold, I lay yesternight with my father:
let us make him drink wine this night also; and go thou in,
and lie with him, that we may preserve seed of our father.
And they made their father drink wine that night also: and
the younger arose, and lay with him; and he perceived not
when she lay down, nor when she arose. Thus were both the
daughters of Lot with child by their father. And the firstborn
bare a son, and called his name Moab: the same is the father
of the Moabites unto this day. And the younger, she also bare
a son, and called his name Benammi: the same is the father
of the children of Ammon unto this day."*

—Gen. 19:1–17, 24–26, 30–38.

The Bible tells the sordid story to the bitter climax and the
sad end. Do not think that the language is too plain. That is
in the Bible. It was put there to be read with solemn warning
for all.

Lot Was a Saved Man, Counted Just and Righteous in God's Sight

Lot was a Christian man. By that I mean just what the
word ought always to mean: he was a converted man, one
who had put his trust in the Saviour who had been promised
and thus had been born again. However dimly he may have
understood the theology now made clear in our Bible, Lot
had looked to God in faith, had been forgiven his sins, and
was, in God's sight, counted just and righteous. Second Peter
2:6–8 tells us that God destroyed the wicked cities of Sodom
and Gomorrah, "and delivered just Lot, vexed with the
filthy conversation of the wicked. (FOR THAT RIGHT-
EOUS MAN DWELLING AMONG THEM, IN SEEING
AND HEARING, VEXED HIS RIGHTEOUS SOUL
FROM DAY TO DAY WITH THEIR UNLAWFUL
DEEDS.)" —II Pet. 2:7–8.

The New Testament, then, makes clear what we might not
see in the account of Lot's life given in Genesis. He was really

a "righteous man," although the wickedness of those cities day by day "vexed his righteous soul." The regenerated heart of Lot did not fit in down in Sodom. The sin there made him miserable; even what he himself did, did not fit in with the new heart that had been put within him by faith. So the story of Lot is the sad story of the failures of a saved man and the ruin that his failures brought upon his own family and upon the entire city where he lived.

And from the mere fact that Lot was saved, and fell unto such sin, ought to come to us two very solemn warnings. The first one is: Do not judge those about you! "Man looketh on the outward appearance, but the Lord looketh on the heart" (I Sam. 16:7). The Saviour has strictly commanded us, "Judge not, that ye be not judged" (Matt. 7:1). You would not have taken Lot to be a Christian, but you would have been mistaken. Samson with his head in the lap of Delilah did not appear to be a judge of Israel who really loved God and God's way. David in his sin with Bathsheba acted as a heathen man or a profligate who did not know God. Peter, denying his Christ and cursing and swearing for fear, did not show the love he really had for the Lord and the fact that he had truly been born again. We know how David and Peter wept over their sins, and it is certain that Lot also grieved over his and that his righteous soul was vexed with his own mistakes and failures as well as with those of the people of Sodom. Do not judge!

And the other solemn lesson is: Christian, take care! "Let him that thinketh he standeth take heed lest he fall" (I Cor. 10:12). I am not warning that you may lose your soul. But I am warning that you may lose everything else that seems dear to a Christian. You may lose property, influence, family, and the peace and joy of salvation though you do not lose salvation itself. O Christian, beware that you avoid the mistakes of Lot!

From the record given above in Genesis, chapters 13 and 19, I call to your attention Lot's worldliness in making money

his god, in calling the wicked his brethren, in settling down
to live in Sodom, and in the use of wine. Then I call your
attention to his powerlessness. He could not win the Sodomites: he was as one that mocked to his sons-in-law; he even lost
his own wife, who probably went to Hell, certainly she died
under the judgment of God; and later he was powerless to
influence even the two poor daughters that remained.

I. LOT'S WORLDLINESS

Prosperous men have always to contend with the problems
that beset Lot. So do others who are not so prosperous. Let us
consider and be warned!

1. Lot Put Money and Business First

All the land of Canaan had been given to Abraham by the
Lord. Abraham brought his nephew, Lot, with him into the
promised land. When there was not room enough for them
to dwell together and quarrels arose over pasturage, Abraham
generously gave Lot his choice of pasture. The rich Jordan
valley had grass in abundance. It had springs of water. It had
shelters from winter's winds. The territory now covered by
a part of the Dead Sea, no doubt, was a rich valley with five
cities: Sodom, Gomorrah, Admah, Zeboim, and Zoar. The
men were wicked exceedingly before the Lord, and yet Lot
chose that valley. There his flocks and herds would pasture
and grow fat. The neighboring cities would furnish a market
for his beef and mutton and wool and camels. The city would
furnish society for his wife and daughters. So Lot, putting
business first, pitched his tent toward Sodom.

I well know that this sin is a respectable sin. Some pastors
have said to their people, "Make all the money you can as
long as you make it honestly, and then give all you can to
God." But that is not wise counsel. No man in the world has
any right to make all the money that he can. Any man who
makes all the money that he can will be making some money
when he ought to be doing something else. No man can make

all the money that he can while he serves God all he can. Take any preacher for an example; should he be thinking first of how much money he can make? Should he accept one of two pastorates that are proffered him just because it pays a larger salary? Should the evangelist go only where the largest offering will be given him? When the evangelist has an opportunity to specify a required remuneration for a revival campaign, should he do so? Of course, the answer is no. No preacher ought to put money-making first. But every other Christian in the world is bought by the same blood of Christ as is the preacher. It took as much of the blood of Christ to keep a business man out of Hell as it did to save the man who is now in the ministry. In many, many ways a minister could increase his income. He could go easy on sin so that a rich deacon might give more money in the offerings. He could sell insurance on the side. He could specially cater to rich people. Or he could specially cater to the multitude, which would be just as bad. But the preacher ought not do it. He ought not to make all the money he can. And neither should anybody else in the world.

Every Christian in the world ought to "seek ye first the kingdom of God, and his righteousness," knowing that "all these things shall be added unto you" (Matt. 6:33).

Any man who puts money-making first is really an idolater, for covetousness is idolatry. It dethrones Christ. It enslaves a man to false ideals. It leads the Christian to compromise with evil for profit. It absorbs a man's mind and energy and thought until he has no time nor passion nor power for soul winning and the things of God. The man who makes money his god loses the joy of the Lord, he loses his interest and delight in the Bible, he loses the intimate fellowship with God that comes of long continued prayer. No wonder that the Scripture plainly says, "The love of money is the root of all evil" (I Tim. 6:10); or as the Revised Version says, "The love of money is a root of all kinds of evil." Any man who puts money first, puts his business first, puts his job first, is

on the way to the ruin of his Christian life! He is travelling
the road that ruined Lot. It will lead to the loss of his precious
influence, will lose for him many, many joys, is likely to
damn the souls of his family and of his friends that he might
win. For the Scripture says that those who covet after money
"have erred from the faith, and pierced themselves through
with many sorrows" (I Tim. 6:10).

But this is not simply a rich man's sin. A man may be as
covetous as Lot and make only twenty dollars a week. It is
not wicked to have such money as God gives legitimately.
Abraham was rich, and so was David, and so was Solomon.
But to love money, even though it be only for necessities, and
though one have his heart set on his job or on his business
only to make an honest and legitimate business for his family,
is yet a sin and a terrible mistake. It is much better to trust
in the living God and lay up treasures in Heaven. Jesus makes
it clear in Matthew 6:25–34 that a Christian's real prosperity
and real happiness is to be found in having no care about
food nor drink nor clothes, but seeking first the things of
God and depending on the God who clothes the lilies and
feeds the sparrows to care for His own dear children bought
by the blood of His Son.

Many a man says in defense of his worldly-minded attitude,
in defense of putting his business first: "Well, a man has to
live." No, he does not! A man has to die. And if he puts the
living first, he will come down in sorrow to his grave as Lot
did. There is not a particle of evidence that any man lives
better or cares for his family really better by putting his business or his job first. There are sweet and precious promises
for the Christian who does not put his business first. "Trust
in the Lord, and do good; so shalt thou dwell in the land, and
verily thou shalt be fed" (Psa. 37:3). There is sweet assurance
for the burdened family man. There is a solid rock he may
rest his feet upon. God will not let the man go hungry who
really trusts in Him and does His will. And in the same Psalm
David says, "I have been young, and now am old; yet have I

not seen the righteous forsaken, nor his seed begging bread"
(Psa. 37:25). What did Lot gain by putting business first? He
would have had more than enough if he had stayed outside
of Sodom, if he had sacrificed some gain. As it was, he lost not
only his family but his property as well. And, alas, his whole
town went to Hell because his testimony had failed and he
could not win nine other people to God! God had promised
Abraham to spare the city of Sodom if ten righteous people
could be found (Gen. 18:32).

Christian, if you are a slave to your job, your business, to
making money, I warn you of two things: first, that you are
guilty of a horrible sin that God hates; and, second, that you
are sowing to the wind and will reap the whirlwind as did
Lot!

2. Lot Called the Wicked His Brethren

When the angels of God were in his home and the wicked
Sodomites would have raped these holy visitors, Lot said, "I
pray you, brethren, do not so wickedly" (Gen. 19:7). Lot,
whose righteous soul was vexed and troubled by the enormity
of the Sodomites' sins, and who had evidently vowed that he
would never live there permanently but only came in as a
sojourner; yet Lot, who was a saved man, called these wicked
Sodomites his brethren! They were so wicked that even then
God had sent heavenly messengers to take Lot out of the city
so it could be burned with fire and brimstone from Heaven.
They were beastly in their sex perversion so that even today
a horrible sin is called by the name of their city. Yet Lot lived
among them; saw their wickedness; heard their filthy language; called them his brethren; and no doubt made a tem-
porary financial profit from his association with these wicked
men who were marked for destruction and Hell. O Christian,
have you, too, moved into Sodom?

Lot never intended to move into Sodom. He only "pitched
his tent toward Sodom." When the grass grew shorter and he
must move his herds again, perhaps he pitched his tent a little

closer still to Sodom, in the rich Jordan River valley. But after living near the city a bit, Lot's conscience was dulled. He was not quite so much offended by the wickedness of the city after he became accustomed to it. So, only temporarily, he thought, he moved as a sojourner into the city. And now he sat in the gate of the city as one of the rulers; and the Sodomites accused him, "And he will needs be a judge." How subtle, how stealthy, is the ruin wrought by evil company!

If Samson had not lain with his head in the lap of wicked Delilah, had he never dallied with her and teased her, he would not have finally given away his secret and lost his hair, lost the power of the Holy Spirit, and found, too late, that God had departed from him! He would not have had his eyes put out and would not have made sport for the Philistines. And he, a judge of Israel, would not have died as a captive slave of the Philistines if he had not kept bad company.

David sat on his palace roof and gazed at a beautiful woman as she took her bath. He looked too long! Then he sent for the woman to meet her. Then followed adultery, then murder, and then the long train of evils that resulted in the death of his baby, the ruin of his daughter, Tamar, the murder of Amnon, and the rebellion and death of Absalom. Bad company caused a great sin and great sorrow in David's life.

Peter was the boldest of all the apostles, the most outspoken. He had vowed to the Lord Jesus, "Though I should die with thee, yet will I not deny thee!" And he meant it from the bottom of his soul. But this same Simon Peter had only to sit for a little while warming his hands by the fire with the wicked soldiers who would crucify Jesus, and with the servants of the high priest—had only to hear for a little their taunts and their jeers, and to keep silent, till all the courage Peter had was gone—gone! And then when a maiden pointed her finger in his face and said, "Thou art also one of them!" Peter denied and then cursed and swore saying, "I know not the man." Bad company broke Peter's heart, and it must have broken the heart of the Saviour Himself, too. It put Peter temporarily out of the ministry. It has brought a shameful reproach on the cause of Christ from that day to this. Bad company ruined Lot. It broke down the integrity of Samson, of David, of Simon Peter. It will ruin anybody in the world, if long continued!

For this reason God plainly commands,

"Be ye not unequally yoked together with unbelievers: for what fellowship hath righteousness with unrighteousness? and what communion hath light with darkness? And what concord hath Christ with Belial? or what part hath he that believeth with an infidel? And what agreement hath the temple of God with idols? for ye are the temple of the living God; as God hath said, I will dwell in them, and walk in them; and I will be their God, and they shall be my people. Wherefore come out from among them, and be ye separate, saith the Lord, and touch not the unclean thing; and I will receive you, And will be a Father unto you, and ye shall be my sons and daughters, saith the Lord Almighty." —II Cor. 6:14-18.

It was for this reason that New Testament Christians were commanded plainly, "But now I have written unto you not to keep company, if any man that is called a brother be a fornicator, or covetous, or an idolater, or a railer, or a drunkard, or an extortioner; with such an one no not to eat" (I Cor. 5:11). Even if a man is a Christian, but if he goes on in the wicked sins of the world, Christian, do not eat with him as with a Christian, do not have fellowship with him as an equal, do not bind yourself with him. Paul in that same I Corinthians, chapter 5, was expressly commanding that Christians should withdraw membership and fellowship from a man in the church who was living a sinful life. Oh, how careful God's Word is to teach that Christians must come out and be separate and have no fellowship with the evil works of darkness!

Lot had no business living in Sodom. He had no business calling the wicked his brethren. Bad companionship and an unequal yoke with the wicked were his ruin.

To be sure, Lot should have loved the men of Sodom. If he

had gone there to witness against their sins and to warn them to repent, God would have greatly blessed him. But when he went there to curry their favor, to enjoy their society, to make money out of business with them, then he compromised his testimony, his religion became a joke, and he lost his influence even with them.

How many a Christian today has been guilty of the same worldly mistake as Lot by joining lodges with unconverted people. Some who read this, no doubt, join in with people who do not love the Lord Jesus, who have never professed to take Him as their own Saviour. And you bound yourself with them with a bloody, horrible oath! You swore to keep their secrets, to favor them above other men or women. That oath many of you count as more binding than the marriage vow, because you bound yourself that you would not discuss even with your wife, or with your husband, the secrets of your lodge. That wicked oath you regard more binding than your duty to your church or to God, and many a matter you have solemnly sworn that you would not reveal to your pastor, the closest spiritual advisor. And all that despite the plain command of Jesus Himself who said, "But I say unto you, Swear not at all" (Matt. 5:34). And again the Scripture has said, "But above all things, my brethren, swear not, neither by heaven, neither by the earth, neither by any other oath: but let your yea be yea; and your nay, nay; lest ye fall into condemnation" (Jas. 5:12). I say, some of you who are God's own, some of you who have been born again, some of you who long to serve Christ, have yet violated His command and have bound yourselves by wicked oaths with unconverted people. You call your fellow lodge members "brother," or "sister," just as Lot called the Sodomites "brethren." I remind you that when one said to Jesus, "Behold, thy mother and thy brethren stand without, desiring to speak with thee," Jesus answered him, "Who is my mother? and who are my brethren? . . . For whosoever shall do the will of my Father which is in heaven, the same is my brother, and sister, and

mother" (Matt. 12:47–50). Jesus said that his brethren were
only those that did the will of His Father. And how, then,
can any Christian properly call the unconverted, those who
do not pretend to know or to love the Lord Jesus, those who
have never trusted Him for salvation—how can a Christian
call them his brethren?

If you look again at II Corinthians 6:14–18, printed above,
you will notice that God teaches that a Christian ought not
to be yoked with unbelievers; because righteousness should
not have fellowship with unrighteousness, and light should
not have communion with darkness, and Christ cannot have
concord with Belial, and he that believeth should not have
part with an infidel, and the temple of God (and each Christian is that) should not have agreement with idols. So the
dear Lord pleads with the Christian, "Wherefore come out
from among them, and be ye separate, saith the Lord, and
touch not the unclean thing, and I will receive you" (II
Cor. 6:17).

O dear brother Christian, come out of Sodom! Break
your partnership, your yoke with the unbelievers.

God certainly has commanded that a Christian should
marry only a Christian; that a child of God ought not to
marry one of the devil's children. And in I Corinthians 7:39
the Christian widow is plainly told that she may be married to
whom she will, but "only in the Lord." You cannot, you
ought not to break the marriage that is made. But, oh, I beg
you, Christian, do not join yourself for life with those who
do not know the Lord Jesus! To do so will bring trouble and
heartache and sin.

Some of you have a business partnership with unconverted
people. Day by day you must bend your convictions to fit
those of unsaved people. You must hear ungodly talk and do
business on ungodly principles, perhaps. Certainly your asso-
ciations are with the unsaved in that case. Then I beg you to
come out and be separate!

Christ ate with publicans and sinners, but He never played

with them. He never went into business with them. The only
times that Jesus ever had fellowship with poor lost, wicked
men was when He was earnestly trying to win and to bless
them. Yes, we ought to love sinners, we ought to weep over
them, pray for them, visit them, teach them, plead with them!
But we ought not to call them our brethren, we ought not to
bind ourselves with them in business or pleasure or marriage.
Lot committed a wicked sin in moving into Sodom. He sinned
even further when he counted the wicked there his brethren.
He said, "I pray you, brethren, do not so wickedly." But he
was not their brother in his heart, and he should not have
compromised and have appeared to be. By his living among
them, his outward compliance with their ways, his seeking
to please them, he endorsed their ungodly lives and was a
party to their eternal damnation when God destroyed their
city with fire and brimstone from Heaven. You never win
souls by compromising, by going with the wicked their way
into sin. Lot's compromise with the people of Sodom lost his
only chance to save them, forfeited his influence over his own
loved ones, and led to the loss of everything he held dear;
wife, children, in-laws, grandchildren, property, reputation, a
good conscience—all, all swept away because Lot put money
first and then mixed with the wicked, compromised with
them, and called them brethren.

3. Lot Let the World Get His Children

Some of his daughters, certainly, married in Sodom, absorbed the Sodom viewpoint, and burned to death in the
wicked city. The two unmarried daughters were taken out of
Sodom, but Lot could not get Sodom out of his daughters!
They were lost to respect for their father, lost to morality,
and lost to God! There is evidence that they were poor lost
sinners. The world got Lot's daughters. We are not told
whether he had any sons.

Perhaps the most shameful incident that ever happened in
Lot's life was when the men of Sodom beat at his door—sex

perverts, seeking to attack the angels inside—and Lot went out to these licentious men and offered to bring his two innocent daughters out to them, to pacify their anger and satisfy their lust! He said, "Behold now, I have two daughters which have not known man; let me, I pray you, bring them out unto you, and do ye to them as is good in your eyes: only unto these men do nothing, for therefore came they under the shadow of my roof" (Gen. 19:8). Did ever a father make a more shameful compromise, a more pitiful effort to conciliate wicked men whose friendship he wanted, than Lot made when he offered to bring out his daughters to these wicked men! It was likely the most shameful moment in Lot's life.

Once before he had imposed on Abraham's generosity, and for covetous reasons had chosen the richest of the grassland that belonged to Abraham. Then, against the constant pricking of his conscience, he moved toward Sodom, and finally into Sodom. Vexed day by day with the wickedness in seeing and hearing the sins of Sodom, yet he stayed there to make money and to have fellowship with wicked men that he called his brethren. And later, in a drunken debauch, he was to ruin the same two girls while insensibly drunk. But former sins were summed up in his tragic compromise that night with the wicked Sodomites, and the later drunkenness and incest were but the natural outcome of his climactic failure.

Lot evidently put the spiritual welfare of his children last when he put business first and when he first pitched his tent toward Sodom and then moved into Sodom. More and more, no doubt, he had let down the bars, permitting other daughters to marry the wicked Sodomites, allowing the lives of his wife and children to be colored by the sins of Sodom. Little by little he had given up the standards of separation which kept Abraham out in his tent with his wife and God, the standards that would not even allow Abraham's son, Isaac, to go back for his own bride, Rebekah, but sent a servant. The worship of God, the whole-souled surrender to His will, the altar, the sacrifices, the prayer life—these Lot had bit by bit forsaken, no doubt. Up to this tragic night, perhaps, he had never faced it squarely. He was already losing his children, losing them for righteousness and losing them for decency and losing them for God; losing their immortal souls, before this, but he did not recognize it. And here tonight, facing a mob of sex perverts outside his own door, Lot suddenly made the decision that had been forming unconsciously in his mind. His business was dearer to him than his children. The friendship and favor of wicked men, his standing in their eyes, meant more to him than the virtue of his children. So Lot offered, "Behold now, I have two daughters which have not known man; let me, I pray you, bring them out unto you, and do ye to them as is good in your eyes."

Christian families who let their children go to the movies, who let their children dance, who let their children smoke, who allow them out at all hours of the night and with any kind of company, without chaperonage and without supervision—such families usually give this simple excuse: "Well, everybody does that now, and you can't expect our children to be different from all of our neighbors' children." But the real truth is that such parents simply do not want to be thought strange. They do not want to be ostracized. They do not want to be called fanatics, or "old fogies." They really want the esteem of the wicked world. They want the social favor and the business patronage of their ungodly neighbors, and are willing to damn the souls of their children, if need be, to get it!

One of the most potent reasons for the cowardice of fathers and mothers these days in the matter of disciplining their children is that they fear the comments of neighbors, and even of relatives. They dare not do what they know is right, because they live in Sodom, and they long to have the fellowship and the approval of the Sodomites!

When I held my first baby daughter in my arms, a little mite weighing six and three-quarter pounds, the loveliest baby I ever saw, I felt the weight of an immortal soul which

God had put in my care. And there I made God a solemn vow to raise the little one for Him. I have often failed, I know, and yet it is a recurring vow, a solemn covenant I have made with God and have made about and in the presence of every one of my six daughters. I have repeated that vow again and again on my knees, and my good wife has joined me. The vow is: "By God's grace, Satan shall not have one of my children—not one! He shall not have their souls. He shall not have their lives. He shall not have their testimonies. Satan shall not have a one of my children!" Oh, we have felt ever so weak and frail. A thousand times I have felt that the duties and responsibilities of fatherhood were beyond me. But by godly example, by earnest entreaty, by many tears, by repeated instructions, by severe punishment that brought the disapproval of many, I have sought to keep my vow to God. And praise His name, He has wonderfully helped.

The fake science teaching of the high schools which says that man came from brute beasts instead of being made in the image of God, which says that the Bible is out of date and not scientifically true, has not deceived my older daughters. Both from the spiritual and the scientific viewpoint they had been carefully instructed and their faith was not shaken. The family daily Bible readings and much prayer have helped, I am sure.

The jazz-crazy world has not yet gotten my daughters, and I have full confidence that it will not. Everywhere good Christian people are shamed by painted, bobbed-haired, dancing, movie-going, petting and smoking daughters, or sons just as worldly. Claiming Proverbs 22:6, "Train up a child in the way he should go: and when he is old, he will not depart from it," we have the assurance that God will preserve our loved ones. It is not easy. The battle is not yet all won. But God is faithful. Christians do not need to let children stray away, and let the world of sin poison and besmirch their young people. I know that a strong, vigorous, really Christian family life, with plenty of prayer, plenty of Bible teaching, plenty of supervision, plenty of real discipline and real love and patience can, by the blessing of a God who answers prayer and keeps His promises, out-pull the world and keep our precious young people from being ruined by worldliness.

Everywhere, I see Christian parents who put the children's school work before the church and revival. Everywhere, I see Christian parents put the child's popularity with playmates or the young man's or woman's social ambitions before their duty to God. On every hand I see parents compromising with the world, lowering the standards, letting down the bars. If that is your case, then you, like Lot, are living in a fool's paradise. One day you will wake up as he did with your influence over your children gone and with the possibility that some of them may go to Hell, and all of them be failures in this life, ruined by the worldliness to which you surrender them now. O father, mother, do not let Satan have your children!

◄ Egypt is a type of the world, and Pharaoh sought to allow Moses to lead the men of Israel out into the wilderness to worship God, but insisted that the Israelites should leave their little ones. Pharaoh said, "Go, serve the Lord your God: but who are they that shall go? And Moses said, We will go with our young and with our old, with our sons and with our daughters, with our flocks and with our herds will we go; for we must hold a feast unto the Lord" (Exod. 10:8, 9). Then again we read,

"And Pharaoh called unto Moses, and said, Go ye, serve the Lord; only let your flocks and your herds be stayed: let your little ones also go with you. And Moses said, Thou must give us also sacrifices and burnt offerings, that we may sacrifice unto the Lord our God. Our cattle also shall go with us; there shall not an hoof be left behind; for thereof must we take to serve the Lord our God." —Exod. 10:24–26.

Bold, noble Moses! Not a child, no, not an animal was to be left behind!

The other day a man of God told me how his saintly father

used to pray for his children, one by one, and again and again he would say in his prayers, "O God, there shall not an hoof be left behind!" He simply meant that Satan should not have a one of his children, nor anything else of his. Oh, may parents today say the same thing! "There shall not an hoof be left behind."

It is as sweet and happy for a young Christian to serve wholeheartedly, out-and-out, without compromise, as it is for an older Christian. It pays now just as much as it paid in other days. The only way to be a happy Christian is to mean business about it and serve God with all your heart. And, oh, parents, I beg you, do not let the world have your children. DO NOT MAKE THE MISTAKE THAT LOT MADE!

4. Lot Fell Into the Habit of Sodom

Lot drank wine in Sodom, no doubt; for when he was hiding out in a cave in the mountains, he had with him his two daughters, and he had his wine! Nothing is said about Lot's drinking wine when he was with Abraham. It is proper to infer that the habit of drink began in Sodom. But it ended up in a drunken debauch and incest, with ruined daughters and illegitimate children. This was another worldly mistake of this saved man, Lot.

I am sure that Lot was very moderate in his drink while he lived in Sodom. We are expressly told that Lot was "vexed with the filthy conversation of the wicked. (For that righteous man dwelling among them, in seeing and hearing, vexed his righteous soul from day to day with their unlawful deeds)" (II Pet. 2:7, 8). Lot was no friend of drunkenness. He was vexed with all that sin. He was really a Christian. He loved decency and righteousness. I am sure that Lot thought many a time, "I never would make a beast out of myself that way! I would not get drunk, as these men of Sodom do. Now, a little wine at the table, just a moderate drink now and then, is a different matter."

I say, no doubt Lot was a moderate wine drinker down in

Sodom. I take it he was not a drunkard, because that is not mentioned against him. But on the other hand, wine does not grow in caves in the mountains, and Lot took wine with him when he fled from Sodom. So Lot was a moderate drinker. It was not until disaster came, his property was gone, his wife was turned to a pillar of salt, some of his children and grandchildren were burned to ashes, that in despair Lot may have turned to unrestrained drinking. If so, he was like thousands of other men in that he tried to drown his sorrows and troubles in drink, and found only worse sorrows. Many a man is only a moderate drinker for a time, but when an emergency comes, such as a quarrel with his wife, or the loss of his job, or a big celebration with the boys, then the tiger of habit he has been feeding overmasters him, and the moderate drinker becomes a drunkard!

And so it always is with those who compromise with the world, if they do not take care. Christians who attend the theater, who, with their children, absorb the Hollywood morals, enjoy the lust, the indecency, the low moral standards, the tolerance for drink and cigarettes and divorce and nudity which the movies feed to their patrons, little think that they and their children will follow in the steps of the screen heroes and heroines. But inevitably, to a greater or lesser degree, they will! Drunkenness follows moderate drinking, and so lust, lawlessness, free love, divorce and crime follow the dirty pictures that are customary and common in the best theaters in America. For confirmation and proof that thousands of girls and boys are led into crime and adultery by the picture shows, see my book, *What Is Wrong With the Movies,* or the larger book, *Our Movie Made Children,* by Henry James Forman, who made a scientific study of the matter. That book is published by Macmillan.

How many times Christian people have tolerated the card table in their homes and turned out gamblers and criminals in their children! How many times has the wine at meals or the toddy or eggnog at Christmas in the home turned out the drunkard and the bum! How many dances in nice homes, patronized by church members, have aroused lust, seduced innocent youth, set the fires of Hell raging in the breasts of manly young men and turned innocent girls into prodigals and harlots! The testimony of dancing master and pastor and parent, the testimony of young people themselves, cannot be ignored. Compromise with the habits and the sinful social usages of the world will lead a Christian and his children to ruin, just as it happened in the case of Lot! Oh, I beg you, Christian fathers and mothers, come out of Sodom and bring out your children! I am sure that Lot, an old man, a pauper, sitting in his cave with his illegitimate children playing about his feet, dreaming of his unbelieving wife who was turned to a pillar of salt, dreaming of his daughters and sons-in-law burned up in the fires of Sodom, facing every day the ruin of his own daughters accomplished in his own drunkenness and lust—I am sure that Lot saw at last, when it was too late, that he would far better have been called straight-laced, a fanatic and a radical and a "Holy Roller"; it would have been far better to have been a fool for God and have saved this wife and children from the ruin of Sodom!

Thus far my message has been on the worldliness of Lot, the ways he fell into sin. If you will read again Genesis, chapters 13 and 19, you will see that Lot sinned in putting money first, in calling the wicked his brethren, in letting Sodom get his children, and in taking up the drink habit of Sodom. Those are the sins of this saved man, who, says II Peter 2:8, "vexed his righteous soul" with the deeds of wicked Sodom. We see the tragic ruin to which Lot came; wealth gone, wife turned to a pillar of salt, married children and grandchildren burned to death in Sodom, (and gone to Hell too, as far as we know), and his two single daughters both having illegitimate children by his drunken incest! Oh, be warned, reader, of the results of sin, even in a Christian's family.

Now we continue God's message about Lot. After his worldliness, we discuss

II. THE POWERLESSNESS OF THIS SAVED MAN

The worldliness of Lot was tragic. But it had its fruitage in a far worse and more deadly sin, that is, his powerlessness.

We Christians need never be without power to win our loved ones and many of our associates. A surrendered, godly Christian, living in the will of God, seeking His favor, can be so filled with the Holy Spirit that he will have a supernatural influence on his wife and on his children and on his associates. Jesus said, "Follow me, and I will make you fishers of men" (Matt. 4:19). And anyone who closely follows Jesus will have power to win souls.

Jesus also said,

"Ye are the salt of the earth: but if the salt have lost his savour, wherewith shall it be salted? it is thenceforth good for nothing, but to be cast out, and to be trodden under foot of men. Ye are the light of the world. A city that is set on an hill cannot be hid. Neither do men light a candle, and put it under a bushel, but on a candlestick; and it giveth light unto all that are in the house. Let your light so shine before men, that they may see your good works, and glorify your Father which is in heaven."   —Matt. 5:13–16.

A Christian who does not have salt cannot save anybody. A Christian whose light is under the bushel of worldliness cannot light the darkened hearts and minds of his own children or his neighbors. But when a Christian has no influence for God, sin is to blame. Powerlessness is wickedness. In Ephesians 5:18 we are commanded, "Be not drunk with wine, wherein is excess; but be filled with the Spirit." That verse proves it is a sin to get drunk. Then the same verse proves that it is a sin not to be filled with the Spirit!

Lot was responsible for the destruction of his whole city, and for the fact that the entire town went to Hell. For in the eighteenth chapter of Genesis we are told how God told Abraham of His plan to destroy Sodom and how Abraham interceded and how God promised to spare the city if there were ten righteous persons in it. And the ten righteous persons were certainly to have been just saved people, like Lot; not perfect people, but people who in their hearts had trusted in the Lord and loved Him. If Lot had won his own wife, his two younger girls, and three married daughters with their husbands, then the whole city of Sodom would have been spared so that some, at least, might repent and be saved. Or if Lot had won a few of his own servants, the city would have been spared. Lot was such an enormously wealthy man that he had many herdsmen, and perhaps he, like Abraham, had hundreds of slaves. But Lot had not won one of them to love and trust the true God! Or if Lot had spent his time when he sat in the gate of Sodom and would "needs be a judge" in really winning his immediate associates, the city would have been spared. But Lot did not do it. There is not any evidence there was a single person in the entire city, not one even in Lot's family but himself, who was truly saved and truly loved God.

1. First, Notice the Powerlessness of Lot in Regard to the Men of Sodom

Lot called the Sodomites brethren. He sought their favor. He listened to their profanity, saw their drinking and perhaps drank with them. He saw their lewdness and did not specially rebuke it, though it grieved him. He even offered them his innocent daughters to keep their favor and to turn them from molesting the angels. But these wicked men, for whom Lot gave up so many principles and committed so many sins, despised his testimony. They said, "Stand back. And they said again, This one fellow came in to sojourn, and he will needs be a judge: now will we deal worse with thee, than with them. And they pressed sore upon the man, even Lot, and came near to break the door" (Gen. 19:9).

The Christian who drinks cannot win his drinking companions to Christ. The girl who dances will never win her dancing boy friend! You may think to gain favor and influence with the unsaved by joining with them in the lodge, or attending with them the movies, or by smoking or drinking or playing bridge with them, but you cannot! Worldliness means powerlessness! And that means that every Christian who sells out is guilty of the murder of the poor lost souls that go to Hell because he lost his influence.

Lot could not win the Sodomites. They despised him. Any one among them would probably have listened respectfully to Abraham, who would not live in their cities, who abhorred their evil practices, who would not associate with them. But to Lot, their worldly-minded friend, they would not even listen with respect! And so the whole wicked city went to Hell because Lot, the only man God had at hand, had sold out and did not have the power of God.

2. Next, Lot Had No Influence With His Sons-in-Law

Genesis 19:14 says, "And Lot went out, and spake unto his sons in law, which married his daughters, and said, Up, get you out of this place: for the Lord will destroy this city. But he seemed as one that mocked unto his sons in law." That is one of the saddest verses in the Bible. Lot's religion was a joke to his sons-in-law. They laughed at his urgent entreaties. They did not believe that destruction was coming on the city. While they stayed and mocked, they died, and Lot was responsible. Lot let them go to Hell because he had sold his influence.

Some of you who read this cannot get your children and your sons and daughters-in-law even to go to church. You cannot get them to read the Bible. They do not want you to talk to them about their souls. Your religion, like Lot's, is a joke to them. Then, dear friend, I'm afraid I know why! You, like Lot, have lived in Sodom. You, too, have chosen the things of the world rather than the things of God. Your powerlessness is a wicked sin. You will be to blame if your loved ones go to Hell because you did not clean up your life, you did not wait in the secret closet, you did not surrender wholly to the power of the Spirit so that you could win your loved ones. Oh, no surrender, no sacrifice, no waiting on God, no loss of friends or money or time is too much, if you keep your children and your loved ones out of Hell!

It may be that was the first time Lot ever realized he had no influence with anybody as a Christian. It may be then he was like startled Samson first awaking from his sleep with his hair cut off, "And he wist not that the Lord was departed from him" (Judg. 16:20). So many, many Christians drift along aimlessly, thinking themselves very good Christians indeed. They do not steal, they are not outrageous sinners, they are greatly respected for morality and uprightness. But, alas, they have no power with God, and hence they have no influence with men, in the matters of God. Abraham, living in his lonely tent in the hills, had time to look out at the stars and remember that God had promised that his seed should be so many, innumerable; and he had time to talk with God. But Lot with his business, his wine, and his fellowship with wicked "brethren" had lost his touch with God, and hence had no power with men. At last it came home and his own sons-in-law, and perhaps his married daughters, had no confidence in his testimony, did not even take him seriously, thought him a joke!

3. Third, Lot Did Not Have Spiritual Power Enough Even to Save His Wife

Lot's wife's heart was in Sodom. Though she was led away by the merciful hands of the angels, she resisted, her heart turned back, and so she lingered behind and looked back toward Sodom. Sodom held all that was dear to her: her daughters, her society companions, her rich neighbors, her fine home, and the enormous property that Lot had accumulated. But, alas, Sodom held also the curse of Almighty God. And so Lot's wife was turned to a pillar of salt for violating God's command not to look back or linger.

No man ought ever to live so that his wife will not follow

him anywhere for God. No woman who is a Christian ought ever to be so powerless that she cannot win her own husband. The other day a woman said to me, "Brother Rice, my husband won't listen to me. He has no confidence in my Christianity. He will not let me talk to him about his soul. He will not go with me to church. Oh, what shall I do!" I answered, without intending to be too severe, and I think I answered honestly, "Your husband knows you better than I do. If your life does not ring true, he knows why, but I do not. But I know that you can so live and so pray and so wait on God and be filled with His Spirit; you can so live out the fullness of God's presence that your husband will have confidence in you and will listen to you."

A mother said to me, "Brother Rice, will you talk to my boy? You know how boys are, they will not listen to their own mothers." And I answered, "I listened to *my* mother." I know many boys who listen to their mothers. That depends on what kind of a mother you are. The mother who is the right kind of a mother, out-and-out for God, against sin, filled with the Spirit, loving, prayerful, waiting on God, filled with the love and kindness and patience and gentleness of Christ—such a mother boys will listen to. I know that fathers and mothers can have influence over their children if they begin early. And I believe that wives can always win their husbands, if they really mean business and do not wait too long. But Lot lost his wife and, as far as we know, she went to Hell.

4. And Then Again, Lot Had No Spiritual Influence Over His Two Younger Daughters

Consider Lot's daughters. Their mother was dead. They lived alone with him in the cave. It would seem that there had never been an opportunity for father and daughters to be drawn so close together. They had suffered together, no doubt had wept together over their loved ones. The young admirers of Sodom were all gone. The distractions of the social whirl were not there. Surely Lot could now gain the confidence of his daughters and win them to know and love the true God. But he did not. He had his daughters out of Sodom, but he did not have Sodom out of his daughters. Lot had his wine with him there in the cave. They knew his life. They had no confidence in his testimony for godliness. So they plotted to get him drunk, which they did, and completed their own ruin!

But the most real sin of Lot in this case was not in his wine-drinking. It was not in the adultery he committed. That was horrible, but he knew nothing of it. Back of all that was the greater sin; he had lost his touch with God, he had lost his influence with his daughters. Lot was a Christian, but he did not have the marks of a Christian. He did not have the joy of a Christian. He did not have the fruit of a Christian.

Some Conclusions

Surely, dear reader, you see that Christians ought to come out and be separate. Oh, I pray that as you read this some of you may make up your minds to come out of Sodom. Bring family, bring business, bring all you can bring with you for God, but COME OUT OF SODOM! For the sake of your own happiness, for the sake of your loved ones, for the sake of poor, lost souls whom you will never be able to win unless you come out and be separate, I beg you, leave off the worldliness and be out-and-out for God. And above every other reason is this, that you are not your own. You are bought with a price. You belong to Jesus Christ, and you owe Him every breath, every heartbeat, and all the love and passion and adoration of your soul. Won't you, for Jesus' sake, come out into the surrendered life, the separated life, before the curse of God falls upon you?

And someone may have read this who is a poor, lost sinner, one who has never been born again, one who does not know Christ as your own personal Saviour. You do not have the peace of sins forgiven. You do not have the assurance that you have a home in Heaven. Your conscience has not been purged, and your heart does not cry out to God, "My Father." Then I call your attention to the fact made so plain in the case of Lot that God hates sin and must punish it. God sent fire and brimstone on Sodom and burned it down. Men, women and children were utterly destroyed. So long, so long His mercy held on to them; but when there was no hope that any would be saved, He blotted them out in His great wrath! I warn you now, God must punish sin.

God punishes even His own children. Lot did not lose his soul, but he lost everything else he had that he counted dear: wife, children, property, reputation, peace of mind, and surely he lost much of his reward and joy in Heaven. For the Christian, in Heaven, must stand at the judgment seat of Christ to give an account, and rewards and joys vary, according to a Christian's works after salvation. Only Lot's unhappy life was spared. It is significant that God would not destroy Lot with the wicked Sodomites.

But God chastened His child. Sin did not pay for Lot, and it will not pay for anybody else.

That is the reason that Christ-rejecting sinners must go to Hell. O dear sinner, I beg you today, flee from Sodom! Repent of your sins. Trust Jesus Christ to save you. Surrender your will to His will. Open your heart and take Him in to be your Saviour and your Lord today!

Chapter 2

LUKEWARMNESS
—The Sin That Makes God Vomit

"I know thy works, that thou art neither cold nor hot: I would thou wert cold or hot. So then because thou art lukewarm, and neither cold nor hot, I will spue thee out of my mouth. Because thou sayest, I am rich, and increased with goods, and have need of nothing; and knowest not that thou art wretched, and miserable, and poor, and blind, and naked."

—Rev. 3:15–17.

I WILL SPUE thee out of my mouth!" These are the words of the Lord Jesus, and our word *vomit* would seem to be a good translation of the word *spue*. The message is given by Christ to the church of Laodicea, the last mentioned of the seven churches in Asia Minor to whom the Spirit sent messages by John, the writer of Revelation. The message seems especially given for the last days. The message to Laodicea just precedes the story of the coming of Christ for His saints as pictured in Revelation 4:1. "I know thy works," Jesus said. He knows the human heart, and that which seems all well to the casual observer is nauseating to God.

"I know that you think you are well off," says Jesus. "You say, 'I am rich, and increased with goods, and have need of nothing,' and knowest not that thou art poor and wretched and miserable and blind and naked."

Who are these that make God vomit? Who are these that

He must spue out of His mouth with disgust? Not the infidel! Not the atheist! Not the self-confessed, unregenerate sinner! He does not mean the man who denies His deity and His atonement for sinners. He does not mean those who are out-and-out for the devil, those who are unconverted. They have never been in intimate touch with Christ; how can He spue them out? They have never known His conscious and happy presence; then how can they lose it? They have never had the sweet communion that a child of God may have, nor the power of the Holy Spirit, nor soul-winning influence; how then can Christ spue them out?

One who is not a branch of Christ can never wither as Christ's branches sometimes do (John 15:6). Unless one has preached the gospel, he could not become a castaway, that is, laid on the shelf with his ministry ruined as Paul feared he might be (I Cor. 9:27).

No, it is not because they are cold that they nauseate the Saviour. It is because they are neither cold nor hot, but lukewarm. The people in the churches, not those on the outside, nauseate God. To lukewarm Christians God says, "I will spue thee out of my mouth."

This does not mean, of course, that a saved person thereby becomes lost nor that Christ forsakes the soul of any of His redeemed ones. One who has believed in Christ already has everlasting life and shall never come into condemnation but is passed from death unto life (John 5:24). One who trusts in Christ shall "not perish but have everlasting life" (John 3:16). No one, now nor hereafter, self nor others, angels nor demons, can separate a Christian from the love of God which is in Christ Jesus (Rom. 8:35–39). What Christ has purchased is His. One who is born again cannot become unborn. One saved by grace will not be lost by works. Christ did not mean here to deny all His precious promises of perfect and eternal salvation given freely to those who believe.

Yet, though a Christian cannot lose his soul, never think that he has nothing to lose by sin! He can lose the joy of salvation, can lose the conscious daily fellowship with Christ. He can lose his influence, his happiness. Lukewarm Christians lose their joy, lose their victory over sin, lose enjoyment of the Bible, lose the answers to their prayers, perhaps lose the souls they might win, and certainly lose much of the reward they might have had in Heaven.

Better Be Cold Than Lukewarm

Would Christ prefer that you be an out-and-out sinner rejecting Him, despising the Bible, insulting the Holy Spirit, refusing to believe, than to be saved but lukewarm? Strangely enough, that seems to be exactly true. Jesus said, "I would thou wert cold or hot. So then because thou art lukewarm, and neither cold nor hot, I will spue thee out of my mouth." Christ desired that all His own be on fire for God, filled with the Spirit, endued with a holy fervor for God. But if you are not red hot, then Jesus prefers that you be cold. "I would thou wert cold or hot."

Of course, you feel that it is better to be a lukewarm Christian than to be a lost sinner going to Hell. And for YOU it is better. YOU had rather go to Heaven though by your indifferent living, your lukewarm heart, your pallid Christianity you sent a thousand others to Hell! And that is what many Christians really do. If you have truly trusted in Christ and so have been born again, you will go to Heaven. But if you are a lukewarm Christian, you thwart the gospel and damn other souls. All some people ever will know of Christ is what they see in you. And what they see in you, many do not want. They see no victory over sin, no Christian joy, no sincere testimony. They see no evidence of a changed heart, no proof of the reality of Christ and salvation to the believer. The gospel as you live it contradicts the gospel preachers preach. Lukewarm Christians are the alibi of sinners, the decoy ducks of Satan. Lukewarm Christians are double-crossers of Christ, spiritual adulterers who do more harm than good. A fervent, godly missionary in a foreign field alone can often win more souls than an equally earnest preacher in America with the assistance of a church of a thousand members. Why? Because most of the members hinder and do not help. A lukewarm church may insulate a whole community against the gospel, or an indifferent family make it impossible to win unsaved loved ones. So, for the sake of others, Christ says, "I would thou wert cold or hot." He would rather you would be cold if not hot, that you would be out-and-out for the devil if you are not out-and-out for God. You would do less harm as an infidel than as a lukewarm church member. The damning blight of America today is too many Christians —that is, too many of the kind that we have, too many indifferent and lukewarm, nominal Christians. If there were only one-tenth as many people in America who made any pretense of faith in Christ, and if every one of these were spiritually on fire, filled with the Spirit of God, joyful, victorious, loving, witnessing, sacrificing Christians, then what a revival there would be!

Self-Satisfied Lukewarmness

How well pleased we are with ourselves! Our complacency is, in fact, the very heart of our sin! If we were burdened about our own faults, if we could see our own shallowness, our own insincerity, our own spiritual poverty, our own blindness, then God would not be so nauseated and disgusted with us. But Jesus said to the lukewarm Christians of Laodicea that He would spue them out "because thou sayest, I am rich and increased with goods, and have need of nothing; and knowest not that thou art wretched, and miserable, and poor, and blind, and naked." That is the reason He must vomit us out of His mouth!

Oh, the sin of our self-satisfaction! We have beautiful church houses, we have more modern church equipment than ever before. We have splendid organizations. We have preachers with doctors' degrees. We have large budgets. We have literature and radio programs. We have denominational schools, and hospitals and missionaries. The most influential people in town are members of our churches. We are rich and have need of nothing! So we think, but to God, our smirking self-righteousness, our being so well pleased with ourselves, is an abomination. We do not know that we are wretched and miserable and poor and blind and naked! Our lukewarmness is simply a phase of our unbelief, of our unconfessed sin, of our love for the world. It proves our estrangement from God, our disregard of the Holy Spirit's leading. We are so full of self and the world that we have no hunger for God. We do not have, and God help us, we do not want!

In Binghamton, New York, in 1936 in revival services in the Binghamton Theatre sponsored by a number of churches, I preached on "Sodom, Gomorrah, and Binghamton; Three of a Kind." A group of learned preachers, meeting in the city, took heated exception to my sermon subject. A prominent denominational official said that for Binghamton, with its schools and hospitals, art and industry, its progressive and intelligent people, to be compared with ancient Sodom was unthinkable! His remarks were printed in the daily press. However, the same night in a big club, within a block of the theater where I preached, was held a very saturnalia of debauch and sin. Fifty prostitutes were brought in from New York City. The most prominent men in the city bought tickets to the banquet and show. By midnight many of the men were drunk and many of the women were naked, and by 4:00 o'clock in the morning, I was told, officers had to stop the breaking of furniture and had to interfere with the wild carousal. Literally hundreds took part. Many were members of the churches where these pious and complacent preachers held forth. Investigation revealed that such orgies were frequent affairs. Many of the preachers were openly modernistic, denying the deity of Christ, the blood atonement, the new birth, and the inspiration of the Bible, and yet they were shocked at the comparison of Binghamton to Sodom and Gomorrah. They were rich, increased with goods, and had need of nothing, they thought. But God knew that they were "wretched, and miserable, and poor, and blind, and naked."

I announced the same sermon subject for the following night. Still larger crowds heard me with blessings from God the second night on the same subject, and the revival continued with hundreds saved.

That incident seems to me the more remarkable, in that newspaper men came to me with shocking revelations about the wickedness going on in the city, while most of the preachers either did not know or did not care.

I say we are a self-satisfied lot. We are lukewarm Christians. And may God forgive us, for that self-satisfaction is the thing that makes us hopeless of the blessings of God. We feel we have need of nothing, so we seek nothing and find nothing! We are not hungry; so we will not eat! We are not thirsty; so we will not drink! We are not conscious of lack of power; so we do not seek power. We do not realize how our sins grieve God; so we do not confess them nor forsake them. We do not feel any special need to pray; so we do not pray, we do not weep, we do not fast, we do not confess our sins! May God awake us self-satisfied Christians before we are spued out of the mouth of God, before we are permanently laid aside, never to be used in His service any more.

Long ago I heard devout Christians talk about "heart-felt religion." (By religion, of course, they meant the true religion of the Lord Jesus Christ.) And they were right about it, that we need our faith and our love and our service to be felt in the *heart*.

How God does want fervor of the heart! Perhaps you once had this zeal, but it has slipped, unnoticed, away. Samson lay with his head on the lap of Delilah, and when he awoke "he wist not that the Lord was departed from him" (Judg. 16:20). Many a car owner leaves his automobile standing without any thought until, suddenly needing it, he finds to his astonishment that the tires are flat, or someone has stolen the gasoline from the tank! How like a Christian that is!

Indifferent About Holiness

Sadly I say it, but with profound conviction: the average Christian is really indifferent about personal holiness. Oh, to be sure, we want to be respectable. We want to stand well in the sight of men. We make clean the outside of the cup and the platter, just as the Pharisees of old. We whitewash the sepulchres, which are sometimes beautiful to behold, and perhaps others do not know all the rottenness and uncleanness inside. We pay tithes, sometimes, of mint, anise and cummin; but we neglect the weightier matters of the law, judgment, mercy and faith. Surely it is true of us, as the Lord said through the prophet Isaiah (Isa. 29:13), and as Jesus quoted about the people of His day (Mark 7:6), "This people honoureth me with their lips, but their heart is far from me." We *talk* a good religion, but how much heart-hunger do present-day Christians have for personal holiness, to be pure in the sight of God, to be set apart altogether and absolutely for Him? How many do you know that seem to hunger and thirst after righteousness and long with unspeakable burden to be like Jesus?

We scorn those mistaught people who claim to have attained sinless perfection. Their claim is foolish, to be sure. But shame upon us—while we scoff at their doctrine we might well be more concerned to hunger after God as many of them do. I know that correct doctrine is important, but I feel sure that in God's sight heart-hunger and contrite hearts, longing to be exactly what God would have them be, are much more important.

Paul himself frankly confessed that he was not perfect and that he had not yet attained what he sought (Phil. 3:12). But nevertheless, Paul followed hard after the Lord Jesus. He said, "Brethren, I count not myself to have apprehended: but this one thing I do, forgetting those things which are behind, and reaching forth unto those things which are before, I press toward the mark for the prize of the high calling of

God in Christ Jesus" (Phil. 3:13, 14). Paul frankly confessed in the seventh chapter of Romans that he was a wretched man, serving the law of God with his mind, to be sure, but with his flesh the law of sin. But Paul makes that confession with an agony of heart and cries out, "O wretched man that I am! who shall deliver me from the body of this death?" (Rom. 7:24). Paul was not perfect, but he grieved and mourned over his sins. Paul was not sinless, but he longed to be, prayed to be, tried to be. Oh, that Christians today would hunger for personal holiness!

We do not believe in the monasteries where Catholic monks go aside from the world. We think it is not the will of God that they should scourge themselves, and lie on rough beds, and keep long hours of fasting on bended knees merely as self-punishment. We do not believe it pleases God for people to climb long stone stairways on their knees, nor that any such punishment of the body is necessary to please God. Yet I think we should be greatly humbled to consider that such monks are oftentimes really with all their hearts seeking to be holy, seeking to be free from sin. There is an easier approach to God than their way—it is through the shed blood of Jesus Christ; and yet I know that God would have us hunger, as they sometimes do, for the Lord Jesus and His purity and power to have absolute control of our lives. We do not wish our daughters to go into convents as nuns and to take upon them the garments that say, in their eyes, that they are "married to Christ," so giving up all plans and hopes of human husbands and homes and children of their own. But at least we ought to have some of that earnest burden of heart for holiness that drives people into convents and monasteries.

They shame me everywhere I go, these Christians who throng the theaters and movie houses, Christian people who use tobacco, Christian women who bob their hair and dress like the unsaved world. It shames me to find Christian men just as absorbed in business, just as covetous as their godless competitors. It is a shameful fact that Christians lie—they lie to their children about Santa Claus, both at home and in the churches; they lie when they threaten to punish. Christians often lie when they say, "I am glad to see you." We preachers often lie when we say, "Yes, I will pray for you."

Understand, I am not saying that Christians are altogether cold on morals. That is not what God tells you. That is not what disgusts Jesus Christ. Christ did not say that you have no scruples, that you do not try to live upright lives in general. He simply said that we are not red hot about it. We are not cold, but we are not hot either. We are only lukewarm about personal holiness.

I have just been reading again the story of Adoniram Judson and how he even withdrew from ordinary cultured society to seek Christ, returned the doctor's degree he had well earned by his labors, how rigorously he brought in every penny of money he himself earned outside of his mission work. He cared about holiness. And George Mueller burned the French novels he had translated and might have sold for much money. He gave up the girl he loved so well, sought out every idle longing or foolish turn of mind. General Stonewall Jackson walked several miles in the dark one night to correct a chance misstatement. "I said that it was on Tuesday night, but I have learned I was mistaken—it was on Thursday night," he said. How he longed and hungered to tell the truth! If you read John Wesley's journal you may find that there were many searchings of his heart as he longed and sought for personal holiness. I mean that Christians ought to seek to do good and be good in their hearts with an intense longing. With fervor of heart we ought to seek goodness, seek purity, seek personal holiness, and beg daily for such an abundant cleansing as will take away every evil thing that grieves the Spirit of God.

It is one thing to be an upright, respectable, moral Christian of good character and standing, and an entirely different matter to be a holy man or woman, that is, set apart for God, longing and praying, with heart searchings, with confession, with tears, with self-crucifixion, to be free of every secret thought and aim, every touch of worldliness that would grieve the Holy Spirit of God. I do not say we are cold Christians, but I say we are not hot Christians.

We are only lukewarm on the matter of personal morality. The average Christian intends to pay his debts, and will if it is convenient. He will pay his rent, if he doesn't get angry with the landlady, or if he does not have some disagreement and move off without paying, with the excuse that the landlord did not keep his part of the contract. When the average Christian buys furniture, he intends to pay for it by the time promised, and will—provided he has plenty of money left after his vacation and after all the ice cream and cake and entertaining and new automobiles and fine clothes are paid for. We are nominally honest. We are not cold toward honesty, but then we are not hot. We are only lukewarm. Almost every retail grocer who sells on credit could give you a shocking list of names of church members who have not settled their accounts. Physicians and dentists could show you the same alarming list, or worse. No retail business that sells to church members would be safe without a regular collection service, careful reminders, and sometimes threats of law! Christians are only lukewarm in honesty.

May God forgive us preachers who are lukewarm on the sin question. We say, "Peace, peace," but there is no peace. We say to the people smooth things. We do not, like John the Baptist, face Herod, saying, "It is not lawful for thee to have her." We do not challenge the Ananiases and Sapphiras of our churches. We do not make people angry. Many preachers, I understand, attend the movies regularly. A leading theater offered my wife and me season passes free. They meant it as a kindness, not as an insult. They had little reason to believe that a preacher would be offended with an offer of free theater tickets. At a meeting of Oak Cliff pastors in Dallas, Texas, where I was a pastor some years ago, I was shocked to note that out of twenty-seven present, thirteen smoked cigars publicly after the meal as they heard their prepared program! And yet we wonder why the spirit of revivals has left our churches! We wonder why the churches and the preachers have not influence over the nation. Like Samson, we have lost the hair of our separation and therefore our power with God! Like Lot, we have mingled with Sodom until we have taken their ways and called them "brethren," so we are as those that mock when we talk about God, even as Lot was as one that mocked to his sons-in-law (Gen. 19:14).

Oh, that God would give to every preacher a red-hot pitch-fork or a sword of fire. Oh, that God would give to every preacher then the fervor of heart, the holy conviction, the boldness of John the Baptist and Elijah to go up and down this land making Christians either get in or out, get on one side or the other, be for God or for the devil. Jesus wishes that we were either cold or hot. For the cause of Christ it would be infinitely better for church members to get out of the churches, take their names off the rolls, quit all pretensions of serving and trusting Christ, if they are only lukewarm.

In April, 1939, in revival services at the Walnut Street Baptist Church at Waterloo, Iowa, I preached on "The Sin of Lukewarmness," or "Church Members That Make God Vomit." God blessed and a good many came, Christians admitting their backslidings and some sinners being saved. When the service was dismissed, the pianist came to me with tears and said, "I ought to have come. I will come tomorrow night. I am a pretty kind of a Christian, playing the piano at church and living for the Devil! I will be the first one to come tomorrow night!" The next night when the invitation began, she played just a chord or two until the song was started and then almost ran to the altar to take my hand so that she might be the first. Christian, do you play the piano for God and live for the Devil? Or do you teach a Sunday School class or lead young people or sing in the choir and live for the Devil? Half-hearted Christianity is an abomination to God and Jesus wants you either hot or cold.

Indifferent, Insincere Christian Service an Abomination to God

Today it is popular to do "church work." Organizations have multiplied in the churches. People are glad to be named chairman of this, or president of that, or secretary of the other. It is especially easy to get a good social committee for entertainment purposes, and it is not so hard to get someone to bake a cake or to sing a song. Church people like "activities." And in our churches the youth are taught speech-making and social entertainment as if that would make them the finest Christians in the world!

But suppose that very strict rules began to be enforced for Christian service. Demand that every Sunday School teacher give up the card parties, the movies, and cigarettes; that women teachers, in hair and dress, be different from the world—demand that Sunday School teachers actually be present at teachers' meeting every week, that they look up every absentee. Hold them to account for every boy and girl. Then you will begin to see that many Christians who are willing to be active are not willing to be really on the altar, on fire for God.

It is no trouble to get people to sing. But most of the singing touches no hearts, leads to no conviction or salvation. It does not bless Christians, it does not warn nor invite sinners. It is singing of words or notes, but it is not testifying nor preaching. How often do you see someone saved through a song? What singers do you know that expect God to save souls through the singing of the song? How many singers do you know that weep as they sing? Oh, no, the idea these days is to sing correctly, to sing circumspectly, to excite admiration and perhaps enjoyment. But all such singing, whether of one or many, is an abomination to God. Congregational singing or special singing must alike offend Him when it does not come from fervent and contrite hearts. But we are commanded to "be filled with the Spirit; Speaking to yourselves in psalms and hymns and spiritual songs, singing and making melody in your heart to the Lord" (Eph. 5:18, 19). Strange that we never connect being filled with the Spirit and Christian singing, but God does. And really no one is fit to sing for God unless he is filled with the Spirit. No singing is acceptable or helpful if one does not sing really in the heart. Oh, may God put a melody ringing in our souls, so that we may sing with gladness, sing with urgency, sing with feeling, sing with tears. We ought oftentimes to break into hallelujahs as we sing. We sometimes have an animal enthusiasm, enjoying the rhythm when we sing these songs, but how little we really sing in the power of the Holy Ghost. Our singing must be so lukewarm as to be an abomination that nauseates God. Be careful never to sing what you do not mean. Singing that is insincere, and hypocritical singing, does not please God. May He forgive our lukewarmness in our singing.

And the Scripture quoted above from Ephesians 5:18, 19 includes speaking as well as singing. We who speak for God should speak in the fullness of the Spirit. I do not know any qualification so important in preaching the gospel as a holy earnestness, a fervor that is born of the Spirit. The Spirit of God is not lukewarm. He Himself yearns over sinners with unspeakable burden. He carries to sinners the invitation of a heart-broken Christ. If the Holy Spirit really speaks through us, surely we cannot but have tears and burdens and fervor.

When I first began to preach, I was shocked at the difference in preaching and in other public speaking. I had carefully worked out every detail of my speeches, often memorizing them, polishing them, trimming every word to suit. They were logical and well ordered. But when I began to preach, some way the Spirit of God got hold of me and I would oftentimes leave the prepared thread of discourse, with this illustration or that, or with entirely new material that I had not prepared. And I found that again and again the tears ran down my face as I spoke, and my voice would choke with emotion. I was sometimes greatly embarrassed, and I once asked God to let me preach without so many tears. He took me at my word and the next time or two I tried to preach it was cold and barren and powerless as if I knew nothing of God. I had no joy in my own heart; how could I rejoice others? I had no tears over sinners, and why should sinners weep? On my face I asked God to give me back again the tears, the broken heart, and He did. And I say to you solemnly that all the preaching without tears, without fervor, without a holy abandon such as a man must have if he is possessed and driven by the Spirit of God—all such preaching is a mockery. God forgive us poor, lukewarm preachers!

Actors on the stage portray only fiction, and yet they so enter the story that they laugh or weep, and eyes and voice eloquently combine as servants of a fervent heart. Even an imagined tale, a bit of fiction, becomes deadly real to them. Yet preachers are talking about a real Hell, Hell that has fire, a Hell that some poor sinner enters every moment because he rejected Christ. Every real preacher has a weight of responsibility upon him that might well drive him to his knees, or else drive him mad. And yet—with platitudes, dull tones, and with eyes that have no fire, and no tears—we preach a powerless gospel. While lost souls scream in Hell for a drop of water, we have no tears! While angels rejoice and shout in Heaven over sinners saved, we have no hallelujahs! So many of us preachers are wells without waters. We go without being sent. We are preachers without being prophets.

The country is full of "unemployed" preachers! How in the world could a preacher be unemployed? There are people to preach to in parks, on street corners, in country schoolhouses. There are children that play in the streets. There are prisoners, hungry-hearted, in the jails. There are homes where death has been. There are drunkards who need a friend, and dying sinners everywhere. And yet preachers are unemployed! Sometimes a preacher tells me, "I have no work at present." He means, of course, no work with a regular salary. I was amazed as a child that in our "half-time" country church, with preaching on the second and fourth Sundays, the pastor would never preach if he happened to be present on other Sundays. He was employed only on the second and fourth Sundays, and thus he had done his duty! The pastor usually had half-time employment in other churches, preaching the first and third Sundays. But when a fifth Sunday came, then did the pastor gladly take the opportunity to preach in one of the churches so hungry for preaching in those days? No, of course not. If he did not attend the fifth Sunday meeting, then he had a good chance to rest, or to hear someone else preach. I am reminded that in the days of Malachi God says that priests would not even shut the doors of the temple for nothing, nor kindle a fire on the altar without pay! (Mal. 1:10). So, doubtless, many of us preachers would not preach if we were not paid for it. And for the very same reason many church members will fill a nominal position, but they do not labor and sweat with a holy concern to get people saved. We cannot get workers enough for soul-winning visits in the hospitals, for personal work in the city jail, for visiting, house-to-house soul winning, and giving out of tracts.

Let every one of us search his heart to see if his service for God is from a hot heart. Unless there is a holy fervor, a fervor inspired by the burning Spirit of God, we cannot please Him with our service. He does not want cold work. He does not want inattentive listeners to sermons. He does not want singing with no heart-rejoicing, nor preaching with no tears. Once on Sunday morning I was waked by my alarm clock to go to an early radio service, and I sighed within myself for the burdens of the day. I had not gotten enough sleep. I was to preach about five times. I thought to myself, "The burdens of the day will be so heavy—how I wish I were through with them." And then there came upon me the shamed realization that I was not glad, not happy in the service of God. I ought to have been able to cry out with David, "I was glad when they said unto me, Let us go into the house of the Lord" (Psa. 122:1). I should have rejoiced like Paul that God had counted

me worthy putting me into the ministry (I Tim. 1:12). How
great is my privilege, that I have never a lack of a place to
preach the gospel! How I thank God that I have more calls
than I can fill. How wicked it is that I should ever feel weary
in my heart over it. You remember that is the thing that disgusted God with the Jews, as He warned them through the
prophet Malachi. The Jews said, "Behold, what a weariness
is it" (Mal. 1:13). They sniffed at the table of the Lord, and
brought that which was torn and the lame and the sick, and
God was disgusted with their offerings. And so when I saw my
sin, I confessed it to God and begged Him to let me never
again be weary of the work that is so dear to the heart of
Christ. The angels in Heaven would preach it if they could,
and why should I not rejoice with joy unspeakable and full of
glory that God has made me a preacher of His gospel? Lukewarmness in Christian service is an abomination to God. Let
us confess it and forsake it, and wait in the closet of confession
and penitence and prayer until God gives again a hot heart
and a hot messege from the dear heart of God.

Modern Christians Unconcerned About Bible

The lukewarmness of church members toward the Word of
God is shocking. First, people do not believe the Bible. It is
strange how many people call themselves Christians, even
fundamentalists, and yet do not believe certain parts of the
Bible, do not count them infallibly correct. So many believe
in inspiration but not in verbal inspiration. Many think that
the Genesis account of creation is only allegorical and figura-
tive, that no fish really swallowed Jonah, or they do not believe that Jesus literally came out of the grave. I had a long
letter the other day from a Presbyterian pastor, insisting that
Jesus could not have had a physical body after His resurrection. Christian Scientists say they believe the Bible and then
deny even the fact of sin. Bobbed-haired, rebellious wives,
when they read the divine commands about obedient wives
and long hair and women keeping silence in the church and

not usurping authority to teach or preach to men, say that Paul was just an old bachelor who had it in for the women. And more than once church members have told me that they would not follow the plain commands of Proverbs about whipping children to make them obey because Solomon married so many wives and had so many children he did not know. Most of us say that we believe the Bible, but our profession is insincere. We believe the Bible but not that it is scientifically accurate. We believe the Bible but not that it is historically correct. We believe the Bible but not that its prophecies about the literal reign of Christ, the conversion of the Jews, the restoration of David's throne, etc., will take place. We believe the Bible, we say, but we do not believe miracles are possible. We do not believe God's promises about answered prayer. We are insincere hypocrites, really indifferent to the Word of God! We do not take it seriously. We believe it nominally but not with all our hearts. We are not infidels, oh, no. We believe the Bible in general but not in particular. We are partly for it and partly against it. We are not cold toward it but neither are we red hot. *We are only lukewarm and that nauseates God.*

How the Lord Jesus leaned upon the Word of God! His constant passion was to live every moment "that the scripture might be fulfilled." He did not forget it in the garden, and it was repeatedly mentioned concerning the crucifixion. Christ died "according to the scriptures" and rose again the third day "according to the scriptures" (I Cor. 15:3, 4). With the Word of God Jesus defeated Satan at His temptation and declared later that not one jot nor one tittle should ever pass until all be fulfilled.

But Christians today are lukewarm in following the Bible. We follow creeds easily. We follow preachers and leaders. But where is the man who whole-heartedly searches the Bible, not to find argument for his own position but rather to see what says the Word of God?

The fact is that Christians are not interested in the Bible.

The average Christian has never even read the Bible through. All over the nation I have put it to a test, and in the average group of Christians not a third profess they have even read through the Word of God! Only a few Christians know how many books are in the Bible, and very, very few can name them. In dozens of cases I have asked people to name their own favorite book in the Bible, and then, whether it were John or Psalms or Romans or Matthew, they could not tell how many chapters are in the book they loved the best. And repeatedly devout Christians have held their hands to signify that they were familiar with the book of "Hezekiah" or the book of "Samson." The average Christian does not know these are not books in the Bible.

Christians do not know their Bibles even moderately well. If the first, twenty-third and the one hundred third Psalm, and the fourteenth chapter of John and the eighth and twelfth chapters of Romans were taken out of the Bible, and a half dozen others, then two-thirds of all the Scriptures that the average Christian can quote would be gone. Christians know more about Joe Louis than they do about Samson. They know more about MacArthur than about Paul, more about Jeff and Mutt than they do about Paul and Barnabas. Christians simply do not know what the Bible says about baptism nor divorce nor about Hell, and so may be led astray by every wind of doctrine. Very few Christians, if marooned on a desert island with a sinner, could show that sinner how to be saved. Modern Christians do not know the Bible that they claim to love. Some read it, a chapter a day, read it with yawns, and then have to place a book mark at the place they stop so they can remember where to begin the next day because they do not remember what they read.

"Oh, I read it, but I cannot remember it," says many a Christian about the Bible. Yet they remember street addresses, telephone numbers, and names of friends. They remember what baseball team is ahead, remember candidates for office and remember and talk about thousands of events discussed in the daily newspapers. The simple truth is that Christians do not read the Bible because they do not love it, do not read it with a passionate fervor. A Christian will read a chapter in the Bible as a matter of duty and then read through the entire daily newspaper, equal in volume to a book or two or three in the Bible. They read the Bible as a respectable duty and read the newspaper because they enjoy it and love it. Lukewarm church members read a few verses in the Bible as Sunday School lessons and then sit up until midnight reading a favorite novel. The sad truth is that we have no heart for the Bible. We do not love it, we do not search it, we do not meditate in it day and night. It is not to us 'sweeter than honey and the honeycomb,' as it was to David. Surely nothing could show our backslidden state more quickly than our attitude toward the Bible. Prosperity and success in everything we say and do is promised to one who meditates day and night in the Word of God and does not depart from its teachings (Psa. 1:1–3; Josh. 1:8). Yet people read the Bible as a drudgery or not at all. The entire Bible can be read through in about ten months at four chapters a day or in a year by reading three chapters on week days and five chapters on Sunday. Yet we are more interested in our letters, more interested in the daily papers, more interested in the comics, more interested in idle chatter and gossip than we are in the Word of God. Surely God is grieved and angry with us for this criminal and inexcusable indifference toward the holy Word of God!

The Hypocrisy of Coldhearted Praying

In the Capitol Hotel in Amarillo, Texas, some years ago, a small group of preachers talked and prayed at 11:00 o'clock at night. The telephone rang and a man with deep concern asked if he could come to our room for prayer. When he came, in his lounging robe and pajamas, we found he had been drinking. He said, "I know I am drunk, and I am not dressed; but I am lost and I must have somebody to pray. My wife has quit me, I have tried to commit suicide, but I am afraid to die."

Then he told us, "I know lots of preachers. My grandfather was a preacher. I know Dr. So-and-So and Dr. So-and-So (and he named a group of prominent preachers), but I cannot ask them to pray because I am afraid they do not mean it," he said.

Do Christians "mean it" when they pray? Evidently most of us do not. We have a lame kind of praying these days. We have prayer without fasting, prayer without supplication, prayer without tears. Most Christians have never prayed all night nor all day. Most Christians never missed a meal nor missed a day's work to pray. We are skeptics about prayer. Very few Christians expect God to heal the sick in answer to prayer. When I have suggested that we pray for rain in a time of drought, church members and even preachers have hooted at the idea of prayer changing such things and have been openly amazed when God did answer such prayers! We count more on "pull" than on prayer to get jobs. We call the doctor before we call the Lord when one is sick. A dear lady in my church once said to me, "Brother Rice, I believe in prayer, too. If I ever get sick and the doctors fail, I am going to send for you to pray for me." That is the way most other Christians do. They pray only after doctors fail!

We spend very little time in prayer. The average Christian does not spend three minutes a day in seeking God's face. Those who do pray, pray more or less as a form. Once you started returning thanks at the table, your grateful heart looking up to God. Long ago the gratitude was forgotten but you still maintain the form of prayer and say the same words with your heart elsewhere. Or worse, many have left off even the form of prayer.

New Testament Christians fasted and prayed. The disciples fasted before Pentecost, for Jesus said that 'when the Bridegroom is taken away then shall they fast.' (Matt. 9:15). The group of earnest Christians at Antioch fasted and prayed before they sent Paul and Barnabas away. In fact it is said that they fasted and prayed twice (Acts 13:1–4). The Apostle Paul was "in fastings often" (II Cor. 11:27). Jesus, seated by the well of Samaria, did not eat for He had meat to eat that the disciples knew not of. Even the Pharisees fasted. But fasting is out of date with modern Christians. We pray without fasting, we give without sacrifice, we witness without tears, and God knows we sow without reaping, we come in without sheaves!

Where is one like Samuel who cried unto the Lord all night? How many are there like Welch of Scotland, who wrestled on the floor through the night in prayer, saying to his wife, "Leave me alone, woman. I am accountable for some two thousand souls, and I know not how it is with many of them this night"? How many Christians are there who know anything about the labors in prayer that "Praying Hyde" of India endured? Or where is one who prays like John Knox, "O God, give me Scotland, or I die"? Who these days prays like Luther, three hours a day? Our prayer is a mockery, an insincere farce. We feel no need to seek God. We are "rich and increased with goods."

Bible teachers go to elaborate pains to discourage Christians from praying for Holy Spirit power. "No, no," they say, "we already have the Holy Spirit, and why should we pray?" In fact, the devil has always somebody to discourage prayer. Why not just believe and go ahead without prayer? And besides, the Devil always has somebody to say, "Does not God know better than we what we need? Would a little, puny man be able to change the mind of an infinite God?" And the best Bible students find a dozen reasons in the Bible why our prayers cannot be answered unless we meet many complicated conditions. We do not love prayer, we spend little time in prayer, we do not expect blessings in prayer. No wonder the

Lord Jesus counts our weak praying, half-hearted, insincere, dry-eyed praying, as an abomination! *May God deliver us from lukewarm praying!*

A Bogus Christianity, Without Sacrifice, Without Martyrdom, Without Fanaticism

How often have we heard it said that God does not now want people to die for Him but only that people should live for Him. But I warn you, there is no authority in the Word of God for that statement. How do you know that God does not want martyrs to die for Him and the gospel now just as much as He wanted Stephen and Peter and Paul and James and many others to die for Him? He wanted John and Betty Stam to die as martyrs in China a few years ago. Do you think this wicked world has changed and gotten so nice that it will no longer oppose the gospel? Do you believe that men's wicked hearts are now all reformed and that there is now nowhere anyone who would take the life of a true witness of Jesus Christ? Then you surely are deceived. Men's wicked hearts are as bad as ever they were. Some men are demon-possessed now as definitely as some were in Bible times. And the Lord Jesus desires the same love and whole-hearted surrender now as ever before. In fact, the command of Jesus, "If any man will come after me, let him deny himself, and take up his cross daily, and follow me" (Luke 9:23), is a clear command that every Christian should be ready to die. To deny self in this case would mean to be as Jesus going before Pontius Pilate and surrendering Himself to condemnation and death. To take up the cross would mean to be as Jesus heading out toward Calvary with His face set like a flint toward death. Paul said, "I die daily" (I Cor. 15:31). He certainly meant beyond any doubt that he was ready to die, willing to die, and that daily he surrendered anew to die. He counted not his life dear to himself. Why should we be less fully surrendered, less willing to sacrifice self? I say to you that if you want to die for Christ today, today is as good a time as any in the history of the world. In Russia thousands have died just for being true to Christ. Murdered by firing squads in the night, sent to frozen Siberia and starved, condemned to death by withdrawing bread cards—how many, many saints of God in Russia thus went home to Glory to meet the Saviour joyfully! And you and I could well do the same.

As John and Betty Stam died in China, so you might well die there today. If you would really like to die for Jesus Christ, there is no doubt that many a Communist, or for that matter many others would cooperate with you, provided you were bold for Jesus Christ.

Or in Germany, where Martin Neimoeller languished long in prison as a preacher of the gospel, some have died and others could well die today. Certainly some are in prison and anyone could be who would stand boldly for the Bible and for soul winning and for Christ.

People talk about certain mission fields being "closed." They are only closed in the sense that Jerusalem was closed to Paul, in the sense that it was closed to James and Stephen. That is, there was danger there, but they preached the gospel nevertheless. Mission fields today may be "closed" to missionaries, just as Rome was closed to Paul. But Paul went to Rome and died gladly by the executioner's axe. Fields are "closed." Are they closed because there is no need for the gospel? Closed because Christ does not have any work to do there? Are the fields closed because God does not love the sinners there and want them saved? Or are they closed simply because there is no one who is willing to face danger for Christ? As to that, only God can speak to each individual and give orders. I am simply saying that men can die for Jesus Christ now if they are the New Testament kind of Christians.

But you need not leave America if you want to suffer for Christ. No doubt in the Jewish quarter of Chicago one who preached like Stephen would be stoned to death like Stephen. No doubt in many parts of the nation imprisonment, abuse by a mob, and even death would be the reapings if we were true to God. Do you suppose if men preached as they ought to preach against the liquor traffic that no one would object? Do you suppose that sinners everywhere would be unconcerned if men of God who were filled with the Holy Ghost and absolutely careless of personal danger were to oppose sin and to preach to sinners?

Die for Christ, did you say? How will a man die for Christ who will not lose ten cents for Him? How will a woman die for Christ who will not give up her face paint or her movies for Christ? We who were never insulted as Christians, we who never were spit upon, never had a rotten egg hurled at us, how can we talk about dying for Christ?

We modern, lukewarm Christians would not even give up a friend for Jesus Christ. How then would we be nerved to stand with the flames licking about us and sing hymns and rejoice? You would not risk a harsh word even by speaking to a stranger about Christ. You would not risk your job by being the right kind of a Christian at work. Perhaps you would not even give God a tithe of your income—then how can you talk about dying for Christ?

The sad truth is that we lukewarm Christians know nothing about sacrifice. Many of us are not fit to die. We are not the stuff that men tie to stakes. We are not made of material that men light fagots under. Sinners throw no stones at our kind of Christians. Many of us never lost a night's sleep nor missed a meal nor gave up a friend for Christ. How would we feel alongside New Testament Christians? How would we modern Christians act if we were thrown to the lions, or if we were stoned like Paul and dragged out of the city like a horse and left for dead? How would we take the spoiling of our goods? How would we look clothed in sheep skins and goat skins and hiding in the caves of the earth? Would our faces shine like Stephen's as we prayed for our enemies? Could we cry as an ancient martyr did to the martyr beside him as the flames began to lick up about them, "Be of good cheer, Ridley! This day we shall light a fire that shall light all England!" What has gone with our love for Christ and our spirit of sacrifice?

We are not cold, and we are not hot. We love God, but with no fervor. We pray, but with no passion. We give, but with no sacrifice. We testify, but without power. We sow without tears! We make Christ vomit with our lukewarm Christianity.

Will you go alone with God in a time of holy confession, forsaking your lukewarmness, begging of Him the "gold tried in the fire"—a burning heart? Will you seek the white raiment of His righteousness and holiness? Will you plead for the anointing of your eyes to see the doom of sinners and weep for their salvation? Oh, God convict us and heal us of our abominable lukewarmness!

Chapter 3

GOD'S SLAUGHTER CREW

*T*HE PROPHET Ezekiel was a captive in Babylon. Probably he had been carried away in the group mentioned in II Kings 24:10-16, eleven years before the final siege and destruction of Jerusalem by Nebuchadnezzar's army, when most of the remaining population was carried away captive. So Ezekiel lived in a most troublous time. He preached to one group of captives in Babylon and, by divine revelation, gave the reasons for the ruin that was even then falling upon Judah and the holy city, Jerusalem, and he prophesied the coming destruction of the city, when the whole nation of Jews, save a remnant of poor people, would be carried away to Babylon for seventy years.

In the ninth chapter of Ezekiel is recorded a wonderful vision the prophet had, showing the terrible slaughter that must come at Jerusalem, and why. Read it carefully and the mystery of it will become plain, with profound spiritual meaning.

"He cried also in mine ears with a loud voice, saying, Cause them that have charge over the city to draw near, even every man with his destroying weapon in his hand. And, behold, six men came from the way of the higher gate, which lieth toward the north, and every man a slaughter weapon in his hand; and one man among them was clothed with linen, with a writer's inkhorn by his side: and they went in, and stood beside the brasen altar. And the glory of the God of Israel was gone up from the cherub, whereupon he was, to the threshold of the

*house. And he called to the man clothed with linen, which
had the writer's inkhorn by his side; And the Lord said unto
him, Go through the midst of the city, through the midst of
Jerusalem, and set a mark upon the foreheads of the men that
sigh and that cry for all the abominations that be done in the
midst thereof. And to the others he said in mine hearing, Go
ye after him through the city, and smite: let not your eye
spare, neither have ye pity: Slay utterly old and young, both
maids, and little children, and women: but come not near any
man upon whom is the mark; and begin at my sanctuary.
Then they began at the ancient men which were before the
house. And he said unto them, Defile the house, and fill the
courts with the slain: go ye forth. And they went forth, and
slew in the city. And it came to pass, while they were slaying
them, and I was left, that I fell upon my face, and cried, and
said, Ah Lord God! wilt thou destroy all the residue of Israel
in thy pouring out of thy fury upon Jerusalem? Then said he
unto me, The iniquity of the house of Israel and Judah is
exceeding great, and the land is full of blood, and the city
full of perverseness: for they say, The Lord hath forsaken the
earth, and the Lord seeth not. And as for me also, mine eye
shall not spare, neither will I have pity, but I will recompense
their way upon their head. And, behold, the man clothed with
linen, which had the inkhorn by his side, reported the matter,
saying, I have done as thou hast commanded me."*

—Ezek. 9:1–11.

I. BEHIND THE SCENE ON GOD'S STAGE

I saw a Punch-and-Judy show, where on a tiny stage little
puppet dolls, called marionettes, acted out their parts, supported on tiny threads. Unseen hands above the stage pulled
the tiny strings and the puppets moved their arms and feet.
They seemed to talk, but the voices were those of unseen
people who controlled the puppets.

There are those who look upon this world and the events

of history, and believe that people and nations act without any divine supervision or control, that events "happen" according to blind fate or chance. That view is almost as foolish as to suppose that the marionettes are their own masters, doing their walking and talking without unseen control. The events of human history shape themselves under the mighty hand of God. The world is never left alone. We are not puppets, but certainly we are not altogether free from God's control. Only those things happen that are permitted to happen by an all-wise God. You cannot rule out God from the universe He created, sustains and controls.

In this ninth chapter of Ezekiel we are given a look behind the scenes in God's theatre of history. Terrible, evil days had fallen on Jerusalem. The city was ruled by Zedekiah, a wicked king set on the throne by Nebuchadnezzar, and subject to that Babylonian king. Zedekiah rebelled eventually, and the utter destruction of Jerusalem resulted. The casual reader of the history might suppose that the chain of natural causes, without God's direct intervention, caused the destruction of Jerusalem. The above Scripture, however, makes it clear that God Himself deliberately determined on the destruction of the city and the slaughter of its people, that the conquerors were divinely directed and led. Second Chronicles 36:17 says of Jerusalem that *the Lord* "brought upon them the king of the Chaldees, who slew their young men with the sword in the house of their sanctuary, and had no compassion upon young man or maiden, old man, or him that stooped for age: he gave them all into his hand." But in Ezekiel the ninth chapter God revealed the secret background to the prophet. Actually God had sent six men (they were angels) to destroy the people of the city. And among the six was a man clothed with linen, with a writer's inkhorn by his side. And the Lord plainly commanded the man with the inkhorn to "set a mark upon the foreheads of the men that sigh and that cry for all the abominations that be done in the midst thereof" (v. 4). And

then the other messengers of God, angels in charge of God's
work in the city, were to go through the city with their
slaughter weapons, killing all, both men and women, old
and young, in a pitiless slaughter excepting only those that
had the mark on their foreheads. Babylonian soldiers were
really only the agents of the unseen angels of God sent to
slaughter them!

How blind we are! We leave God out of our calculations.
We should remember that back of Hitler there was God.
Back of Mussolini there was God. Back of the Japanese war-
lords and the treachery of Pearl Harbor there was God! Back
of disease and pestilence and bloodshed there is God. Back of
chastising, back of inscrutable problems and unexplainable
tragedies there is God. We see only *men* on the stage. If we
could look behind the scenes of God's theatre of history we
would see *God* giving directions to His angels, and the angels
seeing that His plans are carried out in the lives of men, protecting His own, punishing those who forsake Him, causing
His own to pass through the mills of God which grind so
slowly but grind exceeding fine.

The same emperor, Nebuchadnezzar, the first world ruler
appearing on the scene of history, the man who commanded
the destruction of Jerusalem, later was disciplined by the
hand of God. For his proud and haughty spirit,

*"He was driven from the sons of men; and his heart was
made like the beasts, and his dwelling was with the wild asses:
they fed him with grass like oxen, and his body was wet with
the dew of heaven; TILL HE KNEW THAT THE MOST
HIGH GOD RULED IN THE KINGDOM OF MEN, AND
THAT HE APPOINTETH OVER IT WHOMSOEVER
HE WILL."*—Dan. 5:21.

There is still God to reckon with. God still rules in the
kingdom of men. What is the plan and will of God, the unseen God who moves the characters on the stage, prompts
them in their lines, brings them to their just ends, and, at His
own will, rings down the curtain on their lives and careers?

II. GOD'S PROTECTING MARK ON HIS OWN

In the book of Revelation we are told that in a future time of great tribulation, some wicked men will take "the mark of the beast," the Antichrist, in their hands or in their forehead. But here we find that God Himself has a distinguishing, protecting mark, unseen by men, placed upon the foreheads of His own by angels that do His bidding. At least that was true in Jerusalem. All about them the slaughter went on. It seemed a pitiless slaughter, with both old and young alike dying. The slaying seemed indiscriminate, but it was not. There were certain people in Jerusalem that death could not touch! In the midst of the fury when Jerusalem was utterly destroyed and so many thousands were slain, no doubt many died at the hands of brutal soldiers when it seemed senseless and uncalled for. In the horrible siege before the city fell, mothers cooked and ate their children and hundreds starved. In those terrible days it must have seemed to many that God had forgotten, that God did not care. But back of it all there was a divine pattern. God had a secret list of those who were to be slain, and His angels, at His command, supervised the bloody business. But at the same time God reserved a list of marked persons that were not to be injured, that must not be touched. They bore the invisible, protecting mark of God's angel, 'the man clothed in linen with an inkhorn by his side!'

The three Hebrew children, cast in the fiery furnace because they would not bow down to the great image set up in the plain of Dura, by Nebuchadnezzar, must have had such a mark upon their foreheads. In the terrific heat and flames of the furnace, they walked about unharmed and One like unto the Son of God came and walked with them! And when they were taken out, their hair was not singed and there was not the smell of smoke upon their garments! (Dan. 3:19–28).

Daniel himself must have had such an invisible mark upon his forehead. For when he was cast into the lions' den, the jaws of the lions were locked and they could not harm him. I think it was a restful, calm night as Daniel rejoiced in the Lord, knowing that God's angels protected him. He could not be harmed until God gave His consent (Dan. 6:16–24).

The baby Moses surely had this mark upon him when, by a faithful and praying mother, he was placed in the basket daubed with pitch and left afloat on the Nile River. God did not mean the child to be destroyed, but to be the law-giver and liberator of his nation, Israel.

This unseen mark of protection must have been upon Paul the Apostle when he came through countless dangers unscathed. When he was let down from the wall of Damascus in a basket, through a window, God's angel saw that he was not molested. When he was stoned and left for dead, outside of the city of Lystra (Acts 14:19, 20), the mark was still there and Paul was not to die! When tossed upon an angry sea en route to Rome, sailors and soldiers did not eat for torment of fear, fourteen long days and nights, until God's angel stood by Paul and told him, "Fear not, Paul; thou must be brought before Caesar: and, lo, God hath given thee all them that sail with thee" (Acts 27:24). Satan and all his evil men and demons could not kill Paul until God's time came!

We have just seen a terrible war. In every great battle some die and some are left behind unscathed by bullet and bomb. Why? Because, for God's own reason, He has had His angel put upon them a protecting mark. A Christian soldier or sailor who trusts in God knows the meaning of Psalm 91:7–12:

"A thousand shall fall at thy side, and ten thousand at thy right hand; but it shall not come nigh thee. Only with thine eyes shalt thou behold and see the reward of the wicked. Because thou hast made the Lord, which is my refuge, even the most High, thy habitation; There shall no evil befall thee, neither shall any plague come nigh thy dwelling. For he shall give his angels charge over thee, to keep thee in all

*thy ways. They shall bear thee up in their hands, lest thou
dash thy foot against a stone."*

In every situation God has His marked men and women,
those who cannot die because their mission is not done, those
who cannot be injured except just so far as will be to their
own future good and the glory of God.

Many a saint of God has been comforted by the words of
the blessed old hymn for which my mother asked on her dying
bed, and over which she rejoiced as it was sung.

> When through the deep waters I call thee to go,
> The rivers of sorrow shall not overflow;
> For I will be with thee thy trials to bless,
> And sanctify to thee thy deepest distress.

> When through fiery trials thy pathway shall lie,
> My grace, all sufficient shall be thy supply;
> The flames shall not hurt thee, I only design
> Thy dross to consume, and thy gold to refine.

For years I have felt about me the guardian angels of God.
In Chicago some years ago a truck raced around a milk
wagon and, running through the red light, rammed into the
side of my car. Heavy machinery on the front caved in the left
front door until it touched my body as I sat at the steering
wheel. I received not a scratch. Some years before that Rev.
Sam Morris and I with our wives, in west Texas where there
were only a few trains daily, sat on a railroad track eating a
watermelon when a Texas and Pacific train rushed down
upon us without whistling. It seemed a miracle that I was
moved to look up in time and we jumped from the rails as
the train roared by inches away. But on these and many other
occasions I was conscious of the blessed promise that "The
angel of the Lord encampeth round about them that fear him,
and delivereth them" (Psa. 34:7).

Satan complained that God had set a hedge about Job so

the Destroyer could not get at that tried saint. Well, bless God, Satan can touch none of God's children except as God permits it. How blessed are those upon whom are the invisible marks of protection, put there by the man clothed in linen with the inkhorn at his side, one of God's recording angels!

III. "THE MEN THAT SIGH AND THAT CRY" OVER SIN ARE SO DEAR TO GOD

I have said that, in general, all of God's people have a mark of protection upon them. None can suffer and none can die except as God gives permission. In the particular case of the destruction of Jerusalem, not all of God's people were preserved alive. I can hardly believe that in this city full of people, among the thousands starved or slain, there were no Christians. I feel it likely that many of these knew the true God as a personal Saviour. Many knew the meaning of the passover lamb, of the daily sacrifices, of the promises of the coming Messiah. Many were familiar with Isaiah's chapter 53, telling of the coming Redeemer. Even today on the battlefields of the world many die who have trusted Christ as Saviour. Many were starved in China, or were slain at Hongkong or Singapore or Dunkirk, or died in the cold Atlantic or the peaceful Pacific when their ships went down; yet they knew Christ as Saviour and had trusted Him for forgiveness.

The mark of protection on men at Jerusalem was not for all those who knew the Lord; rather, it was for a particular type of saved people. That mark was for those who sighed and who cried for all the abominations that were done in the midst of Jerusalem. Ezekiel 9:4 says, "And the Lord said unto him, Go through the midst of the city, through the midst of Jerusalem, and set a mark upon the foreheads of the men that sigh and that cry for all the abominations that be done in the midst thereof."

"Do you mean to say," someone may ask, "that God Himself deliberately plans the tragic death of His own children sometimes? Do you mean to say not all of God's children are under the same protection and care?"

That is exactly what this Scripture teaches. God lets certain kinds of Christians die in the midst of lost people so that the outward world may see no distinction. In fact, God sometimes, in a terrifying manner, points out Christians for horrible and tragic deaths.

Some have thought that Ananias and Sapphira, who according to Acts, chapter 5, were struck down by God's almighty power for their presumptuous sin, were unsaved people, but I do not believe it. God would as quickly strike a Christian for lying to the Holy Ghost as a lost sinner. And church members at Corinth who died for their sins, of whom Paul said, "For this cause many are weak and sickly among you, and many sleep" (I Cor. 11:30), were probably truly saved people. The Scripture does not even hint that they were unsaved. Such Christians would certainly have an embarrassing time at the judgment seat of Christ, giving account of the deeds done in the body (II Cor. 5:9, 10). Certainly they would lose a reward and be ashamed before Christ. But such Christians die for their sins, in many cases.

Certainly Christians sometimes die AS PUNISHMENT. Sometimes other Christians are protected from the same slaughter, because their heart attitudes please God.

I do not mean now to infer that death is always a tragedy for a Christian. In every war some great Christians die; in peace time some great Christians die, too. But the best Christians do not DIE AS PUNISHMENT FROM GOD. The best Christians go on, in God's good time, to their happy and blessed reward. Other Christians, sometimes, die along with wicked people because they do not have in their hearts the one great qualification so dear to God and so important in His saints. They do not hate sin and weep over it. They do not sigh and groan in spirit for revival. They are not burdened for a dying, sinning world so dear to the Lord Jesus.

God help us to learn the lesson that what God wants is not primarily the life of a Pharisee. What God wants in His people is not, primarily, the outward marks of respectability, blameless regularity in life, and a fair percentage of public service and worship. No, no! What God wants first in His people is a broken and a contrite heart! God wants people who know how to weep over sinners; who sigh and who cry for the abominations on every hand!

I am not speaking just now of the indignation and the fire of reformers who set out to change political or moral situations. I am for the reformers. We need their work. But it is not the *work* that God looked for most among the inhabitants of Jerusalem. What He sought most of all was people with eyes red from weeping, with hearts that sighed and cried over Jerusalem's sin! It was not first of all public speaking God required, but private burden and heart passion.

God was not looking so much for correctness in doctrine in Jerusalem as He was looking for men and women with broken hearts.

I sat the other day in the services of a fine church. The pastor is sound in doctrine, clean in life, beautiful in character, kindly in spirit. The membership is composed of the finest type of people. They are, manifestly, truly saved. They believe the Bible. They are liberal in their giving. The people are not modernistic in their doctrine and they are not worldly in their living. But the formal services in that church continue week after week, often month on end, with never a sinner finding Christ. Tears rarely fall in the services. There is rarely a public invitation for sinners to come openly to Christ and openly confess Him in the services. I wondered, as I sat there, if the same man clothed in a linen garment, and with an inkhorn by his side, should come to that congregation, how many of us would be marked in our forehead as those that sigh and cry for the abominations on every hand? For years there has been no great ingathering there. How many of us weep over the lost? How many of us have in us that one attitude of heart that can possibly bring a revival— a heart-burden, a travail of soul, a compassion that weeps over sinners?

America is full of church members, principally good men and women, millions of whom have truly been converted, who would not be marked for protection if the angels marched through this land with their slaughter weapons!

Thousands of preachers stand in their pulpits Sunday after Sunday, who, if God brings America to judgment as He brought Jerusalem, would die in the slaughter. They have, in most cases, real sincerity. Thousands of them believe the Bible. Thousands of them are sacrificial, scrupulously honest in their service to their congregations. But most of them do not have the distinction that they sigh and cry! I am persuaded that the average preacher does not weep in the pulpit because he does not weep in the prayer closet.

We preachers are a fat, sleek, comfortable, conforming and well-fed group. We are not Elijahs, fed by ravens and widows, and sought to be slain by the Jezebels and Ahabs. We are not John the Baptists, calling people to repentance, telling Herod of his sins, having our heads cut off! We are not Pauls who could face the elders in the cities where we have ministered three years and say, "Wherefore I take you to record this day, that I am pure from the blood of all men. For I have not shunned to declare unto you all the counsel of God. . . . remember, that by the space of three years I ceased not to warn every one night and day with tears" (Acts 20:26, 27, 31).

Preachers who do not weep, who do not sigh, who do not sweat blood, figuratively, do not bring revivals.

Away with preaching that has no tears! Away with praying that has no tears! Away with teaching that does not come from a broken heart! Away with all the Christian service that is not anointed with tears, that does not include sighs and groans of travail! Churches that have no weeping, no confessing, no fasting and prayers, no deep unrest and burden, do not have visitations of power from on high.

I beseech all who read this message to seek a broken and a contrite heart. I plead with every mother and father who has a lost boy or girl to wait on God until your hearts are humbled and broken. First learn to weep and then you may learn to pray! First learn to weep over sinners and then you may learn to win sinners for "They that sow in tears shall reap in joy. He that goeth forth and weepeth, bearing precious seed, shall doubtless come again with rejoicing, bringing his sheaves with him" (Psa. 126:5, 6). And we need it emphasized again in every church that when Zion travails, sons and daughters will be born into the kingdom and not until then (Isa. 66:8).

I register here and now my heart's vow to God that I will seek to be broken in spirit, that I may weep with the Lord Jesus over sinners, as He wept over Jerusalem. Oh, if God's angel clothed in linen and with the inkhorn by his side, goes through the land today, I pray that he may find me among those that sigh and that cry for the abominations on every hand, and that I may be counted worthy to have the mark, invisible upon my forehead, which those receive who have a broken heart over God's business and over sinners!

IV. THE PITILESS SLAUGHTER AT GOD'S COMMAND

Infidels in the church and out have talked learnedly about the inadequate picture of God in the Old Testament, and have scorned what they call "the low moral standard" there. Such enemies of the Bible, such self-sufficient and self-righteous fools, do not believe in a God of judgment. They do not believe in the God who brought the flood on a horribly wicked race. They do not believe in the God who ordered the destruction of the Amalekites, saying, "Now go and smite Amalek, and utterly destroy all that they have, and spare them not; but slay both man and woman, infant and suckling, ox and sheep, camel and ass" (I Sam. 15:3). They do not care that that wicked nation was set in idolatry and in rejection of the true God. It matters not to them that here was a fountain-head of iniquity poisoning all the nations round about. Modernists, unbelievers may say, "I could not love a God like that." But poor sinner, whether you love a God like that or not, this is the kind of a God you must deal with. The God of creation and the God of salvation is likewise the God of judgment. God hates sin and punishes it. Nothing is clearer in all the Bible than this fact. Nothing is clearer in all human experience than this fact. It is only a Bible-denying, fact-ignoring fool who will deny that a just and holy God must punish unrepentant sinners.

The same wicked people today, modernists and pacifists, are not for putting down Hitler. They are not for punishing crime. They are not for disciplining children. They are not for holy, Spirit-anointed preaching against sin. They do not hate sin, they do not want it punished. But the holy God of the Bible is not like these hypocrites who see no harm in sin and who do not want it punished.

The inhabitants of Jerusalem saw round about the besieged city the Babylonian armies. They feared the swords and spears and firebrands of the heathen nation. But if they had understood the vision of Ezekiel, they would have feared, instead, the angels of God going about with slaughter weapons smiting down the people who had turned their backs on God and gone into sin. They would have feared rather the fierce wrath of an angry God than the war-like prowess of Nebuchadnezzar's soldiers.

In Ezekiel, chapter 8, the prophet was shown in a vision the secret place of worship where the ancient men of Israel offered incense to idols. This represented the imagination of the hearts of the people. Their idolatry may have been kept secret, but God knew it. "Every form of creeping things, and abominable beasts, and all the idols of the house of Israel," were portrayed upon the walls of that secret place of worship revealed to Ezekiel. Then in the door of the gate of the Lord's house which was toward the north, women were weeping for the idol god, Tammuz, (Ezek. 8:14) equivalent to the Greek god, Adonis. The Webster's International Dictionary says, "The festival of Adonis was the *Adonia,* generally held at midsummer, at which the women first lamented his death and afterwards rejoiced in his resurrection." At the door of the temple, between the porch and the altar, Ezekiel was shown in the vision, "about five and twenty men, with their backs toward the temple of the Lord, and their faces toward the east; and they worshipped the sun toward the east." So the people of Jerusalem were guilty of every form of idolatry and religious abomination. For these things came the wrath of God on Jerusalem and fearful destruction.

It is foolish to believe that only the Old Testament pictures God as being angry with sinners and as bringing death and ruin upon them. The same God of judgment is revealed in the New Testament. Jesus, in Luke 13:1-5, tells how Galileans were slain by Pilate for their treachery, and how the tower of Siloam fell on eighteen men in Jerusalem and killed them. And then Jesus warned the public that this was the judgment of an angry God on sinners and He repeated twice the following warning, "Except ye repent, ye shall all likewise perish." Jesus Himself solemnly foretold the coming destruction of Jerusalem a second time, saying, "And they shall fall by the edge of the sword, and shall be led away captive into all nations: and Jerusalem shall be trodden down of the Gentiles, until the times of the Gentiles be fulfilled." This great prediction, given in detail in Luke 21:20-24, was fulfilled literally in A. D. 70 when Titus, with his Roman army, surrounded, besieged and took the city, with a terrible slaughter of over a million Jews (according to Josephus the historian), with the burning of the temple, and with multiplied thousands sold into slavery. Remember that that happened in New Testament times; Jesus foretold it as the judgment of an angry God, and it came to pass terribly. So the God of the Gospels is the God of judgment exactly in the same fashion that the God of the Old Testament is a God of judgment.

The book of Acts tells how God killed Ananias and Sapphira in a direct punishment of His wrath (Acts 5:5, 10); how King Herod sinned, "And immediately the angel of the Lord smote him, because he gave not God the glory: and he was eaten of worms, and gave up the ghost" (Acts 12:23); how Elymas the sorcerer was struck blind (Acts 13:11). The book of Revelation is a book foretelling terrible, bloody judgments upon nations, armies, cities and the whole world. The New Testament portrays the God who judges and punishes sin the same as the God portrayed by the Old Testament. Bloodshed, wars, disasters, earthquakes and pestilences are simply the instruments of God's vengeance on sinners.

May wicked sinners everywhere be warned to repent of their sins and seek the mercy of God before His wrath falls! If one read this who is unsaved, I warn you in the words of the Saviour Himself, "Except ye repent, ye shall all likewise perish."

Read again God's command to the six men (angels) with the slaughter weapons: "And to the others he said in mine hearing, Go ye after him through the city, and smite: let not your eye spare, neither have ye pity: Slay utterly old and young, both maids, and little children, and women."

V. "AND BEGIN AT MY SANCTUARY"

"Slay utterly old and young, both maids, and little children, and women: but come not near any man upon whom is the mark; *and begin at my sanctuary*. Then they began at the ancient men which were before the house" (Ezek. 9:6).

It is remarkable that the terrible sins for which God professed that He was bringing judgment on Jerusalem were largely centered about the temple. The idolatry was in the temple, or on the steps of the porch, or in the gate of the temple. And when judgment was to begin, the angels of destruction were warned to begin their bloody work "at my sanctuary." And we are told that, "Then they began at the ancient men which were before the house." The first to be killed were the people at the temple.

Verse 7 says, "And he said unto them, Defile the house, and fill the courts with the slain: go ye forth." How striking that God gave particular orders that the temple should be ceremonially defiled, that the first place bodies of men should fall would be in and about His own house, the temple! And this is God's behind-the-scenes picture of His own workings in having Jerusalem destroyed and the people slain and carried into captivity. I think Ezekiel's vision was before the siege was finished, before the destruction actually took place. But when it did take place, II Chronicles 36:19 says, "And they burnt the house of God, and brake down the wall of Jerusalem, and burnt all the palaces thereof with fire, and destroyed all the goodly vessels thereof." Actually when the siege was successful, when the Babylonish hordes broke into Jerusalem, the temple of God was the first place destroyed, it is indicated. God was angry at His people, and He had come to feel that the temple was a place of abominations. Similarly, in the New Testament, when Jesus was rejected by the Jews, He wept over Jerusalem that had killed the prophets, had stoned God's messengers, crying out, "How often would I have gathered thy children together, even as a hen gathereth her chickens under her wings, and ye would not!" Then He uttered the terrible curse (though they did not know it was a curse), "Behold, your house is left unto you desolate" (Matt. 23:37, 38).

Again, a few years after Jesus was crucified, Jerusalem was besieged and taken and destroyed with terrible slaughter, and again, this time contrary to the orders of Titus, the great temple was burned to the ground and later not one stone was left upon another! A place of worship where people do not have broken hearts, where they do not weep over their own sins and the sins of the people, becomes an abomination to God, which He is anxious to destroy! How God must hate some of our church buildings where there are no tears, no penitence.

In I Peter 4:17 we are told, "For the time is come that judgment must begin at the house of God: and if it first begin at us, what shall the end be of them that obey not the gospel of God?" Revival begins at the house of God, for II Chronicles 7:14 promises it, "If my people, which are called by my name, shall humble themselves, and pray, and seek my face, and turn from their wicked ways." And so judgment, punishment, begins also at the house of God. Do not blame lost people for the moral decline of this country. First, blame the people of God. First, blame the churches. First, blame us preachers. Do not blame sinners if they do not weep over their sins. First, blame us, the saints who do not weep. How should sinners be convicted when Christians are not convicted? How should sinners seek the church and seek God when the churches do not seek sinners? Oh, first of all, we need a sighing and a crying among the people of God over the abominations in the land, over the sins that grieve.God, over poor lost sinners that are undone and Hell-bound!

Do you think it was wholly incidental and accidental that in Russia at the very first of the revolution, the churches were burned, the priests were killed or sent to Siberia, religion was branded as the opiate of the people, and atheism was made the doctrine of communism? Do you think it was wholly incidental and accidental in Spain's revolution not long ago, that churches were burned and priests and nuns were killed by the hundreds? Remember that God is behind the scenes in these cataclysms. You thought it was the ungodly, atheistic, communistic assassins, hating the Bible and God, who were solely responsible for those horrible murders. They were horribly guilty, but God, who had begun judgment at the house of God, made the wrath of men to praise Him. I hate communism with a holy hatred. Though we were an ally of Russia in the past war, God keep us from condoning the horrible, unchristian, God-hating, undemocratic and inhuman ways of communism; her blood purges, her atheism, her oppression of the poor. Every Christian ought to shudder at the inroads of communism in America. But I solemnly declare that I believe cold, powerless, formal churches with no penitence for sins, no weeping over lost sinners, no burning of compassion for the dying, lost souls for whom Jesus died, are essentially little better than atheism. I believe God wants no churches where there is not a sighing and crying over sins and over sinners. I believe any Christianity without a burning evangelism is hypocrisy and abomination to God!

The declension, the apostasy, the breakdown of morals and character in America is chargeable to Christians, to churches, to preachers. America is now suffering expense, bloodshed and other punishment for our sins, brought on because we have failed God. And by *we* I mean we Christians. If America falls, if America is overrun with communism, if millions are slain in race riots and labor wars and the bloody wars which may come, then judgment will fall first of all upon the Christians in name, who do not sigh and who do not cry over sin and sinners. "Judgment must begin at the house of God." God gave Ezekiel this rule; "and begin at my sanctuary."

O Christians in America, repent! May God raise up brokenhearted Christians to seek God until revival comes, until mercy is poured out, until God's face shines upon us again in peace!

Will You Begin Definitely to Wait on God Each Day Until Revival Comes?

America needs the prayers of men and women 'who sigh and cry' over the sins of America and over lost sinners. Will you set aside a time every day for secret prayer, for confession, plead with God for a broken heart, plead with Him for a blessed revival in your community? If you feel a special burden of prayer we would like to hear from you, and when God answers with a precious revival we hope you will send us that good news.

Chapter 4.

THE CURSE OF HIDDEN SINS

ᴿᴼ⁻²⁶⁻⁸⁷

*"He that covereth his sins shall not prosper:
but whoso confesseth and forsaketh them shall
have mercy."*

—Prov. 28:13.

COVERED-UP SIN cannot get by! Sin unconfessed, unlamented, sin with an alibi,
sin that is excused, sin with no self-judgment, is certain to
bring the curse of a holy and righteous and angry God! It
would be well for you to memorize this text from Proverbs
28:13: "He that covereth his sins shall not prosper: but whoso
confesseth and forsaketh them shall have mercy." There is a
terrible curse, a woe, a plague, a condemnation of God on
hidden sin.

One of the most remarkable illustrations of the fact that
God cannot abide hidden sin, that it is certain to bring failure
and ruin, is found in the seventh chapter of Joshua where the
sin of Achan brought defeat in battle to the nation Israel until
he was hunted down and Achan and his family and all his
possessions destroyed. I want to take you through that entire
seventh chapter of Joshua of twenty-seven verses, and draw
some heart-moving lessons about the curse of God on hidden
sins.

In the preceding chapter, Joshua 6, we are told of the
marvelous capture of Jericho. For seven days Israel had
marched about the city; the seventh day they marched around
it seven times. The priests of God bore the ark, and the people followed. When the trumpets of rams' horns were blown,

all the people shouted, and the walls fell down flat! So they
went in and took the city. But God had plainly commanded
them:

*"And ye, in any wise keep yourselves from the accursed
thing, lest ye make yourselves accursed, when ye take of the
accursed thing, and make the camp of Israel a curse, and
trouble it. But all the silver, and gold, and vessels of brass and
iron, are consecrated unto the Lord: they shall come into the
treasury of the Lord."*

They took the city, by God's gracious blessing, without the
loss of a man. But alas! One man had sinned. As Joshua 7:1
tells us, "But the children of Israel committed a trespass in
the accursed thing: for Achan, the son of Carmi, the son of
Zabdi, the son of Zerah, of the tribe of Judah, took of the
accursed thing: and the anger of the Lord was kindled against
the children of Israel." Sin marred sweet fellowship between
God and His people. Sin stopped the flow of His power, the
smile of His blessing! Let us read the remainder of the chapter, passage by passage, as we find God's lessons for us about
the curse of hidden sin.

1. Sin Brings Defeat, Failure, Ruin!

*"And Joshua sent men from Jericho to Ai, which is beside
Bethaven, on the east side of Bethel, and spake unto them,
saying, Go up and view the country. And the men went up
and viewed Ai. And they returned to Joshua, and said unto
him, Let not all the people go up; but let about two or three
thousand men go up and smite Ai; and make not all the people to labour thither; for they are but few. So there went up
thither of the people about three thousand men: and they
fled before the men of Ai. And the men of Ai smote of them
about thirty and six men: for they chased them from before
the gate even unto Shebarim, and smote them in the going
down: wherefore the hearts of the people melted, and became
as water."*   —Josh. 7:2–5.

There was a sin undiscovered, unrepented, unconfessed between God and Israel! So the boldness that God had put in the hearts of the Israelite soldiers departed. Three thousand men turned and ran like children before the enemy! Thirty-six men were killed. Shame and disgrace and a sense of utter disaster settled upon the whole nation of Israel.

But that is exactly what the Scripture forewarns in Proverbs 28:13. "He that covereth his sins shall not prosper." Covered sins bring failure. And I think we may properly say that the converse of this statement is often true. Failure is caused by sin. Failure, defeat, is God's red light warning us of danger. We have incurred His wrath, His anger, we have grieved His holy heart by our sins, and for that reason, God does not allow us to prosper.

I know that some people, like Job, suffer to the glory of God, and for the good of multitudes, whose sins are not responsible for their sufferings. I know that some people, like the martyr Stephen who was stoned, and like Paul with his thorn in the flesh, suffered to the glory of God when their own sins, as far as we can tell, were not to blame. Poverty and sickness and tribulation are not always the proofs of hidden sins, nor the evidence of God's displeasure. But on the other hand it is only fair to say that Job was truly prospering when he suffered, though he did not know it at the time. And Stephen's highest hour on this earth was when flying stones broke his bones, his face shining like that of an angel when he went to meet his Saviour who stood at the right hand of the Father to receive Him! And Paul's thorn in the flesh was his secret of success. None of these tribulations or burdens could be called a curse; rather they were blessings.

But even physical sickness and trouble is often clearly a sign of God's displeasure for our sins. In I Corinthians 11 we are told that men of Corinth had partaken of the Lord's Supper unworthily and that "For this cause many are weak and sickly among you, and many sleep. For if we would judge ourselves, we should not be judged. But when we are judged,

we are chastened of the Lord, that we should not be condemned with the world" (I Cor. 11:30–32).

Many people at Corinth had already died, and many were
weak and sickly, all as God's judgment on their sins. Though
these were Christians, born-again people, they did not prosper, and it was because of their sins. Their sins were covered,
unconfessed, unjudged. So failure and sickness and even
death came to them!

In James 5:16 those who want healing for the body are
plainly told, "Confess your faults one to another, and pray
one for another, that ye may be healed." This and many other
Scriptures indicate that sickness is often the natural and in-
evitable result of sin. People do not prosper because they
have not confessed and forsaken their sin. Financial failure,
poor crops, broken homes, accidents, disease, financial re-
verses—all these are the natural fruit of unconfessed and unlamented sin. "He that covereth his sins shall not prosper."

And how much more is this true of spiritual matters. Sometimes the most real prosperity is when we are in poverty or
when the body is wracked with pain. So we cannot always
judge by financial failure or success, by physical health or
sickness, whether one is really prospering with God. We may
frankly confess that sometimes it is not best for God's people to prosper too much in physical and material matters.
Money may be a curse; even prolonged good health may not
be the best in some cases.

But always it is God's will that Christians should prosper
spiritually. Always God wants His people to have their prayers answered and their hearts full of joy, for Jesus said,
"Hitherto have ye asked nothing in my name: ask, and ye
shall receive, that your joy may be full" (John 16:24). Always
God wants His people to have singing hearts, for He commanded us, "Be filled with the Spirit; Speaking to yourselves
in psalms and hymns and spiritual songs, singing and making
melody in your heart to the Lord" (Eph. 5:18, 19). The
Saviour wants us always to be conscious of His presence, for
He promised those who would carry out the Great Commis-

sion, "Lo, I am with you alway, even unto the end of the world" (Matt. 28:20). Always it is God's will for Christians to have soul-winning power, the marvelous power of the Holy Spirit. For it is promised, "But the manifestation of the Spirit is given to every man to profit withal" (I Cor. 12:7). And again, "If ye then, being evil, know how to give good gifts unto your children: how much more shall your heavenly Father give the Holy Spirit to them that ask him?" (Luke 11:13). Christians *ought* to be prosperous in spiritual matters all the time. And if we are not, the text in Proverbs 28:13 gives us the reason why. "He that covereth his sins shall not prosper: but whoso confesseth and forsaketh them shall have mercy." If we do not prosper materially, it is sometimes because of unconfessed and unforsaken sins! If we do not prosper *spiritually*, it is ALWAYS the result of hidden sin!

Oh, you who are praying for revival, open your ears to this truth of God's Word! It is sin, unconfessed sin in the hearts and lives of God's people, sin in the churches, sin in the preachers, sin in the Sunday School teachers, sin in the officers of the church, sin in the church members that blocks the power of God! If pastors preach with little blessing, sin is the reason. If the Holy Spirit of God does not move with heavenly fragrance over the hearts of the people in your services, it is because of unconfessed and unforsaken sin! If sinners are not convicted at the preaching, if they do not attend the services, if they will not listen to the invitation to attend services or to hear the gospel or to be saved, then sin in the lives of God's people is the reason! "He that covereth his sins shall not prosper." The churches have covered their sins, and they do not prosper.

The lost note in evangelism is the condemnation, the exposure of sin. The command of Christ we do not emphasize is the command to repent! Some people do not like evangelism. They deplore any preaching against sin, any stirring of guilty consciences, any ferment of unrest in the churches.

Again and again pastors have been fearful and nervous, thinking it would lead to disaster when I preached so plainly and pointedly against sin and when I made the application personal and embarrassing. Pastors are often afraid the evangelist will drive people away, that church members will quit coming or will quit giving, that lost sinners will be offended and will be turned away from the gospel by such pointed preaching against sin. But, praise God, in numberless cases the timid pastors' fears have been proven unfounded and they have learned that only by repentance regarding sin can God's people have a revival. There is no way to get God's favor back on the churches and His revival power in evidence again in America except by getting God's people to confess and forsake their sins.

All over America preachers speak continually about God's love, about Calvary, about grace, about believing on Christ, about being kind and courteous, and loving everybody; and yet they have no revivals. God's people do not feel the breath of Heaven. Lost sinners are not convicted and are not saved. The work steadily declines, the crowds diminish, the influence of the church deteriorates. What is wrong? What is wrong is that these preachers all have the cart before the horse. When defeat and disaster and failure are around the church of God it is because of sin, and we cannot hope for God's blessings until we face that fact and deal with sin. A man has to be sick before you can get him to call a doctor. Dr. Joe Henry Hankins well says, "You must get a man lost before you can get him saved." To bring a revival in any locality. God's preacher and God's people must begin to face honestly the fact of their sins and confess and forsake these things that grieve God and have brought failure and ruin to His cause in that particular locality.

2. There Are Times When Something Else Must Come Before Prayer!

Let us read further in the divinely inspired story.

"And Joshua rent his clothes, and fell to the earth upon his face before the ark of the Lord until the eventide, he

and the elders of Israel, and put dust upon their heads. And Joshua said, Alas, O Lord God, wherefore hast thou at all brought this people over Jordan, to deliver us into the hand of the Amorites, to destroy us? would to God we had been content, and dwelt on the other side Jordan! O Lord, what shall I say, when Israel turneth their backs before their enemies! For the Canaanites and all the inhabitants of the land shall hear of it, and shall environ us round, and cut off our name from the earth: and what wilt thou do unto thy great name? And the Lord said unto Joshua, Get thee up; wherefore liest thou thus upon thy face? Israel hath sinned, and they have also transgressed my covenant which I commanded them: for they have even taken of the accursed thing, and have also stolen, and dissembled also, and they have put it even among their own stuff. Therefore the children of Israel could not stand before their enemies, but turned their backs before their enemies, because they were accursed: neither will I be with you any more, except ye destroy the accursed from among you. Up, sanctify the people, and say, Sanctify yourselves against to morrow: for thus saith the Lord God of Israel, There is an accursed thing in the midst of thee, O Israel: thou canst not stand before thine enemies, until ye take away the accursed thing from among you."

—Josh. 7:6–13.

Someone has said, "There is nothing you can do as important as prayer, until after you have prayed." In most cases, no doubt, this is true. But the passage above shows us that sometimes prayer is out of order; that prayer will not get results; that something else must come, before God will hear prayer. Here we have the remarkable spectacle of Joshua on his face before God, weeping, praying, and the Lord saying to him roughly, "Get thee up; wherefore liest thou thus upon thy face?" God plainly told Joshua that Israel had sinned, and that all the praying he could do and Israel could do would not receive an answer until they remedied the wrong that had been done. God said, "Neither will I be with you any

more, except ye destroy the accursed from among you," and
again, "Thou canst not stand before thine enemies, until ye
take away the accursed thing from among you" (vs. 12, and
13). There are times when God will not hear. There are
occasions when repentance and restitution are far more important than any words we can utter in prayer, any praises we
can give, any request we can make! There are times when
God demands action instead of words.

Remember how the Saviour said in Matthew 5:23, 24,
"Therefore if thou bring thy gift to the altar, and there re-
memberest that thy brother hath ought against thee; Leave
there thy gift before the altar, and go thy way; first be reconciled to thy brother, and then come and offer thy gift."

If you have anything to offer God, first go be reconciled to
your brother. First, go try with an honest heart to make right
the sin you have done! Before you sing for God, or preach for
God, or give money for God, or pray to God, confess and forsake your sin!

A remarkable book on revival is *"By My Spirit"* by Dr.
Jonathan Goforth. It tells of a great revival that came to the
mission field in China, where Dr. Goforth was a Presbyterian
missionary. Many thousands were saved, the churches were
revived and blessed in a remarkable manner. And everywhere, as Dr. Goforth tells us, the revival started the same
way, with heartbroken confession of sin! His preaching was
about sin, particularly the sins of Christians. Confessing and
forsaking sin brings God's blessings, His poured-out mercy,
His reviving power!

Dear Christian, why beseech God for His blessing, His
power, His manifest presence, when there is sin unconfessed
and unlamented, sin covered up in your life? I say to you
earnestly, that there is no use to pray, no use to read the
Bible, no use to try to serve God, unless you will honestly set
out to uncover the sins in your life that grieve the Holy Spirit
and bring you failure. The way to the fulness of God's bless-

ing is not first in prayer, except as we honestly seek for God to show us the sins that grieve Him and ask for grace to do right in confessing and making restitution for our sins first. After you have honestly faced your sin, have found and confessed and repudiated the thing that is grieving God in your life, then you have a right to pray, to wait on Him for His power and blessing, to beseech Him with tears and pleadings. It is wonderful to pray when we are "on praying ground and pleading terms with God," as our fathers used to say. But many prayers never get as high as the ceiling. To many of us on our knees, God would say, "Get thee up; wherefore liest thou thus upon thy face?" and "Neither will I be with you any more, except ye destroy the accursed from among you," just as He said to Joshua.

In II Chronicles 7:14 the Lord promises that "If my people, which are called by my name, shall humble themselves, and pray, and seek my face, *and turn from their wicked ways;* then will I hear from heaven, and will forgive their sin, and will heal their land." So for revival and blessing, God's people need to have the humility to see their lack and their distance from God, and connected with their praying they must 'forsake their wicked way' and not until then will God hear.

If sin brings failure to the Lord's work, and defeat to His people, then it is also true that only sin—unconfessed, unlamented, unrepented sin—can keep a poor lost sinner from Jesus Christ and salvation! The only people who go to Hell are those who have not confessed and, in their hearts, forsaken their sin.

You can preach until you are black in the face, of the wonderful love that Jesus Christ has, of the great price He paid on Calvary, of His free offer of mercy, and you will not have anybody saved unless you get people to face their sins and repent of their sins. Before Jesus gave Nicodemus the Pharisee that world-famous promise in John 3:16, He had to tell Nicodemus three times that he must be born again or never see the kingdom of God: that that which is born of the flesh is, after all, of the flesh, and cannot see God in peace. Before Jesus could say to the woman at the well of Sychar, in Samaria, that He Himself was the Messiah, He had to probe her heart, to call her attention to her many husbands and the one with whom she was living then who was not her husband. When she was conscious of her sins, so much so that she could say to the men in the city, "Come see a man that told me all things that ever I did," He was then ready to announce Himself as the Saviour for sinners such as she was.

My wife once talked to a lost woman without any results. Later she said to me, "I did not know where to begin. I could not find a point of contact. How should I begin to talk to a woman like that?" And I replied, "Always begin on the point of sin." There every person with a conscience is defenseless. And the matter of sin is where God wants every sinner to begin, in turning to God. In other words, a sinner must repent to be saved. "He that covereth his sins shall not prosper: but whoso confesseth and forsaketh them shall have mercy."

I say, there is no use to pray when there are known sins unconfessed to God, unlamented, unrepented of, that grieve God and turn away His face from us.

3. "Israel Hath Sinned"—A Whole Nation Held Accountable for One Man's Sin Until It Is Exposed and Punished

Do you think God would blame Joshua for the secret sin of Achan, which he had not seen, of which he had not approved, and of which he had not before even heard? That is exactly what God did!

In verse 11 God said, *"Israel* hath sinned, and *they* have also transgressed my covenant which I commanded them: for *they* have even taken of the accursed thing, and have also stolen, and dissembled also, and *they* have put it even among their own stuff."

Although one man sinned, the whole nation was held

guilty, until they uncovered that sin and punished it! A whole army was defeated. Some thirty-six men were killed. A nation was in distress, because of one man's sin.

And later, when Achan died, his sons and daughters were slain also, as if they were parties to the sin. No doubt in some sense they were.

Christians dare not be indifferent to the wickedness that goes on around them. Do you think that God would hold Christian people who never drink and never sell liquor or beer or wine, guilty along with the tavern-keepers and brewers and distillers? Does God hold preachers and devout Christians to blame for America's drunkenness? Yes, He does! We helped elect the politicians who brought back liquor. The evil administration which led in the repeal of the eighteenth amendment could never have been elected without church people. In any local area the sentiment against drink could have been overwhelming if people of God had taken a stand.

How many of you readers eat meals in hotels or restaurants where beer is served, where wine is on the menu? Shame upon you! You are a partner of the liquor business! Your money supports their business. Your influence makes easy the ruin of girls, the debauching of young men, the corruption of government, carried on by the liquor business. You are a helper to those who make paupers and harlots and criminals!

America is guilty. Ungodly people cry out that "preachers must keep out of politics" if we solemnly warn the people of the results of sin, if we condemn the godlessness and immorality and criminality of the liquor interests and of other protected vice. But before God we are wicked sinners, guilty with all America of her sins, if we do not rebuke them. The preacher is a prophet of God. The church should speak out against sin, as Christ would do. Part of the reason the churches have lost their influence with men and their power with God in America is that preachers have turned out to be weaklings who do not hate sin, who are not bold in denouncing wickedness, and who do not call on people for repentance. Any real revival, widespread, in the churches, will require that preachers and churches begin to take the blame for the moral lapses in America and confess their guilt and failure.

How *could* God give a revival in a church holding lewd, licentious dances for soldiers (or for anybody else)? How could God send a revival to churches whose officials own property rented out for taverns, with the church treasury reaping part of the profits? When I spoke along this line once, a pastor, after the meeting, came to me and said, "What can I do? Did you see that large sign of a beer distributor downtown? That business is owned by the most influential Christian man in my church. When we need money, he will give me any amount I need for a good cause." I say to you that God will not pour out a revival on a church where His blessing would make Him a partner in wickedness.

Let us repeat it, that repentance is a duty of preachers and bartenders alike, of church ladies and harlots alike. "Israel hath sinned," said the Lord. We must feel our guilt for the souls around about us, for sinners we have not warned, for sin we have not rebuked, for our complacent toleration of wickedness that has grieved God. See how Daniel and Nehemiah confessed their part in the guilt of their nation, in Daniel 9:3–19 and Nehemiah 1:6, 7.

Joshua knew nothing about Achan's sin. *But he ought to have known!* God's command had been explicit and urgent, that no one should touch the treasure; it belonged to God. Joshua should have set measures in action that would have insured that God's plan would have been carried out. The whole nation knew about God's command. Every individual in it ought to have been carefully watching himself, his family, his neighbors, to help see that all did right and no curse should come from God because of sin. About such matters we cannot say with Cain, "Am I my brother's keeper?" It is not only our business to know how the other half of the world lives: we are accountable to God, in some sense, for their sin.

At first it may seem heartless and cruel that God should have Achan's children stoned and their bodies burned for their father's sin. But how could a Babylonish garment and two hundred shekels of silver, and a wedge of gold of fifty shekels' weight be brought into the tent, a hole dug, and the treasure hidden in the earth in the midst of the tent, without others knowing of it? If they were not active partners in the crime, they were passive accomplices. The Scripture says, "Happy is he that condemneth not himself in that thing which he alloweth" (Rom. 14:22). If we permit sin in those for whom we are accountable, if we ignore sin in those we might influence, yea, if we do not rebuke sin and take sides against it all about us, then we are accountable to God as sinners. The whole nation Israel entered into the curse of Achan's hidden sin because they had not opposed it, had not sought it out, had not punished it. God could not give Israel victory until they brought Achan to judgment.

4. Find the Sin Yourself!

God did not tell Joshua who had committed the terrible sin against God. He would not tell Joshua even to what family, what household, or what tribe the sinner belonged. JOSHUA HAD TO FIND THAT OUT FOR HIMSELF!

The story continues, in the words of Holy Scripture, as follows:

"In the morning therefore ye shall be brought according to your tribes: and it shall be, that the tribe which the Lord taketh shall come according to the families thereof; and the family which the Lord shall take shall come by households; and the household which the Lord shall take shall come man by man. And it shall be, that he that is taken with the accursed thing shall be burnt with fire, he and all that he hath: because he hath transgressed the covenant of the Lord, and because he hath wrought folly in Israel. So Joshua rose up early in the morning, and brought Israel by their tribes; and the tribe of Judah was taken: And he brought the family of

*Judah; and he took the family of the Zarhites: and he brought
the family of the Zarhites man by man; and Zabdi was taken:
And he brought his household man by man; and Achan, the
son of Carmi, the son of Zabdi, the son of Zerah, of the tribe
of Judah, was taken."*   —Josh. 7:14–18.

Are we accountable for sin that we do not know? Yes! It is
our *business* to know. We ought to be so diligently on the
lookout for sin in our own lives that we would know it when
it appears.

A man said to me, "Well, if the use of tobacco is a sin, why
doesn't God convict me of it? When I feel convicted, then I
will be ready to quit, but not before." I told the man that he
was wrong in placing the responsibility on God about his sin.
If he honestly wanted to know whether he was right in de-
filing his body, the temple of the Holy Spirit, or whether
Jesus, our Example, would have used tobacco, or whether the
use of tobacco would be a bad influence on young people and
a bad testimony before the world, he could certainly find out.
It is not God's responsibility to make us know what any one
could see if he sought to know. *We* are the ones who have
broken the contact, the fellowship with God. If God had
wronged us, and so broken fellowship with men, it would be
God's part to find out what was wrong and correct it. Since
we sin against God and break the fellowship it is always our
responsibility to find the hindering cause and make it right.

Israel had sinned; so Israel must find the sinner and punish
the sin and take sides with God against wickedness. God demanded that the whole nation be arrayed, tribe by tribe, to
stand before God, that the guilty sinner who had brought the
curse might be discovered. God would help if they were
willing to search. The tribe of Reuben stood before the Lord,
but the guilty one was not there. He was not found in the
tribe of Simeon, nor of Levi. How relieved each whole tribe
must have been to find the terrible sinner was not in their
ranks! But when the tribe of Judah stood before God, God
said, 'He is in this tribe!' Then family by family, household

by household, and at last, man by man, God went with them through the tribe until Achan was found. I imagine that there was an awe, a sense of solemn fear, as the nation waited before God, earnestly seeking to find who it was had broken God's law, had stolen God's treasure and had the accursed thing hid.

I confess to a sense of sorrow that it was in the tribe of Judah Achan was found. In the very tribe from which our Saviour was to appear, was found the man whose sin had brought defeat to the whole nation of Israel! And so often, in some part of our lives that may seem holy or innocent, something is found that grieves God and blocks His power and has ruined the sweet fellowship of a Christian with the Holy Spirit of God.

If you do not have an overflowing life of blessing; if you do not win souls, many of them; if defeat and failure are yours; then will you be honest with God? Will you set out to seek diligently, in all your habits, in all your heart's desires, in all the things you do and think and love, find the Achan in your heart? I plead with you, be merciless in your search of your own heart and life. Do not excuse! Do not cover up! Do not give an alibi, and do not blame others. Find that hidden Achan in your heart and life and drag him out before God and there pass judgment upon him. Confess and forsake the sin that has grieved God.

Too many people say, "I will quit drinking, if God will take the taste of liquor away," or "I will give my unconverted sweetheart up, if God will take him out of my life." Oh, my friend, hunt out your sin *yourself.* If it is the sin of drink, then give it up, though you may have to fight a flaming thirst until you die! God will help you if you really want to find the Achan in your own life and heart.

5. The Progress of Sin; 'I Saw, I Coveted, I Took, I Hid.'

Achan, faced with the fact that his sin stood open before God, and that he must be punished, shamefacedly told the story of his sin. In Joshua 7:19–21, the story continues:

"And Joshua said unto Achan, My son, give, I pray thee, glory to the Lord God of Israel, and make confession unto him; and tell me now what thou hast done; hide it not from me. And Achan answered Joshua, and said, Indeed I have sinned against the Lord God of Israel, and thus and thus have I done: When I saw among the spoils a goodly Babylonish garment, and two hundred shekels of silver, and a wedge of gold of fifty shekels weight, then I coveted them, and took them; and, behold, they are hid in the earth in the midst of my tent, and the silver under it."

Note the progress of Achan's sin. "When I *saw* among the spoils a goodly Babylonish garment, and two hundred shekels of silver, and a wedge of gold of fifty shekels weight . . ." About some things, at least, it is true that ignorance is the handmaid of innocence. Paul said, "In malice be ye children" (I Cor. 14:20). It is far best for the Christian never to see some things, so he will never want them. The old-fashioned Christian who will not have playing cards in his house will never learn to gamble with them. One who never sees, in movies and night clubs or elsewhere, half-clothed girls, drinking, smoking, gambling, petting, making love to many men, is likely to miss being led into that kind of life by these sirens of sin. It is the Devil's game to make people think it necessary for people to "know the ways of the world," to "sow a few wild oats." How precious is the virgin mind that does not know much about sin! How I thank God that I was saved as a boy of nine! Achan saw, gazed at, admired the Babylonish garment, the two hundred shekels of silver, the wedge of gold, before he coveted and took them and hid them.

But *seeing* led to *coveting*. A Christian might drink only ginger ale at the tavern bar, but there he is already on the way to drinking beer and whiskey. The girl who attends a ball but never dances a step, will soon surrender her body to the lustful embrace of every casual male acquaintance as other dancers do. The boy who hangs about with gamblers will become a gambler. Coveting follows seeing!

And Achan then *took* the forbidden treasures. He doubtless never would have thought he would be guilty of such a sin! The fallen girl never intended to be a harlot. Ask the drunken bum, and he will tell you that he never intended to lose wife and children and job and health and character to become the sot, the bleary-eyed creature without manhood that he is. David was the pure in heart, but when he gazed on Bathsheba taking her bath, and had her brought to his house, then he committed the terrible sin. Mark it down, that there is no limit to the grossness of the sin that any person living may commit, *if only* he puts himself continually under the influence of temptation! The only safety even for Joseph, that stainless hero of the Old Testament, was to flee in fear from Potiphar's wife. The only safety for any Christian is to shun even the appearance of evil, to hate even the garment spotted by the flesh, to flee from youthful lusts. What you never covet, you will not take. If you do not allow yourself to be tempted, you will not fall. So the Saviour taught us to pray, "Lead us not into temptation."

Then Achan *hid* the stolen treasure. After we commit our sins, then we must rationalize them, must excuse them, must make an alibi for them. We feel we must defend ourselves by blaming others, by saying this is not as bad as that. Stealing the treasure was a wicked sin; hiding it was worse. And Christian, that sin which first came between you and God is bad, but that is not the last step in the progress of sin. The most guilty part in this quadruple sin is to hide it, deny it, ignore it, refuse to confess it, refuse to repent of it!

6. Hidden in the Tent

Joshua 7:22, 23 says,

"So Joshua sent messengers, and they ran unto the tent; and, behold, it was hid in his tent, and the silver under it. And they took them out of the midst of the tent, and brought them unto Joshua, and unto all the children of Israel, and laid them out before the Lord."

In public Achan probably seemed as good an Israelite as anyone in the camp! The public part of godliness he may have observed as well as any Levite. Perhaps he did not work on the Jewish Sabbath. Perhaps he was careful never to eat pork. It is probable he brought the tithe of his flocks as sacrifices, just as did other good Jews. But Achan's sin was not in public; it was in private. It was not in the house of worship, but back hidden in his own tent!

A woman who had sung in the choir and taught a Sunday School class, deeply convicted by my preaching, wrote to tell me how she had murdered her unborn babies. So nice, so religious, so faithful in public; so wicked, so black her sin in secret at home! A popular preacher preached to big crowds, was greatly loved and admired for his pulpit eloquence, until it was discovered that he lived a double life; that in his secret life there was a black shadow that made it impossible for his people to listen to him again, except with shame and disgust! A deacon in a north Texas church was an active Sunday School worker, took a leading part in laymen's programs, but it was discovered that for two years he had been living the life of a thief, stealing again and again from the express company. It is not surprising that Achan's stolen property, the accursed things, were hidden in the floor of his tent.

O Christian, do not believe that there is nothing wrong with your life because you attend church, sing in the choir, because you give of your money or testify in prayer meeting. It is not so much in public but in private that our lives dishonor God and our sins bring failure and defeat and the curse of God upon us. Search rather in the secret closets of your heart. See what you love and what you hate. Look at the motives that control your actions. Are you a Pharisee, doing the outward deeds of Christianity to be seen of men? Or are you willing to unroll all the secret thoughts and processes of your heart before the Lord Jesus and with tears beg Him to be Master of them all? Are you willing to unlock every closet door in your being, lay every affection on the altar, as Abraham bound Isaac on the altar of sacrifice? I beg you, do not finish this paragraph without asking God to show you the things in your own deceitful heart that may grieve Him and dishonor Him and withdraw His sweet communion from you!

Some person reads this sermon, no doubt, who has never been born again, who has never known what it is to come to Christ as a poor, condemned sinner, confessing your sin, begging Him to forgive and save you, and trusting Him to do it, once and for all. Well, if you have not come to Christ like that, if you have not been born again, if you have not been converted, if you have not been given a new heart by trusting Christ to forgive you and save you, I know why. I know what is back of your rejection of Christ. It is a black, hideous, wicked thing. Whatever excuses and alibis you make, they are not the real reasons you are not a Christian.

It is true there are hypocrites in the church. Judas, a hypocrite, was among the first twelve disciples. It is true that preachers are not all they ought to be. In fact, they are human beings like everybody else, tempted, falling short, sometimes worldly-minded, never able to be quite the men they long to be, even the purest and best of them. You say, "Well, I am afraid I cannot live right." Perhaps you couldn't. You are not perfect and you never will be until, if you trust in Christ, you are caught up to meet Christ, and are made perfect in His likeness. It may be true, as you say, that you "do not feel like being a Christian." But back of all these silly excuses is one dark, hidden, secret and wicked reason. You really are not a Christian because you do not love Christ. You love your sin. In John 3:19–21 Jesus said,

"And this is the condemnation, that light is come into the world, and men loved darkness rather than light, because their deeds were evil. For every one that doeth evil hateth the light, neither cometh to the light, lest his deeds should be reproved. But he that doeth truth cometh to the light, that his deeds may be made manifest, that they are wrought in God."

You see, Jesus knew your heart, and He knew that there is only one reason you do not come to Christ and be saved. You love your sin. You are not willing for Christ to rebuke your sin. You are not willing for Him to have first place. You want to have your own way. In your case it is true as in the case of every lost man living that "light is come into the world, and men loved darkness rather than light, because their deeds were evil." Christ, the light of the world, has appeared to you, has knocked at the door of your heart. You turn Him down for the same reason that wicked Pharisees crucified Him. In your wicked heart you do not love Him. You do not want what He has. You do not want to give up your sins. You do not want to have a new heart. You hold onto your sins, reject the Saviour, and so damn your own soul!

This is one reason why I believe that preachers and every soul winner ought to go after sinners, hammer and tongs, with tender love, yes, but with bold accusations. We ought to love sinners, oh, yes; but we ought not to believe their alibis, their silly excuses. We ought to know that hidden in the tent of every unconverted man's heart is the wicked, blasphemous, hellish rejection of Christ, the deliberate choice of sin instead of the Saviour. Sinners do not turn down Jesus Christ for any good reason. Always it is this wicked reason of a love for sin, a holding onto the forbidden, a rebellion against the right and good that God has in mind for them. That is the reason Christ-rejecting sinners will go to Hell, and ought to go to Hell. There is the blackest sin in their hearts. And not only is there sin but a *love* for sin in the heart of every unconverted person.

I remember only one man who ever told me the truth about why he was not saved. In a country revival service I asked a man, "Are you a Christian?"

"No!" he bluntly answered.

"Don't you want to be?" I said.

He answered, "Well, if I wanted to be a Christian I could be, could I not?"

I answered, "Yes, of course you could. Christ is willing to save you tonight."

"Then I guess I don't want to be, or I would be," he answered insolently.

Yes, he was right. He was not a Christian because he did not want to be. You, poor sinner, poor unconverted enemy of Jesus Christ, are not a Christian because you do not want to be. You want your sin. You may lie about it, you may cover over your sin, but the fact remains you do not love Christ, you do not want Him; rather you want your sin and hold onto it.

Poor sinner, that course will take you to Hell, for "He that covereth his sins shall not prosper," says the text of Proverbs 28:13. You must uncover that sin, open up that wicked heart, confess your sin and repent of it, if you would be saved.

7. The Terrible Judgment of God Upon Unforgiven Sin

Infidels and modernists who do not want to repent of their sin, are bold in their criticism of the Bible. They say that the Old Testament pictures an angry, vengeful, tribal God. They cannot believe in any God who would bring a flood to destroy a race, or any God who would command the destruction of the Amalekites, or the God who would have Achan and his children stoned and their bodies burned. But frankly, the God of the Old Testament is the God of the New. And the God who demanded judgment on sin in the case of Achan is the same God of whom Christ told us, "Which is able to destroy both soul and body in hell" (Matt. 10:28). Christ Himself spoke more about God's judgment on sin, God's wrath, and the torments of Hell, than did any prophet of either the Old Testament or the New Testament!

This terrible sin of Achan, in boldly disobeying God, in hiding the stolen treasure in his tent, might have been the ruin of the whole nation. Such gross and deliberate sin demanded public punishment. That terrible punishment is told in Joshua 7:24-26,

*"And Joshua, and all Israel with him, took Achan the son
of Zerah, and the silver, and the garment, and the wedge of
gold, and his sons, and his daughters, and his oxen, and his
asses, and his sheep, and his tent, and all that he had: and
they brought them unto the valley of Achor. And Joshua said,
Why hast thou troubled us? the Lord shall trouble thee this
day. And all Israel stoned him with stones, and burned them
with fire, after they had stoned them with stones. And they
raised over him a great heap of stones unto this day. So the
Lord turned from the fierceness of his anger. Wherefore the
name of that place was called, The valley of Achor, unto
this day."*

As Joshua and all Israel took Achan and stoned him, his
sons, his daughters, his oxen, his asses, his sheep and his tent
and all that he had, and burned what was left of them with
fire, no doubt many lips quivered with deep emotion, and
many eyes were red-rimmed from weeping. It was such a
lesson as to impress all Israel with the terrible nature of sin,
and of God's all-consuming wrath on sin when it is covered
and not confessed. In that valley of Achor, they covered the
burned, broken bones of the man they had publicly executed,
with a great mound of stones as a perennial warning to the
people of Israel that sin must be punished.

And I warn you, poor unsaved reader, that the fires of
eternal Hell and torment burn hot today for Christ-rejecting
sinners like you. It is true that God loves sinners, loves the
whole world, as John 3:16 says. But in the same chapter John
3:36 says, "He that believeth on the Son hath everlasting life:
and he that believeth not the Son shall not see life; BUT
THE WRATH OF GOD ABIDETH ON HIM." God's
wrath stays, day by day, on every poor Christ-rejecting sinner!
God's indignation grows over your sin. Punishment must be
yours if you do not repent. And unless you repent in time,
Hell's eternal punishment and ruin must be God's judgment
on your sin. A holy God cannot let sin get by. It is only fair,
only honest, only right, that sin must be punished. Every law

on the statute books, every courthouse, every jail, every policeman on the corner, adds its testimony to the deliberate opinion of all mankind, that sin must be punished.

8. Achan Need Not Have Died!

The story in the seventh chapter of Joshua is done, but I revert to the text in Proverbs 28:13: "He that covereth his sins shall not prosper: but whoso confesseth and forsaketh them shall have mercy." Achan covered his sin. He hid his stolen treasures. He did not confess his sins until they were already discovered. He never seemed willing to admit, even then, the terrible nature of his guilt. So Achan died in a public execution, at the direct command of God. But Achan need not have died!

Our text says that "Whoso confesseth and forsaketh them shall have mercy." God is a just God, but He is also merciful. God is a righteous, a holy God, but He loves sinners. God must judge and must punish unconfessed, unrepented sin; but praise His merciful name, He is willing to forgive us when we confess our sins!

After all, it was not sin alone that led Achan to his terrible doom. It was holding onto his sin, covering up his sin.

Let us imagine a scene that did not happen. I see Achan come in with his guilty treasures, hastily dig a hole in the dirt floor of his tent. I see him wrap the wedge of gold and the two hundred shekels of silver in the Babylonish garment, then wrap the whole bundle in a skin, perhaps, then cover it up. But suppose Achan had suddenly begun to weep, and frantically dig his buried treasure out of the earth. Suppose he had taken it in his arms and run to Joshua, weeping and saying, "Oh, God forgive me; what a sin I have committed; Joshua, please pray for me. I stole a Babylonish garment, and two hundred shekels of silver, and a wedge of gold. They belonged to God, and when we were sacking the city of Jericho I took them, against God's command. I will bring a lamb for a sacrifice. I will restore the things I stole. I confess my sin before God and before all Israel. Oh, pray for me, that I may have mercy and forgiveness!"

Does any reader here believe that God would have commanded Achan to be stoned? No, no! "He that covereth his sins shall not prosper: but whoso confesseth and forsaketh them shall have mercy." Achan, if he had been willing to turn from his sin, confess his sin, forsake his sin in time, would have been forgiven. Achan need not have died. He could have repented and so have been forgiven and saved.

Dear Christian, your failure is not simply that you have sinned. Every child of God sins. Jesus Himself taught us to pray every day, "Our Father which are in heaven . . . forgive us our sins" (Luke 11:2, 4). So He knew that this matter of sin would be a daily burden to honest Christians. But failure and defeat and the curse of God does not come upon us so much because we have sinned, as because we *cover* our sins. We do not hate them. We do not take sides against them. We do not weep over them. We do not try to make restitution for them. God forgive us, our sins come between us and God because we do not honestly repent of them with all of our hearts!

There is only one way for daily cleansing and daily victory for a Christian, and that way is by daily confessing and daily turning from our sin. First John 1:9 is for Christians, and in it we are plainly given this beautiful promise: "If we confess our sins, he is faithful and just to forgive us our sins, and to cleanse us from all unrighteousness." We can have daily mercy, daily cleansing, if we daily confess our sins and turn our hearts away from them. Thank God for the forgiveness; and thank God again for the cleansing! We can have not only forgiveness for our sins day by day, but we can have such cleansing as will help us overcome the things we hate that dishonor God.

Every Christian ought to be able daily to look up into the heart of God and cry out, in the words of the familiar and beloved old song,

Return, O heavenly Dove, return,
  Sweet messenger of rest.
I hate the sins that made thee mourn
And drove Thee from my breast.

The dearest idol I have known,
  Whate'er that idol be,
Help me to tear it from Thy throne
And worship only Thee.

God's children do not have to be chastised if we confess and forsake our sins. "For if we would judge ourselves, we should not be judged," says I Corinthians 11:31. If we will not judge ourselves then God must chasten His children.

Dear lost sinner, if you are a wicked sinner, yet you do not have to die and go to Hell forever. If you are a criminal or a harlot, a blasphemer, a drunkard, a convict, or a dope fiend, God does not want you to go to Hell. People do not go to Hell simply because they are sinners. Rather they go because they will not repent of their sins! If you today will confess your sins to God, and in your poor, helpless heart, will, as far as you know how, turn away from your sin, God will have mercy and will forgive and save.

You have your choice. You may cover your sins, make alibis for them, hide them from the face of men. You cannot hide them from God. You cannot deceive God. Sooner or later you must answer to God if you try to cover your sins. Be sure of this, you will not prosper. Be assured that one day you will be bound forever in Hell, away from God and in the lake of fire, if you try to cover your sins and get by without repenting, without turning to Christ for mercy and pardon.

On the other hand, "Whoso confesseth and forsaketh them shall have mercy." What a sweet offer! Here is the only way a sinner can have forgiveness. Here is the only way a smiting conscience can find peace. Here is the only way a poor lost soul can be saved. Oh, confess your sins and come to Christ for the mercy He promises so freely today! Simply confess your sins to Him. Never mind about stammering words. Never mind the theological language. He knows your heart. If you honestly admit your sin and want mercy, you may have it. Just the moment you turn your heart to Him in faith, trusting Jesus Christ who died for you, willing for Him to forgive and cleanse you, that moment God takes you in His arms as His own child. That moment the Holy Spirit works a change in you and you become a born-again Christian, converted, forgiven, saved!

I hope that many a reader will go to the quiet place of prayer and there confess the sins God knows in your heart and honestly forsake them. If there is anything you can do to make them right, oh, do it—do it at once! But look to Christ now, this moment, for forgiving and cleansing as you confess and forsake your sins in your heart.

If some poor sinner today repents of his sins and trusts Christ, how glad I would be to know it. Will you write me a letter or card and tell me so? If you like you may use the words given here. Sign your name today, and tell the Lord you mean it and will depend on Him for the forgiveness and mercy He promised every sinner who honestly confessed and forsook his sins. You may copy it in a letter or card, or write in your own words. But when you trust Christ, then claim Him today.

My Decision for Christ

Dr. Curtis Hutson
P. O. Box 1099
Murfreesboro, Tennessee 37130

Dear Dr. Hutson:

I have read the sermon on "The Curse of Hidden Sins" in the book *The Ruin of a Christian*. I realize that until today I have been a poor, lost sinner. But today I have honestly confessed to God that I am a sinner, and the best I know how I trust Him to

forgive my sins and give me a home in Heaven.   I would ap-
preciate any of your free literature that would help me as I set
out to live a successful Christian life.

Date _____

Signed _____

Address _____

_____

Chapter 5

THE SIN OF LYING

1. *"Thou shalt not bear false witness."*—Exod. 20:16.

2. *"For he* [the Devil] *is a liar, and the father of it."*—John 8:44.

3. *"Lie not one to another."*—Col. 3:9.

4. *"Lying lips are abomination to the lord."*—Prov. 12:22.

5. *"A lying tongue . . . a false witness that speaketh lies . . . doth the lord hate."*—Prov. 6:16–19.

6. *"Putting away lying, speak every man truth with his neighbor."*—Eph. 4:25.

*L*YING AND DECEIT are one of the marks of the close of this age. Second Timothy 3:13 declares that "evil men and seducers shall wax worse and worse, DECEIVING AND BEING DECEIVED." We are told that "FALSE prophets shall rise, and shall deceive many" (Matt. 24:11), and I Timothy 4:1, 2 says, "Now the Spirit speaketh expressly, that in the latter times some shall depart from the faith, giving heed to seducing spirits, and doctrines of devils; Speaking lies in hypocrisy; having their conscience seared with a hot iron." Being seduced by evil spirits and speaking lies in hypocrisy is one of the marks of "the latter times," and "false accusers" will be many and strong in the perilous times of "the last days" (II Tim. 3:1, 3). In these days we may expect "false teachers" who shall come

in "privily," that is, secretly, deceitfully, with damnable heresies denying the Lord, and the language of these preachers
and teachers will be "feigned words" (II Pet. 2:1–3).

Lying and deceit are becoming most prevalent sins, as
Satan, the god of this world, more and more makes himself
felt. When the Man of Sin appears, the Antichrist, he will
come "with all deceivableness of unrighteousness" (II Thess.
2:10) and with "lying wonders" (II Thess. 2:9), and if it were
possible he would deceive the very elect (Matt. 24:24).

Christian people are so swept off their feet by the worldliness around them that we need especially to beware of the
sin of lying.

All Lying Is of the Devil

Many people believe a lie is a very small matter, but they
do not realize that it is one distinctive qualification of the
Devil. Jesus said in John 8:44,

*"Ye are of your father the devil, and the lusts of your father
ye will do. He was a murderer from the beginning and abode
not in the truth, because there is no truth in him. When he
speaketh a lie, he speaketh of his own: for he is a liar, and the
father of it."*

Satan is himself a liar. There is no truth in him. When
Satan first spoke to man in the Garden of Eden, he spoke with
a lie, and from that time on, he has brought men to sin,
misery, shame and eternal damnation by teaching them lies.
He will continue to do so until the millennial reign of Christ,
after which he will be allowed to go out and deceive the
nations for the last time (Rev. 20:8, 9). Satan is back of every
lie that was ever told. He is the father of lying. Every man
and woman and child who lies, follows the Devil in it, pleases
the Devil, is led by the Devil in this respect. Lying, then, is a
fearful business. Satan is the great deceiver and the men who
are the most accomplished liars are the closer to Satan. The
Man of Sin, who will be Satan incarnate, will be the most
brilliant liar, the most attractive deceiver, the most person-

able and magnetic and plausible falsifier the world has ever seen. All lying is of the Devil, Jesus said. Every lie, then, is of Satan; and every man who lies, whether he be saint or sinner, does it under the influence of Satan. There are no good lies, no white lies, no excusable lies, since all lies are from Satan.

Lying Is of the Carnal, Wicked, Fleshly Nature

Every Christian has two natures, the old carnal, fleshly nature, and the new, spiritual nature, the divine nature. If you do not constantly mortify the deeds of the flesh, judge, condemn, and crucify that wicked, lying self, your light will be put under a bushel, your testimony will be hindered, and the natural man will rule. Jeremiah 17:9 says, "The heart is deceitful above all things, and desperately wicked: who can know it?" That is the heart of every person in the world. Again we are told that "The wicked are estranged from the womb: they go astray as soon as they be born, speaking lies" (Psa. 58:3). And Romans 3:13 says, "With their tongues they have used deceit." That is true of all, both Jew and Greek, saved and lost, Paul tells us.

Dear Christian, it is your constant duty to watch this sinful tendency to lie and deceive, and keep it under, mortify it. In the third chapter of Colossians, we are told that since we are counted risen with Christ, we should seek the things that are above and mortify our members which are upon the earth (vs. 1–5). Then we are commanded to put off certain sins and "lie not one to another, seeing that ye have put off the old man with his deeds; And have put on the new man" (Col. 3:9, 10). Every time a Christian lies or deceives, he is giving way to the old fleshly nature which was crucified with Christ and which ought day by day to be reckoned dead and crucified afresh.

Lying Is an Abomination to God

The sin of lying is so terrible that God put, "Thou shalt not bear false witness" as one of the Ten Commandments.

Lying ranks alongside idolatry, murder, adultery and stealing in God's sight, and He put it in the same Decalogue.
Lying is such an abomination to God that He mentions it
repeatedly in the Bible as a terrible sin. We are told that
    *"These six things doth the Lord hate: yea, seven are an
abomination unto him: a proud look, a lying tongue, and
hands that shed innocent blood, An heart that deviseth
wicked imaginations, feet that be swift in running to mis-
chief, A false witness that speaketh lies, and he that soweth
discord among brethren."*   —Prov. 6:16–19.
    God hates lying so much that of the seven things that are
an abomination to Him TWO OF THEM ARE LYING!
Notice that among the seven things that the Lord says He
hates are, "a lying tongue," and "a false witness that speaketh
lies." That is the reason that this list is called "six things"
and then "seven." There are six sins, but lying is mentioned
twice. We are told again that "Lying lips are abomination
to the Lord: but they that deal truly are his delight" (Prov.
12:22). If God is delighted with them that deal truly, how
horrible in God's sight it must be for a child of God to speak
lies. God even commands us not to respect those that turn
aside to lies (Psa. 40:4), and we have the solemn warning that
"the mouth of them that speak lies shall be stopped" (Psa.
63:11). God has set Himself forever against a lie and must
bring it to exposure, to judgment and punishment. How
tenderly the Lord pleads with Christians in Ephesians 4:25:
"Wherefore putting away lying, speak every man truth with
his neighbor," and then in verse 30, He explains that such
sins grieve the Holy Spirit of God who dwells within us and
by whom we are sealed into the day of redemption!
    Lying is of the Devil, it is an outbreaking of the leprous,
carnal, wicked nature, it is an abomination to God, it grieves
the Holy Spirit who dwells within God's people and it must
always bring sorrow, rebuke and failure. Lying is a terrible
business!

Modern Excuses for Lying

Doctors are sometimes taught that lying is permissible under certain circumstances—that to tell the truth would sometimes do more harm than good. So they sometimes deceive patients and deceive the families. I will say frankly that I want no doctor to wait on me or my family who is a lying agent of Satan. A man who will lie about one thing will lie about another if he has enough to gain by it, and a liar can never be trusted.

Lawyers customarily feel that lying and deceit are a proper part of the practice of their profession. How low, then, their profession has fallen! No wonder that *liar* and *lawyer* sound so much alike! We can well understand how any group of men who have been willing to approve lying have largely sold out to criminals, defeat justice on any technicality and have led the people to despise the laws, courts and government which they are sworn to uphold. I am sure there are honorable, upright lawyers who scorn and hate a lie, but the public generally has been led to adopt the attitude of the Irishman who wandered in a graveyard reading the epitaphs. On one headstone, he read, "Here lies a lawyer and an honest man." And he exclaimed in astonishment, "Begorra, here are two men buried in the same grave!"

Lying and dishonesty have brought great reproach on the legal profession.

Modern business makes the frequent excuse, "You can't make a living and be absolutely truthful. You can't get by in this modern world with all its wickedness unless you lie as others do." So some used car dealers turn back the speedometers to read thousands of miles less than the actual mileage on the cars they sell. Clothing stores insist that "Yes, it is absolutely pure virgin wool," when often it is not. Or "It is the latest style" when it was kept over from last year. The fish in the market are "absolutely fresh, just received this morning" but the careful buyer knows he must watch for the sunken eyes and the softened flesh or the strong odor that belie the butcher's words. Lying is a part of modern business —not always, but far too often. In most cities the government has to wage a constant warfare against crooked scales, short weight and adulterated products. And the daily papers a little before the war reported that "The Federal Trade Commission charged twenty-one automobile manufacturers and financiers with obtaining a higher rate of interest on deferred car payments than they have advertised they charge." "The Commission said that the complaints alleged the company advertised they sold their cars on an annual 6% payment plan. Actually, the Commission charged, the interest payments total about 12%." Then follows the names of the principal automobile makers of America!

Lying, straight-out falsehood, is the commonly accepted business practice in a large part of modern business. Actually that simply means that men sell out to Satan hoping to gain by lying and deceit.

Parents, especially, feel that lying is permitted in their case in dealing with children. Children ask so many questions that parents do not want to answer, so lying is a customary business in the average home. Parents think that lying threats are better than honest punishment and discipline, they think that pleasant lies are sometimes better for small ears than unpleasant truths. So parents lie. They glibly explain that storks bring babies, that Santa Claus lives at the North Pole, that rabbits lay Easter eggs, that "the 'booger man' will get you if you don't go to sleep." An adult's idea of a joke on children is, "I am going to give baby sister to the neighbors." In fact, books and magazines even have helpful hints to parents on how to deceive their children. The churches help all they can, and pastors and Sunday School teachers faithfully propagate the lie about Santa Claus and reindeers at Christmas, liking that better than the truth about the Babe born in a manger, the shepherds in the fields, the wise men from the East and the angels who praised God saying, "Glory to God in the highest." Churches have their Easter programs where children are taught not about the resurrection of the Saviour, but about Easter eggs, little chickens, and baby rabbits. Children's classes are given miniature gifts of rabbits with their little nests of candy eggs which they presumably have laid. Thus the whole background of a child's life is formed of a tissue of lies! Small wonder that he soon learns to have no confidence in the opinions of the mother and father who dealt with him so falsely. If any parent reads this, I suggest that you check and see which one your child will believe first, you, or his high school teacher! Children instinctively know that one who brazenly lies about Santa Claus and babies and "booger man" and whipping, can't be trusted when they express opinions about dancing and drinking and gambling and picture shows.

Preachers and Lies

Anybody who talks as much as a preacher does, is in deadly danger of lying. Preachers are human, and they must watch themselves lest the carnal nature that is in all of us, that evil deceitful nature, lead them to lie. Every preacher knows the temptation to exaggerate, to color falsely, to boast overmuch, to tell only one side of what happened. Preachers very properly long to be loved and respected, and are tempted to lie to make a good impression. How easy it is for a preacher to miss the truth! The preacher must illustrate his message from a thousand sources. How can his memory always be accurate? And would the message not be more impressive if the incident were repeated as if it happened to the preacher himself? You who are not preachers do not know the terrible pressure Satan brings upon every speaker to exaggerate or to tell only part of the truth, or to intimate more than is true or less than is true.

I suppose the most obvious matter about which preachers lie is the size of the crowds they have preached to. This is a painful and embarrassing matter, but practically every church auditorium is greatly overrated in capacity, and preachers are responsible for that. A preacher feels that if he can tell that he has had big crowds to preach to, it will prove that he is a great preacher. Every preacher wants to be known as a great preacher. Therefore many preachers lie about the size of their crowds.

It must be said in fairness that many preachers have very hazy ideas on this question and do not know how to accurately estimate the capacity of a building. But they could find out. I have preached in many theatres and have uniformly found that theatre owners know accurately how many people their buildings will hold and that they almost never exaggerate the seating capacity. (They do certainly exaggerate their attractions.) Preachers in the matter of crowds cannot be trusted like theatre men, probably because the theatre man is thinking about money and the preacher about reputation.

In a leading religious magazine when I lived in Dallas, Texas, I saw a report of the Gipsy Smith revival in Dallas. It was a great revival. I attended a number of services. The crowds were really enormous and the results, I believe, were blessed.

But the reporter of the meeting stated that the First Baptist Church seats 6,000 people, when in fact it seats considerably less than half of that. I counted the opera chairs in the various lengths of rows in the entire balcony, then the number of such rows very carefully. I counted the number in the choir. I carefully counted the number of persons closely packed in the Gipsy Smith meeting in a row of seats across the entire auditorium and multiplied by the number of such rows in the entire lower floor. I estimated that way that the building seated 2,540 people. A church auditorium actually seating 2,500 people, as that does, is a magnificent auditorium. Why stretch it to the enormous and mythical capacity of

6,000? I do not know who made the report, and I was in the heartiest sympathy with the great Gipsy Smith revival. The crowds were really enormous. But I know that whatever preacher reported that revival ought to have taken five or ten minutes and found out at least the approximate capacity of that wonderful church building before making such a terrible blunder; a false statement that will bring reproach upon preachers and churches.

If he was dealing in hearsay, he should have said so. I use this case only as an illustration of a very general and widespread habit which preachers have of misrepresenting the size of their crowds. That habit is so general that a preacher feels if he tells the real number he has it will appear small in comparison with crowds of other preachers. I suppose there is no church auditorium in America that will seat anything in the neighborhood of 6,000 people. Certainly the great ones that I have seen do not. The great Moody church in Chicago will seat 4,040 people. The Church of the Open Door in Los Angeles seats about 4,000. Very few preachers in America regularly preach to congregations of a thousand people. Only a handful of the world's greatest preachers do. Spurgeon's great tabernacle in London, England, is said, by careful judges, to have seated only about 3,000 or a little more. The same building now seats less, I am told.

It is a wicked shame that preachers have been so notorious in their exaggerations that "ministerially speaking" to many people means telling a whopper!

"Ye Are My Witnesses"

Christians, we are witnesses of the Lord Jesus Christ. Our usefulness to Christ depends upon the faithfulness of our testimony. Peter and John said, "We cannot but speak the things which we have seen and heard." The integrity of a Christian's testimony is one of the most important things in the world. I beg you, dear reader, so speak the truth that the unsaved man near you will believe what you say about Christ and about being born again, about Heaven and Hell and judgment.

In the first great church at Jerusalem, the integrity of Christian testimony was so important that the first man and woman who were publicly known to have lied were struck dead by the Holy Spirit! Peter said, "Thou hast not lied unto men, but unto God." Oh, may God give us a tender, sensitive conscience that burns and hurts under falsehood and will speak nothing but the truth, and that in love! We do not need, always, to tell all we know, but certainly what we do tell should be absolutely true. A Christian should never need to swear, but should say, "Yea," or "Nay" and be believed, like an unconverted man under oath. "Let your yea be yea and your nay, nay."

We need to have among the children of God a wholesome time of repentance and confession. D. L. Moody tells that a woman once came to him asking prayer and advice concerning a habit of exaggeration. Moody advised her that the next time she exaggerated she should simply confess to her friend that she had lied! When you confess that exaggeration, false insinuations and half truths are really wicked lies, and that every lie is from Satan, the father of lies, then you will find it easier to quit this terrible sin that God hates, this sin which grieves the Holy Spirit, this sin of those who will be left outside the gate of Paradise!

All of us need to remember that "Lying lips are abomination to the Lord; but they that deal truly are his delight," and that two of these things which God hates are a lying tongue and a false witness that speaketh lies.

Nearly all the slanders that break someone's heart are composed of lying half-truths, insinuations, hearsays and exaggeration. If Christians will follow the command of the Bible which says, "Putting away lying, speak every man truth with his neighbor," a peace will fall upon the churches of the land such as we have never had before.

Let every preacher, every teacher, every parent promise God now that they will tell no lies in the name of the Lord next Christmas, about Santa Claus or reindeers or anything else. That does not honor God. Let us make a solemn vow to God that we will earnestly try to "Lie not one to another." Let us have no respect for liars as God commanded (Psa. 40:4). And let us earnestly try to keep in subjection these wicked, deceitful hearts of ours. We should earnestly long for the time to come when our Saviour from Heaven will release us from our carnal, lying dispositions and make us like Jesus who is *"The Truth"* and like *"God that cannot lie."*

And let us warn sinners everywhere that outside the gate of the New Jerusalem will be "whosoever loveth and maketh a lie"!

Chapter 6.

"BREAK UP YOUR FALLOW GROUND, AND SOW NOT AMONG THORNS"
—Jer. 4:3

The Way to Revival for the Backslider, the Worldly, the Powerless, the Fruitless

"If thou wilt return, O Israel, saith the Lord, return unto me: and if thou wilt put away thine abominations out of my sight, then shalt thou not remove. And thou shalt swear, The Lord liveth, in truth, in judgment, and in righteousness; and the nations shall bless themselves in him, and in him shall they glory. For thus saith the Lord to the men of Judah and Jerusalem, Break up your fallow ground, and sow not among thorns. Circumcise yourselves to the Lord, and take away the foreskins of your heart, ye men of Judah and inhabitants of Jerusalem: lest my fury come forth like fire, and burn that none can quench it, because of the evil of your doings."

—Jer. 4:1–4.

WE NEED A REVIVAL, even as Israel did in the time of Jeremiah. Jeremiah lived in the time when the people of Judah and Jerusalem were carried captive. Most of the book of Jeremiah is the impassioned pleading and warning of the inspired prophet of God, begging the people to repent, and solemnly prophesying the certain captivity of the people and destruction of Jerusalem

125

and the temple if they did not turn from their sins. Many times Jeremiah gave combined warnings and promises as he did in Jeremiah 4:1 above: "If thou wilt return, O Israel, saith the Lord, return unto me: and if thou wilt put away thine abominations out of my sight, then shalt thou not remove." That is, if Israel would repent and turn from sin she would not be carried captive to Babylon, moved out of her holy land.

Idolatry cursed the land. Covetousness was the ruling motive of the people. Religious teaching was generally in the hands of false prophets and worldly priests, whose teaching and preaching tickled the ears of a worldly and pleasure-loving people. Jeremiah cried (Jer. 5:30, 31): "A wonderful and horrible thing is committed in the land; The prophets prophesy falsely, and the priests bear rule by their means; and my people love to have it so: and what will ye do in the end thereof?" There was shocking need for a revival in Jerusalem and Jeremiah earnestly pled with them to "BREAK UP YOUR FALLOW GROUND, AND SOW NOT AMONG THORNS."

This is a message to backsliders, that is, a message to nearly every reader of this book. Are we not backslidden? Was there ever a time when you were nearer to God than you are today? Was your heart ever happier than now? Was your life ever more fruitful? If you need to answer yes to any of those questions, then today you are, of course, a backslider.

But with most of us I dare say there would be little argument as to whether or not we are backsliders. Does not your own heart tell you that you need a visitation from Heaven? Does not your own soul hunger and cry for more of God's presence and power in your life? Are you having the fruit that you ought to have? Is your life in some sense a failure? Jeremiah speaks to most of us when he says:

"Thine own wickedness shall correct thee, and thy backslidings shall reprove thee: know therefore and see that it is an evil thing and bitter, that thou hast forsaken the Lord thy

God, and that my fear is not in thee, saith the Lord God of hosts." —Jer. 2:19.

Most of us have committed the two evils God's people so many times commit—we have forsaken Him who is the fountain of living waters, and hewn us out cisterns, broken cisterns, that can hold no water (Jer. 2:13). Praise God His invitations to backsliders, then, are for us today! Our Heavenly Father cries: "Turn, O backsliding children, saith the Lord; for I am married unto you" (Jer. 3:14). And again, "Return, ye backsliding children, and I will heal your backslidings" (Jer. 3:22). Some, at least, of the Jews did, saying, "Behold, we come unto thee; for thou art the Lord our God!"

The Scripture teaches us to take up our cross *daily* and follow Christ (Luke 9:23). We must come *daily,* according to the model prayer, to ask forgiveness for our sins (Matt. 6:11, 12). The proper attitude for a child of God every day is the attitude of penitence, confession and turning from sin, judging ourselves so that we need not be judged in the wrath of God (I Cor. 11:31, 32; I John 1:8–10). Yes, if you had a revival only yesterday, you need one today! If you won many souls this week, you ought to win more. You are not all that God wants you to be. Not yet is your life a garden, every bit of which bears perfect fruit for God. You have fallow ground to be broken up. You have thorns to be digged out so that your life may be perfectly fruitful for Christ.

Fallow Ground!

The Jews were accustomed to allow their fields to lie fallow every seventh year. Fallow ground means hard soil, unbroken by the plow. Fallow ground means soil growing up in thorns, briars and weeds. Fallow ground means, saddest of all, fruitless ground.

Break It Up!

Dear reader, if you are to have a revival, if God is to get fruit from your life, your ground must be broken up. And that is not as easy as it may seem.

Really breaking up the ground is the hard way. I remember that when I was a boy on the dry west Texas farm I called my father's attention to the way a farmer nearby prepared his ground for sowing grain by using the disc harrow. With four horses to his disc harrow, this farmer prepared the surface of the ground. Small weeds and grass were destroyed and the farmer was soon over his field, cutting a swath six or eight feet wide each round. How much faster that was than our slow way, with four horses hitched to a double-disc plow, cutting fourteen to eighteen inches of soil! The easy way was four or five times as fast as our way! We plowed six to ten inches deep while our neighbor simply stirred the crust for two inches or so. On our neighbor's farm the shallow scratching of the harrow did not open the hard soil, baked under a west Texas sun, to soak in the winter rain. The soil was not loosened so that roots could dig deep for the plant food needed. Large weeds were not destroyed by the disc harrow. Johnson grass roots were never disturbed. The yield of grain was not nearly so great on our neighbor's field who planted without breaking up deeply the fallow ground.

How the plow jolted as great clods of hard, dry dirt were turned up by the plow! Then the clods must be broken by a harrow, or dragged. But when it rained, nearly all the water soaked in and the deep, soft seedbed was prepared. And, my friend, your life must be broken up if God is to send a revival and make you bear fruit.

Very often in God's plan a deep breaking up is necessary for usefulness. Ground never brings forth much fruit until it is broken up. Corn or wheat can never make bread until it is broken fine, ground to flour or meal. Olives do not yield their oil until they are pressed. Incense never gives its sweetest odor until it is burned. Flowers smell sweetest when they are crushed. If you avoid the breaking up of your ground, you miss the secret of fruitfulness and blessing!

Did you ever notice how many things God broke up when He blessed men in the Bible? We are told three times concerning the five loaves and two fishes, when Jesus fed the five thousand, that Jesus "blessed, and brake, and gave the loaves to his disciples, and the disciples to the multitudes." Blessed and brake! Blessing means breaking. God never smiles on a field as when it is plowed deep. God never rains righteousness upon a life in fullness until it is broken up, broken deep. Break up your fallow ground!

The pitchers that Gideon used to free Israel from the Midianites were all broken. Whole pitchers would not let the light shine that was inside. If God wants the pitchers of our lives to be broken, then let's offer them freely, to be broken and be blessed and bring forth fruit. The lambs that were sacrificed had to die before they could fulfill their destiny as pictures of the coming Lamb of God whose blood should take away the sins of the world.

God had to break Moses, the son of Pharaoh's daughter, learned in all the knowledge of the Egyptians and high at court. Moses' whole life was broken up. His wealth was gone, his honor was gone, his pride was gone, his friends were gone, his ambition was laid in the dust. Moses was broken before God used him.

What a successful farmer Elisha, the son of Shaphat was, plowing his plantation with twelve yoke of oxen before him! But it was all broken up when God called him to be a prophet. He killed oxen for sacrifices and burned the plow and yoke for fuel and left all, his past life broken and gone, simply that he might pour water on the hands of the prophet Elijah and some day be used of God!

Jesus broke up the fishing business when He called Peter, James and John and Andrew to preach. It was good-by to nets and profit, good-by to father and ship if one were to follow Jesus and become a fisher of men. And Matthew, sitting at the receipt of custom, was a rich publican, making money hand over fist, doubtless, when Jesus came by and said, "Follow me." Jesus broke up his income, broke Matthew away from his friends and occupation. Oh, I tell you, it takes a breaking-up of the ground, if God is to find fruit in your life!

The slave girl healed of her demon in Acts, chapter 16, lost her power to tell fortunes and God broke up the money-making business of her masters when He saved that soul. When the legion of devils was cast out of the poor maniac of Gadara, our Lord almost broke up the hog business on that countryside! It cost two thousand hogs drowned in the sea, to put one poor sinner in his right mind, clothed and at the feet of Jesus, and to send him happy-hearted and glad back to tell his kindred and friends how great things the Lord had done for him. How foolish you are and how little you know of God's way, if you think you can have a revival without a deep breaking-up in your life, if you can have blessing and fruit-fulness without sacrifice and cost! No, no! If you want a re-vival, if you want to be near to God, if you want to win souls, if you want to bear fruit, then BREAK UP YOUR FALLOW GROUND!

Our ease must be broken. We are too self-complacent. We are too well satisfied with ourselves, our families, our homes, our churches. God knows, it is likely that many of you who read this do not count yourselves backsliders at all! It may be you are satisfied well enough with the few sheaves you gather, the few fish you catch, the occasional brand that you pluck from the burning, if any at all. That complacency and ease must be broken up, I tell you, if ever you are to have the re-vival God has for you and to bear the fruit that He plans for your life.

It is one of the most terrible curses of the churches today that we are neither cold nor hot. In the words of the Saviour, in Revelation 3:15–17, we are told:

". . . I would thou wert cold or hot. So then because thou art lukewarm, and neither cold nor hot, I will spue thee out of my mouth. Because thou sayest, I am rich, and increased with goods, and have need of nothing; and knowest not that thou art wretched, and miserable, and poor, and blind, and naked."

We are content with crowds whether we have souls or not. We are content with sermons whether we have anointing from Heaven or not. We have socials instead of revivals. We have *supper* rooms, instead of *upper* rooms. We have enter tainment when we ought to have agonizing. Fasting, prayer, confession, tears of repentance—these are out of date in the average church.

What shall we say for ourselves, we preachers? We please our churches very well! They pay our salaries very well! We dress very nicely. We read the best books. We stand well enough in the community, we think. But God knows that most of us preachers do not have the fire in our bones that Jeremiah had. We do not have the "Woe is unto me, if I preach not the gospel!" that Paul had. Many of us have never had the coal of fire from off the altar of God touch our lips and cleanse us from our impurities. Oh, may God revive the preachers of today! Tobacco-using preachers, picture-show-going preachers, nice, polite, well-fed, well-dressed preachers! Preachers with soft, flabby faces, with big laughs, with ready jokes on the street, with inoffensive ways, with cultured speech in the pulpit, but no fire, no tears, no compassion! We are preachers but not prophets! We preach Heaven but little of Hell! We raise money from men but we cannot pray down a revival from God! We are a sleek, smug, well-satisfied bunch, we preachers! No camel's hair for us unless it be woven into the finest overcoat! No locust and wild honey diet—we live on the fat of the land! No Philippian jail with beatings and stocks for us successful modern preachers! No, the judges and bankers are members of our churches. We can get our traffic tickets "fixed" when other people would have to pay a fine. No Mt. Carmel Elijah experiences for us. It is too sensational, and too dangerous! And besides, our voices will never do to speak in the open air! Let the Salvation Army officers and the Pentecostal people hold their street services and preach from the back of trucks and over loud-speakers on the square, denouncing sin and calling men to repentance—but that is too fanatical, and too embarrassing for us successful, modern, college- and seminary-bred preachers! God in Heaven, wake up the preachers!

Preacher brother, if you lead your church in revival, your life must be broken up, your hard ground broken, your hard will bent, your pride humbled, the fountain of your tears broken. Break up your fallow ground!

Break Up Your Hearts

To break up your fallow ground means to break up your heart! Strange as it may seem, one can break his own heart. One can be burdened, can be penitent, can mourn over his sins, if he will. All spiritual emotions and acts that please God must come from the human will surrendered to the will of God. There is a moral quality in believing and it is wicked not to believe in Christ, not to believe the Bible, not to trust God to keep His promises. So we can set ourselves to seek God, to turn our hearts from sin, to afflict ourselves in godly sorrow for sin. James 4:9 commands: "Be afflicted, and mourn, and weep: let your laughter be turned to mourning, and your joy to heaviness." In the same passage Christians are commanded to "submit" to God, to "draw nigh to God," to "cleanse" hands, to "purify" hearts, to "humble" self. In all these matters, turning to God, seeking his face, man deliberately acts. The Spirit of God does move on our hearts, and leads us to repentance, but repentance does not come unless the sinner himself repents, so we will not be turned to God unless we wish to turn. We will not be revived unless we seek revival. Our hearts will never be broken up in a way pleasing to God unless we set out to have them broken. It is proper for a Christian to be afflicted and mourn, to weep and to humble himself. It is proper for every Christian who wants a revival, a transformed life, who wants to "sow to yourselves in righteousness, reap in mercy" (Hos. 10:12) by all means to seek a broken heart, literally to break up the fallow ground of his own heart. I beg you, Christian man, woman, and child who reads this to break up the fallow ground of your heart!

As we study to be joyful when happiness is proper, so let us study to mourn and be penitent when we should have broken hearts to seek revival.

On Thanksgiving day we have feasts, public services of praise. We assemble ourselves with laughter and fellowship and rejoicing in every home. At Christmas time we decorate with lights and evergreens, with tinsel and color and holly. We send presents one to another. We make merry with feasts and holiday visiting. We cultivate joy when it is time for joy, so why not cultivate sorrow when it is time for sorrow, time to seek God, to mourn over sins and to have broken hearts?

The Lost Art of Mourning and Repentance

Bible Christians knew the now-forgotten art of seeking after God. They were accustomed to prayer and fasting, to periods of mourning over sin. Daniel is an example. As he considered the desolation of Jerusalem during the captivity, Daniel was led to have a broken heart and seek after God. He said: "And I set my face unto the Lord God, to seek by prayer and supplications, with fasting, and sackcloth, and ashes: And I prayed unto the Lord my God, and made my confession, and said . . ." (Dan. 9:3, 4); and then follows the most heartbroken out-pouring of confession, confession of Daniel's sins, confession of the sins of his people and the kings, that one ever read. *Daniel set himself* unto the Lord God "to seek by prayer and supplication, with fasting, and sackcloth and ashes." If we set ourselves that way we can have broken hearts, can have the fallow, idle, barren, thorn-infested, fruitless ground of our lives broken up in a way that can please God. Then when we sow the fields we will sow in good ground that will bring forth fruit to God.

Study the prayer of Daniel when he set his face to seek God, to seek by *prayer, supplication, fasting, sackcloth and ashes and confession.* That prayer is continued in Daniel 9:4–19.

In it Daniel reminded himself and reminded God of all the sins that had broken the heart of God, had brought his grief and wrath upon Israel and Judah and Jerusalem. Daniel did not forget, did not cover up, did not minimize sin, but rather, he dwelt upon it and mentioned the sins, the wickedness, the rebellion, the departing from God, the refusal of Israel to hear. He repeated before God the curses, the evil, the reproach, the displeasures that were upon God's people for their sins! In that prayer Daniel mentioned the sins of Israel twenty-one times. It is certain that Daniel's heart was more broken at the close of the prayer than at the beginning. His pride was more humbled, his will more surrendered, no doubt, after a review of Israel's departure from God and God's wrath upon Israel. So all those who set themselves deliberately to mourn before God until their hearts are broken up and their fallow ground is plowed and the thorns removed can seek and find broken hearts in a way that is pleasing to God. O ye Christians, break up the fallow ground of your hearts!

All the things that are wrong with us are wrong in the heart. Our sins, our prayerlessness, our worldliness, our absorption in trival things, our carelessness about souls, our spiritual blindness, these all proceed from our hearts, stubborn, carnal, sin-cursed, unbroken hearts! Our lack of revival does not proceed from circumstances. Our fruitlessness, our barrenness is not a fault of the head; it is a black sin of the heart! It is not so much that our minds need to be taught, but rather that our hearts need to be broken up. May God give us grace to set about to seek the broken and contrite heart that God will not despise.

David's Broken Heart and How He Got It

David knew how to seek God and Psalm 51 gives the picture of his heart as he sought God after he had fallen into the horrible sin with Bathsheba. I suggest that if you are yourself backslidden, with not the same joy or fruitfulness that once was yours, not quite the same fervor in prayer, the same interest in the Scripture, nor the same zeal in soul winning that you once had, that you set yourself to quietly meditate over this fifty-first Psalm. Read it prayerfully, read it with tears, make its confession, its burden, its shame, its pleading, its holy vows, your own. How many times I have gone back to this Psalm to weep over my own cold heart and to beg God, "Hide thy face from my sins, and blot out all mine iniquities. Create in me a clean heart, O God; and renew a right spirit within me" (Psa. 51:9, 10).

When David had first committed adultery with Bathsheba and had caused her husband to be killed that the sin might not be known, David tried to cover up the sin. He did not confess it to God, he did not lament it, he did not even frankly face the matter in his own heart until the faithful prophet, Nathan, came and said, "Thou art the man," according to II Samuel 12. Only then did David really face his sin. But when David saw how far he had gone from God he deliberately set himself to realize the enormity of his sin, to probe the wickedness of it, to lay it all out before God. David set himself to break up the fallow ground of his heart. David made confession, he fasted, he prayed, he wept. But II Samuel 12 does not tell all the story so we turn back to Psalm 51 again. There David said: "For I acknowledge my transgressions: *and my sin is ever before me*" (v. 3). David comforted Bathsheba concerning the sin and over the death of their baby; and God gave them another child, the dear Solomon, "and the Lord loved him." But David had not dismissed the matter of sin: rather he could cry out to God, "and my sin is ever before me!" David knew how treacherous was his heart and what shame his sin had caused; so David held his sin before his face until his heart should be thoroughly broken, until God should revive him and cleanse him! No one will ever beg God for a clean heart until he himself faces thoroughly the shame, the terrible wickedness of his sin!

David could have given sacrifices of sheep and oxen. He

said, "For thou desirest not sacrifice; else would I give it: thou delightest not in burnt-offering" (Psa. 51:16). But David set himself to offer sacrifices to God that would bring a real revival in his own heart, a revival of fruitfulness and righteousness, so David continued his prayer. "The sacrifices of God are a broken spirit: a broken and a contrite heart, O God, thou wilt not despise" (Psa. 51:17). David offered the sacrifice that God wanted, the one that would please Him, that is, the sacrifice of a broken spirit. Oh, may God give us grace to seek and find and offer willingly this sacrifice so pleasing to God, a broken spirit and a broken heart!

My brother preacher, what you need is a broken heart! What your ministry needs is the contrite humility, the sackcloth and ashes of spirit that must precede all great revivals of blessing. "They that sow in tears shall reap in joy," and "He that goeth forth and weepeth, bearing precious seed, shall doubtless come again with rejoicing, bringing his sheaves with him" (Psa. 126:5, 6). No gentle rain from Heaven ever mellowed the earth and made it fruitful as the moisture of tears will soften your own heart and make it fruitful. Beloved reader, let us offer the sacrifices of a broken spirit, for a broken and contrite heart God will not despise.

It is good then for Christians to have a time when they take no delight in clothes. Indeed we should not appear unto men to fast as hypocrites wearing long faces, but for seasons we should turn ourselves away from all delights of the flesh. Days of fasting help the heart to seek God. If we follow the example of Esther and Mordecai (Esther 4:16), of Ezra (Ezra 8:21, 23), of Nehemiah (Neh. 1:4), of the people of Nineveh (Jonah 3:5–10), the example of King Hezekiah, Isaiah and others (Isa. 37:1–4), the example of Paul and Barnabas and other New Testament leaders (Acts 13:1–3), then we will set times of fasting. Then our hearts will truly seek God, we will turn our hearts away from laughter and rejoicing that we may afflict ourselves and mourn. In such cases it is proper for husbands and wives to separate themselves for brief periods and by consent, that they may fast and pray (I Cor. 7:5). Sometimes we should take particular time to get down on our knees when we pray and even on our faces and thus encourage our hearts to be humble. Sometimes we should take particular pains to mortify the deeds of the flesh (Rom. 8:13), to carefully practice self-denial. George Mueller, the great English man of prayer, tells how when a ship went down at sea with great material loss, the owner made a love gift to the Lord of thousands of dollars seeking thereby to show his love and trust and to miss none of the sweetness of God's reproof. "Break up your fallow ground, and sow not among thorns."

Pride, Self-will, Self-centered Plans Must Be Broken

Many lives are set in a routine that leaves God little control. There was not room for Jesus to be born in the inn in Bethlehem; just so, many are so self-controlled, so absorbed in our own plans and ways that we do not have time nor heart for the will of God to be done. Our ears are not sensitive to the call of the Holy Spirit. Perhaps you are so accustomed to rising by the alarm clock at a certain hour that you would never dream of getting up in the wee small hours for a vigil of prayer. I know not how it is with others, but when I am nearest to God, frequently in the early morning long before others are up, I feel the sweet wooing of the Spirit calling me to read and pray and meet God. I believe in definite times for prayer, but sweeter are the times when we feel a call to pray and break up our plans and leave work undone to meet God.

Every Christian should lay plans to win souls, but happy is the Christian whose eager heart waits sensitively for the Spirit's leadership, "Speak to this man, he is lost," or "Go now to the neighbor for whom you have been praying."

God help us never to make any plans except subject to His will and such as we will gladly break, or change, or abandon, at the slightest indication that His sweet will is otherwise. Let us not withhold from God our businesses, our friendships, our ambitions, our hopes, our plans, our hearts —let us, O Lord Jesus, break them up, every one, after Thy will.

Help us to break up our fallow ground!

Sow Not Among Thorns

Fallow ground, barren ground, unbroken ground, brings forth weeds. As my father and I rode horseback along a road in west Texas years ago, he said to me, "Son, that man will lose his cotton crop if he doesn't watch out."

"Lose it?" I said, "How could he lose it?"

"If he doesn't kill those weeds and that grass soon," my father said, "they will get higher than the cotton plants, will overshadow them and crowd them out and there will be no cotton crop."

Sure enough, it turned out as my father said and that field was abandoned as that farmer desperately tried to kill out weeds in another patch and save what he could of his crop. It is almost useless to sow among thorns and weeds on fallow ground. So are religious services with hearts unbroken, hearts preoccupied with the thorns of worldliness and sin. One reason for breaking up our hearts, plans, and hopes and breaking up our wills is that we may root up these absorbing thorns of sin.

One day when I was five years old my bare feet pattered down the furrow following my Uncle Tom. To my distress he plowed up some beautiful flowers among the corn rows. I asked him, "Uncle Tom, what are these pretty flowers climbing on the fence, and on the corn stalks?" He told me that they were morning glories and I liked the name then, as I do now.

I said, "Aren't they pretty, Uncle Tom?"

He answered back, "They are not pretty to me. I wish every one in the field were dead. If I grow morning glories I can't grow corn."

Some of the things in which you delight seem sweet as a

morning flower; but I wonder, dear reader, if they can prevent your growing corn for the Lord? Are the things you love and hug to your bosom like thorns on a barren field, an abomination to the Lord of the harvest?

About the hardest work I ever did as a boy, was "grubbing." In west Texas the mesquite trees do not grow high, but have gnarled and twisted roots growing big and strong, deep into the ground. What digging with the mattock, what tugging with team or stump-puller or tractor before the land was ready to be put in cultivation! But it would be useless to try to cultivate the soil otherwise. Roots would break the plow. The sprouts would shoot out of the ground, the bushes would take the ground again if they were not dug out.

"Sow not among thorns" if you want fruit for God. Dig out that sinful habit! Confess and forsake that wicked grudge against your neighbor or loved one—forgive today and be forgiven! With penitence, with confession and tears give up that amusement that seems "no harm." Break up your ground, dig out the thorns, and then God will make your ground fruitful.

Chapter 7

THE SEVEN-FOLD SIN OF THOSE WHO DO NOT WIN SOULS

1. *The Sin of Disobedience to Christ*
2. *The Sin of Little Love for Christ*
3. *The Sin of Not Following Christ*
4. *The Sin of Not Abiding in Christ*
5. *The Sin of Dishonesty in a Sacred Trust*
6. *The Sin of the Short-Sighted Fool*
7. *The Sin of Blood-Guilt—the Manslaughter of Souls!*

*T*HE WINNING of souls to trust in Jesus Christ and be saved from their sins is the principal duty of every Christian in the world.

That is the thing nearest to the heart of God. For this He sent His Son, Jesus Christ, into the world to live a sinless life and die on the cross. Jesus said, "I came not to call the righteous, but sinners to repentance" (Luke 5:32). And Paul said in I Timothy 1:15, "This is a faithful saying, and worthy of all acceptation, that Christ Jesus came into the world TO SAVE SINNERS!" And even now, in Heaven, "joy shall be in heaven over one sinner that repenteth, more than over ninety and nine just persons, which need no repentance" (Luke 15:7). The thing nearest to the heart of God is the winning of precious souls. It is the thing Christ died for. It is the one great matter of rejoicing in Heaven. It ought to be the unceasing, principal business of every Christian.

The preachers in the New Testament churches were set on

winning souls. Every one of them did the work of an evangelist, covering the Roman Empire with millions of believers in the first century after Christ died!

The ministry of Jesus was largely one of personal soul winning. He won Nicodemus one night. He won the woman at the well of Sychar in Samaria. He won the woman taken in adultery in the eighth chapter of John. He won the woman who was a sinner who wept over His feet at the home of Simon the Pharisee. He won the Gadarene demoniac, Mary Magdalene, and the woman who stooped to touch the hem of His garment in a throng. He won Zacchaeus, the publican, and Levi, another of the same kind. It was His daily business.

Soul winning was the normal thing for every individual Christian in Bible times. John the Baptist pointed Andrew and John to Jesus. Then Andrew won Peter. Jesus won Philip, then Philip won Nathaniel. The woman at the well of Sychar, a new convert, won many in her own town, the same day she was saved. The jailer at Philippi found Christ at midnight, and before morning had his whole family saved and baptized! When persecution began at Jerusalem, scattering all except the preachers, then "they that were scattered abroad went every where preaching the word" (Acts 8:4).

The Bible makes it clear that soul winning is the business of every Christian. One who does not win souls is guilty of a horrible list of sins which block revival, deaden the churches, grieve the Spirit of God, cause Christians to miss the joy and manifestation of the Holy Spirit, and damn millions of souls! Consider the seven terrible sins of every Christian who does not win souls as he ought.

1. The Sin of Disobedience to Christ

Christ plainly commanded every Christian to win souls. His Great Commission as given in Matthew 28:18–20 says:

"All power is given unto me in heaven and in earth. Go ye therefore, and teach all nations, baptizing them in the name of the Father, and of the Son, and of the Holy Ghost:

*Teaching them to observe all things whatsoever I have com-
manded you: and, lo, I am with you alway, even unto the end
of the world."*

To these eleven disciples Jesus explained that all authority
was His, and that therefore they were commanded to go and
make disciples in all nations, winning souls and getting them
baptized. But it is obvious that eleven disciples could not win
souls in every nation. The commission as given in Mark 16:15
says, "Go ye into all the world, and preach the gospel to every
creature." To preach the gospel to every creature in all nations, even to the end of the world, was obviously more than
those eleven disciples could do. They were simply to begin
this work, doing what they could, then others were to carry
it on.

And that is exactly what these eleven disciples were commanded to teach others. After they made disciples (got people
to trust in Christ and be saved) and got them baptized, they
were to continue, "teaching *them* to observe all things whatsoever I have commanded *you*." They were to teach the new
converts to set out to carry out the Great Commission *just exactly as the apostles were commanded to do it.* That means
that every Christian in the world has exactly the same command as the apostles had, *to get people saved!* Every new-
born soul ought to be taught to observe all things whatsoever
Jesus commanded the apostles to observe, as the plain words
of the Great Commission say.

So Jesus commands every Christian to win souls. Every
Christian is equally responsible for taking the gospel to every
creature.

This command is repeated again in the last chapter of the
Bible. In Revelation 22:16, 17 Jesus Himself gives this plain
command:

*"I Jesus have sent mine angel to testify unto you these
things in the churches. I am the root and the offspring of
David, and the bright and morning star. And the Spirit and
the bride say, Come. And let him that heareth say, Come.*

And let him that is athirst come. And whosoever will, let him take the water of life freely."

Jesus plainly said He had sent His angel to testify unto us in the churches, "And let him that heareth say, Come." Everyone who hears the gospel is commanded to tell lost sinners to come!

If you are not a soul winner, then, you are not obeying Jesus Christ, the One to whom all authority is given in Heaven and earth. You are not carrying out His commands. You are a disobedient child of God, if child of God you are. You are a rebel. However much money you give, however well you may teach the Bible, no matter how separated and unworldly you are in your life, you are not right in your heart; you are disobeying Christ if you are not a soul winner.

Remember that for disobedience and rebellion, Saul lost his kingdom, and he and his house were rejected by the Lord. God had the prophet Samuel say to Saul, "Hath the Lord as great delight in burnt offerings and sacrifices, as in obeying the voice of the Lord? Behold, to obey is better than sacrifice, and to hearken than the fat of rams. For rebellion is as the sin of witchcraft, and stubbornness is as iniquity and idolatry. Because thou hast rejected the word of the Lord, he hath also rejected thee from being king" (I Sam. 15:22, 23). No sacrifice you can make will be pleasing to God as long as you disobey Him. Rebellion is as the sin of witchcraft, stubbornness is as iniquity and idolatry. The sin of not winning souls is a sin of direct disobedience to the main command of Jesus Christ. It is disobedience of the last command Jesus gave His people before He went away. It is disobedience in the matter that is nearest to His heart. Oh, wicked sinners that we are, when we Christians do not win souls!

2. It Is the Sin of Lack of Love for Christ

Those who do not win souls as they ought are disobedient Christians, but that is not all. Their disobedience proves their lack of love for Christ.

In John 14:15, Jesus said to the same apostles to whom He first gave the Great Commission, "If ye love me, keep my commandments." And then in John 14:23, the same night He was betrayed, Jesus continued, "If a man love me, he will keep my words." Then in the next verse, John 14:24, Jesus said, "He that loveth me not keepeth not my sayings: and the word which ye hear is not mine, but the Father's which sent me."

There it is as clear as it can be, that if you love Christ you will obey Him, you will keep His words. If you love the Father, you will keep these words, because they are really the words of the Father as well as of the Son. Disobedience is evidence of lack of love.

All of us can well be ashamed that we do not love our Saviour better. But those who love the Saviour best are the best soul winners. Those who win fewer souls and work less at winning souls, love the Saviour less. Those who do not win any souls to Christ at all love Him, oh, so poorly! For Jesus Himself plainly said, "If a man love me, he will keep my words," and again, "He that loveth me not keepeth not my sayings."

In Dallas, Texas, I was called, at about 3:00 in the morning, to the bedside of a dying saint. "Daddy Hickman," with cancer of the liver, was about to go to meet his Saviour. He called his grown sons to his bedside, and took their hands and asked them a solemn question, one after another; "Son, are you going to meet me in Heaven? You can't tell me a lie on my deathbed, and I must know!" One by one the boys promised that they would take Christ as Saviour then and there, or declared that they had done so already and would live for Him. They made other holy promises. And I remember how moved one young couple related to the family were, when he called them and placed their hands together and solemnly urged them to quarrel no more but to have peace and a happy home.

How solemn are the parting words of a loved one! How

earnestly we would take to heart the last command of a dying father! But how much more earnestly we should take to heart the last command of Jesus Christ, to go and preach the gospel to sinners, to make disciples, to win souls.

Many a young man has all his life avoided the gambling table or alcoholic drinks because he promised a dear mother on her deathbed, and felt he must keep his promise. A late king of England read the Bible every day because he promised his mother, Queen Victoria, that he would. He loved his mother and so he could not ignore that sacred request. And if we love Jesus Christ we cannot ignore the plain command, the last entreaty of His heart, to go after poor lost sinners for whom He died and for whom His heart yearns, even yet, with inexpressible longing and love!

If you, then, do not win souls, your love for Christ has grown cold. Perhaps once you loved sinners, prayed for them, warned them and plead with them, but now you, like the church at Ephesus, have lost your first love. You do not win souls. Evangelists sometimes become "Bible teachers" because their love for Christ has grown cold. And Christians everywhere content themselves with the mere outward forms of worship and giving and praying and reading and doing "church work" when they ought to be winning souls. Oh, the trouble is, they are guilty of the sin of little love for Christ. For, "If a man love me he will keep my words," Jesus said.

Do you love Christ? If you do, then you will win souls. If you make small effort to win souls, then your love is small. If you make none, how can you say you love Him at all?

3. It Is the Sin of Not Following Christ

In Matthew 4:19 Jesus said, "Follow me, and I will make you fishers of men." In Mark 1:17 Jesus said, "Come ye after me, and I will make you to become fishers of men." These promises were made to the apostles, but remember, He has given us the same commission, command and promise.

This matter of following Jesus, being a disciple or learner of His ways, is a matter often mentioned in His teaching in the Gospels. In Luke 9:23 Jesus said, "If any man will come after me, let him deny himself, and take up his cross daily, and follow me." And to the rich young ruler who thought he had kept the law from his youth, Jesus said, "If thou wilt be perfect, go and sell that thou hast, and give to the poor, and thou shalt have treasure in heaven: AND COME AND FOLLOW ME" (Matt. 19:21). We are to have the mind of Christ (Phil. 2:5). And I Peter 2:21 tells us, "For even hereunto were ye called: because Christ also suffered for us, leaving us an example, that ye should follow his steps." In John 12:26 Jesus said, "If any man serve me, let him follow me," and in John 14:12 we are promised that one who believes in Christ, "The works that I do shall he do also." So every Christian ought to follow Christ. But if you are not winning souls you are not following Christ. For He plainly says in Matthew 4:19, "Follow me, and I will make you fishers of men." The one who fails to win souls is sinning in the matter of not following Christ.

As a boy preacher I went with a dear old pastor through one summer, singing in five or six short country revival campaigns. When I started out to preaching I found I used some of the same texts and illustrations and ideas he did. Later I went with an evangelist to sing in one or two campaigns, and I learned all I could from him and used his methods and some of his sermon material. I was later assistant pastor to a godly man, a fine preacher, and to this day I acknowledge his help in many of my sermons. I followed these men, and so learned to do the work as they did it. One of the best ways to be an evangelist is to go with an evangelist and learn how he does it. But the very best way to be a soul winner is to follow Jesus, the Master Soul Winner, and get His passion, His burden for dying sinners, and be led by His Holy Spirit in winning them. No one really follows Jesus except as he becomes a soul winner. Jesus makes every true disciple, every learner, every one who follows in His steps, into a soul winner something like Himself.

If you, then, are not a soul winner, you are not following Jesus. What a sin!

4. Not to Win Souls Means That You Are Not Abiding in Christ

In John 15:1–8, the Lord Jesus gave a precious teaching about fruit bearing. Christ Himself is the true vine, and we are His branches. He said, "Every branch in me that beareth not fruit he taketh away: and every branch that beareth fruit, he purgeth it, that it may bring forth more fruit." You see, the idea is that every Christian should be in such close touch with Christ that, as the sap comes from the vine into the branch with life-giving, fruit-bearing power, so the Holy Spirit may flow from Christ through us, making us fruit-bearing Christians, really making us soul winners.

Again He said, *"Abide in me, and I in you. As the branch cannot bear fruit of itself, except it abide in the vine; no more can ye, except ye abide in me. I am the vine, ye are the branches: He that abideth in me, and I in him, the same bringeth forth much fruit: for without me ye can do nothing."*—John 15:4, 5. There is no way to win souls except by abiding in Christ, being in touch with Him, knowing His will, feeling His heartbeat, being wholly committed to His will and work! But every one that really abides in Christ brings forth fruit, yea, much fruit! "He that abideth in me, and I in him, the same bringeth forth much fruit." In the same chapter verse 8 says, "Herein is my Father glorified, that ye bear much fruit; so shall ye be my disciples."

Remember that the Lord Jesus wants souls saved. That is what He died for. That is what preaching the gospel is for. That is what the Great Commission means. That is the work of the churches. That is what preachers are called to do. That is what every Christian is commanded to do. Christ 'came to seek and to save that which was lost.' "Christ Jesus came into the world to save sinners." If I abide in Christ, my aim, my purpose, my burden, my business, my work, will be that same precious work. And my fruit will be that same precious fruit. Soul winning is the business for which every Christian is called. Precious souls are the fruit we should bear. The fruit of a Christian is another Christian.

If you are not a soul winner, then the Bible makes it clear that you do not abide in Christ. Your heart is not at one with His heart. Whatever your activity, whatever your reputation, however sanctimonious you feel and however much of a Pharisee you are in your life, *you do not abide in Christ, if you do not win souls!* What a sin for a Christian not to abide with surrendered heart and perfect union, and so help in His blessed and main business of winning souls!

5. Not to Win Souls Is the Sin of Dishonesty in a Sacred Trust

In Matthew 25:14–30 is the parable of the talents. There the Saviour illustrated His own coming and kingdom in the future by the story of a man who had gone into a far country and left his affairs in the hands of his own servants. To one he had given five talents, to another two, to another one talent. And you remember that the first two men doubled the money left with them by trading; the third man hid his talent in the earth, accusing his lord of reaping where he had not sown. But his master answered the servant, "Thou wicked and slothful servant . . . . Thou oughtest therefore to have put my money to the exchangers, and then at my coming I should have received mine own with usury." In the similar parable of the pounds in Luke 19:11–27, Jesus told how a lord went away to receive for himself a kingdom. First he gave his ten pounds to ten servants, saying to them, "Occupy till I come." When he returned, as Jesus will one day return, he called to them for an accounting. Again one man had laid up his pound in a napkin and had no increase, and Jesus called him, "Thou wicked servant"!

The idea in each case is that Jesus has given us His affairs for which we are to care. As honest stewards of that committed to our care, we must bring fruit; we must win souls. Every man who has received the gospel and all the blessings of salvation and has not passed them on is wicked, dishonest—a servant who has robbed his master of the proper increase he has a right to expect for his investment. Those whose pounds multiplied were to rule with their lord when he returned. How guilty was the wicked man who cheated his lord and had no increase to bring! So every Christian who does not win souls is a dishonest servant, and will face Christ with shame.

Sometimes we hear of the frightful scandal of a man who has been made executor of a will and stolen the funds he handled. Some man before his death appointed a friend to administer his estate, and to see that his widow and his orphan children were properly cared for. But the unfaithful administrator has been known to use the money for his own ends, or to waste it in speculation. Sometimes the widow lives in poverty, and the children, instead of being provided for as the father intended, must leave school. The administrator who wastes the estate committed to his hand, or who uses it for his own selfish gain, is a crook, a thief, a dishonest man. And that is exactly the kind of person a Christian is who takes salvation, takes all the blessings that God gives him freely, and then, instead of passing them on to others as he has been commanded to do, makes his Christian life only a matter of his own safety and comfort and blessing, and never wins the souls for whom Christ died! How wicked, how dishonest is the Christian who is an unfaithful steward of the gospel!

But the sin of the Christian who does not win souls is also dishonesty toward *men*. Paul said, "I am debtor both to the Greeks, and to the Barbarians; both to the wise, and to the unwise. So, as much as in me is, I am ready to preach the gospel to you that are at Rome also" (Rom. 1:14, 15). Paul was a man, one of a race of men. Paul could not wash his hands of his fellow men. Every man that lives owes something to the race. Every child receives from mother and father more than he can ever pay them. If he pays his debt at all it must be to the rest of the world. It is only a murderer like Cain who can say, "Am I my brother's keeper?" We owe a debt to every poor dying sinner! We are crooked, dishonest, unfaithful to a trust, if we do not share with others the precious gospel we have.

Dr. H. A. Ironside in 1943 was in Dallas, and in a letter to me enclosed a circular announcing his engagements in a number of colored churches with striking names. Across the top of the circular Dr. Ironside simply wrote, "Trying to pay my debt to my colored brethren." Every Christian has a debt to sinners. He has received that which is not his alone. If he selfishly takes for himself all the blessings of God he receives and does not lead others to know Jesus and have peace and forgiveness and a home in Heaven, if he does not keep others out of the torments of Hell, he is a dishonest man, an unfaithful steward, a wicked sinner against both God and man!

6. Not to Win Souls Is the Sin of a Short-Sighted Fool

These are strong words, but consider the words of the Scripture and see if they are not true. Proverbs 11:30 says, "The fruit of the righteous is a tree of life; and he that winneth souls is wise." Christians should bear fruit as a tree of life, and every wise Christian wins souls.

The same thing is taught in Daniel 12:2, 3 which says:

"And many of them that sleep in the dust of the earth shall awake, some to everlasting life, and some to shame and everlasting contempt. And they that be wise shall shine as the brightness of the firmament; and they that turn many to righteousness as the stars forever and ever."

Oh, the bright shining of soul winners in Heaven! They that turn many to righteousness shall shine "as the stars forever and ever." Here we see that the true wisdom takes the long look. A Christian who has any spiritual wisdom can see it is not best to center his endeavors on things that pass away with his life. To make money, to make friends, to enjoy the pleasures of life—to be much concerned about these passing pleasures and this passing wealth is not good sense. It is not spiritual wisdom. When "them that sleep in the dust of the earth shall awake," when Christians come before Christ to receive their awards, when God's bonfire burns up the wood, hay and stubble of wasted lives, then every Christian who did not win souls will find that he has played the consummate fool!

Psalms 53:1 says, "The fool hath said in his heart, There is no God." No Christian can be that kind of a fool. Jesus said to the two disciples on the way to Emmaus, "O fools, and slow of heart to believe all that the prophets have spoken." These were Christians, but they were guilty of a kindred folly to that of the atheist. And the Christian who never wins souls is a fool, too, and for a very similar reason. The man who denies God and eternity is a fool. The man who does not believe the Bible is a fool. And so the man who lives as if this world were the only world; as if it were better to make money than to win souls; as if it were more important to fill his belly and clothe his back and live in a fine home and drive a nice car and make a name for himself, than to lay up treasures, and meet there in Heaven a host of those he has won to Christ, that man is a fool!

Oh, the short-sighted folly of those who neglect eternal things for temporal things! Oh, the sin of those who do not accept the value that Christ put upon a soul! Oh, how wicked is the sin of us poor foolish Christians who do not win souls and thus who miss the chance to shine forever and rejoice forever with the heart of the Saviour we have made so glad, by bringing sinners for whom He died to love and trust Him and be saved!

7. Not to Win Souls Is the Sin of Blood-Guilt; the Sin of Soul-Manslaughter

In Ezekiel 3:17–19, the word of the Lord came to Ezekiel, saying:

"Son of man, I have made thee a watchman unto the house of Israel: therefore hear the word at my mouth, and give them warning from me. When I say unto the wicked, Thou shalt surely die; and thou givest him not warning, nor speakest to warn the wicked from his wicked way, to save his life; the same wicked man shall die in his iniquity; but HIS BLOOD WILL I REQUIRE AT THINE HAND. Yet if thou warn the wicked, and he turn not from his wickedness, nor from his wicked way, he shall die in his iniquity; BUT THOU HAST DELIVERED THY SOUL."

If Ezekiel did not warn the Israelites about their iniquity, and if they died in their sins, then God required their blood at the hand of Ezekiel! What a staggering thought is this, that God says to a man about sinners, "His blood will I require at thine hand"! But if Ezekiel warned the wicked, even if the wicked did not turn, then God said, "Thou hast delivered thy soul."

That strange commission was given to Ezekiel for the nation Israel. Surely it implies that God still holds people to account for the souls of those that they do not warn! Surely we are guilty of the blood of every poor lost soul who goes to Hell if we had a chance to warn them, to weep over them, to woo them tenderly and win them and get them to come to Christ, and we did not!

Paul had this in mind when he came to Miletus, the little port of the great city Ephesus, and had the elders of Ephesus meet him there. Solemnly facing these preachers, Paul told them that after his three years' ministry in Ephesus they would see his face no more, and then said, "Wherefore I take you to record this day, that I am pure from the blood of all men. For I have not shunned to declare unto you all the counsel of God" (Acts 20:26, 27). Then he said again, "Therefore watch, and remember, that by the space of three years I ceased not to warn every one night and day with tears" (Acts 20:31).

Paul could solemnly say, 'After three years in Ephesus I

am not to blame if any person here goes to Hell. I have no blood on my hands! I have gone night and day with tears, publicly and from house to house, carrying the whole counsel of God. I am not to blame if anybody goes to Hell!'

O Christian, is there blood on your hands? Are you guilty of the death of immortal souls for whom Christ died, because you did not warn them?

A missionary to China tells how, when a boat overturned in a Chinese river, he urged some near-by Chinese fishermen to bring their boat quickly and help him rescue a man who was struggling, drowning. The fishermen said it was none of their business. "How much?" they asked. They insisted on a price of fifty dollars before they would rescue the drowning man. The missionary gave them all the money he had, about forty dollars, and at last persuaded them to try to rescue the drowning man, but when he was brought out of the water it was too late. Life had already fled. The callous hearts of the fishermen took no responsibility for their drowning country- man. But they were guilty of murder, as certain as there is a God in Heaven to hold men to account!

But are you much different, Christian, when you let people near you go to Hell and you never warn them, never weep over them, never see that they have the gospel?

In Roosevelt, Oklahoma, I promised to go see a dying woman who was distressed about her soul. But I waited until the second day, and she died before I ever saw her. In Dallas, Texas, an old man, past eighty, heard me on the radio and wrote, saying, "I am dying with cancer and I am not ready to die. Brother Rice, please come and pray with me and help me to get ready to die." But I had so many burdens each day I postponed it, and finally after two weeks I sent a young preacher to visit the old man and help him prepare to meet God. When no one answered the doorbell a neighbor came to tell the young preacher that the old man had died and the family were then gone to his funeral! I have hopes that in their extremity these two people may have turned to the Lord and may have trusted Him. I say I have some hopes, but no certainty at all. And oh, what will I say to the Lord Jesus when I see Him, if He asks me to give an account for the souls of these two who sent for me and I did not get there in time!

The sin of not winning souls is the sin, the blood-guilty, terrible sin of soul-manslaughter. I beg you in Jesus' name, consider how guilty you must be in God's sight if you do not put your very best and all your heart's strength and love into the one precious business of soul winning!

So, Christian, if you do not win souls, you are not right with God. You may be saved, but you are not a good disciple. You are a backslider. You may be born into God's family, but you are a poor, disobedient, wilful child. If you are God's child you are a disobedient one. If you are God's servant you are an unfaithful one. If you follow the Saviour at all, you follow afar off.

Consider again, this seven-fold sin of failing to win souls. It is the sin of disobedience, of lack of love, of failing to follow Christ, of not abiding in Christ, the sin of dishonesty in a sacred trust, a sin of short-sighted folly, missing eternal rewards, and a sin of blood-guilt for which we must give an account!

May God convict His people of their sin in not winning souls dying all around us.

Chapter 8.

> ## "SPEAK NOT EVIL ONE OF ANOTHER, BRETHREN"
> —Jas. 4:11

*M*ORE PEOPLE sin with the tongue than any other way.

People sin *more often* with the tongue than any other way.

The terrible sin of the tongue is dealt with in detail in James, chapter 3. There we are told that, "If any man offend not in word, the same is a perfect man." God says that the tongue is a little matter but it is full of deadly poison, that it sets on fire the course of nature and is set on fire of Hell. And James 4:11 commands, "Speak not evil one of another, brethren."

It is wrong to speak evil of another Christian when you do not tell the truth.

It is wrong to speak evil of another Christian when you do not know whether it is so or not.

It is always wrong to speak evil of a Christian, even when you feel sure you are telling the truth. The Scripture plainly and emphatically commands, "Speak not evil one of another."

Many Christians pride themselves on telling the truth and the whole truth no matter what anybody thinks about it. They say, "Hew to the line and let the chips fall where they will." Other people say, "I say just what I think, no matter what people think about it. I am no hypocrite. I am not mealy-mouthed." But Christians need to learn the Christian grace of not telling all the truth and not saying all that they think. The sin of criticism is a bitter, wicked, guilty sin that brings the wrath of God. The critical tongue is one that is "set on fire of hell."

157

There are many reasons why God condemns the critical spirit as unchristian and wicked. There are many reasons why all of us ought to confess and forsake our habit of criticism which grieves the Holy Spirit, makes others unhappy, breaks peace and fellowship among Christians, and brings shame and reproach on the cause of Christ.

"Judge Not, That Ye Be Not Judged"

Jesus said on this matter in Matthew 7:1–5:

"Judge not, that ye be not judged. For with what judgment ye judge, ye shall be judged: and with what measure ye mete, it shall be measured to you again. And why beholdest thou the mote that is in thy brother's eye, but considerest not the beam that is in thine own eye? Or how wilt thou say to thy brother, Let me pull out the mote out of thine eye; and, behold, a beam is in thine own eye? Thou hypocrite, first cast out the beam out of thine own eye; and then shalt thou see clearly to cast out the mote out of thy brother's eye."

First, a Christian ought not to stand in judgment on another Christian because he does not know all about it. Most gossip and most criticism is based on hearsay and rumor. Your criticism of other people is usually simply quoting that old liar, "they say." Before you pass a criticism that will break somebody's heart or bring tears or shame or arouse anger or cause some weak Christian to stumble, you had better consider carefully whether you absolutely know what you are talking about. Eli thought that Hannah, a broken-hearted woman in tearful prayer for a child, was drunk. He thought that he *saw* her drunk. But he did that woman an injustice and would have committed a terrible sin to have reported anything of the kind. The apostles at Pentecost were accused of being drunk when in fact they were filled with the Holy Spirit (Acts 2:13). Those who saw them sinned against God when they criticised the Spirit-filled Christians. So you had better be mighty careful before you criticise people even when you think you know they are wrong. "I saw it with my own eyes"—how many false and cruel slanders are started with such a statement! But Eli's eyes deceived him (I Sam. 1:13–15). Hannah was not drunk though she appeared to be. The apostles at Pentecost were not drunk though the prejudiced observers thought they saw convincing evidence.

A woman once said to me, "Why have you got it in for me? You passed me on the sidewalk and deliberately looked the other way and wouldn't speak!" Poor, dear, sensitive soul! I am so absent-minded I must often offend in that way. My burdens and problems are so many that I sometimes forget the most ordinary courtesies and often do not see people when I look them square in the face. I never remembered even seeing the woman just mentioned. Yet she sinned when she judged me. And about all such cases the Bible says, "Judge not, that ye be not judged." Do not feel free to criticise with unchristian license, for all of us are so human and weak and ignorant that we do not know enough to pass judgment fairly.

Every lawyer discovers that among obviously honest people, witnesses sworn to tell nothing but the truth and obviously trying to tell the truth, differ in their reports of things to which they were eye witnesses! If three people see the same automobile accident they will yet not agree on what really happened. One reason we cannot tell things straight is because we do not see them straight. Our capacities are so limited and our sin-cursed human nature so frail that a prayerful Christian dare not judge others on his own judgement. For God knows we do not want others to judge us by appearances. "Appearances are deceitful" and "all is not gold that glitters."

I was once forcefully reminded that even sincere, intelligent people do not see things as they are. My dear friend, Rev. P. B. Chenault, was killed when his car was rammed and wrecked by a drunken driver. When the drunken killer was tried I was brought to the stand to identify the car. Mr. Chenault had just concluded a two-weeks' campaign in the

church of which I was pastor in Dallas. On the stand the
prosecuting attorney asked me, "What kind of car did Mr.
Chenault drive?"

"A 1938 two-door Buick Sedan," I replied.

"Did you know the car well?"

"Yes; the car sat in my driveway for two weeks, I often rode
in it, I even drove it," I replied.

The district attorney then asked, "What color was the car?"

"It was black," I replied.

"Are you sure?" asked the prosecutor.

"Yes, I am sure; the car is black. I have seen it since the
wreck."

I went back to the witness rooms and the case proceeded.
That evening I discovered that the deputy sheriff who had
seen the wreck, arrested the drunken driver, called the ambu-
lance, and had the car towed in to a garage, had sworn on the
stand that the car was green. The district attorney asked that
I see the car again and I was summoned as a witness the
following day. I went to the garage a block away to see the
car and discovered that it was not black, nor green; it was
dark blue! I had been misled because the car was very dark,
and got the impression that it was black. The deputy sheriff,
equally sincere, was misled by his remembrance of the green
smear of paint left on the car driven by the drunkard. The
undercoating of paint on Mr. Chenault's car was dark green
and that color was left on the other car. And that glaring impression overruled in his mind the true color which he saw
repeatedly with his own eyes.

Both of us swore to tell the truth, the whole truth, and
nothing but the truth. Both of us sincerely intended to do so.
But neither of us did. So every Christian should be humbly
conscious that he cannot trust even his own sight, his own
hearing, and his own memory when criticising others. How
foolish, then, how wicked, to speak evil of another even when
we think we tell the exact truth.

No critic, for example, could tell the exact truth about

David's sin with Bathsheba if he had never read the fifty-first Psalm. And any Jerusalem gossiper might, with his own ears, have heard Peter deny Christ, and yet he could not possibly have related the thing as it was if he did not see Peter go away in the dawn of that sad, sad day, weeping bitterly, or who did not know the import of that holy meeting by the sea of Galilee a few days later as recorded in John 21:15–17. In either case the exact facts, outwardly, those that could be seen and heard and measured, could not possibly be judged truly without a heart-knowledge of the unseen factors of those loving, impulsive, sinning but truly devoted Christians —David and Peter.

"Speak not evil one of another, brethren," even if it is true or if you think it is true. You dare not trust yourself to judge.

How blind our criticism often is! We speak evil of people and quote what they said, only we do not quote *exactly* what they said. On the same basis Jesus was cruelly and bitterly criticised. Witnesses came and swore in the trial which condemned Him to be crucified that they had heard Jesus say concerning the temple at Jerusalem, "I will destroy this temple that is made with hands, and within three days I will build another made without hands" (Mark 14:58). They swore that therefore Jesus was an enemy of the Jewish religion and of the temple. Actually, Jesus had said something very similar to that but "he spake of the temple of his body" (John 2:21), that is, that He would rise from the dead after three days in the grave.

Evil speaking concerning others is always unkind, usually it is silly and foolish and often it is downright vicious. When you do not know exactly what a man meant by his words, and often you do not even remember the exact words, then it is foolish to do him harm and sin against Christ by hurtful criticism.

And if we are not fit to judge people by what we ourselves see and hear, then how can we judge them by hearsay and gossip?

When I was very young I was greatly impressed with the silliness of gossip by a game people used to play, called "gossip." We would sit in a big circle around a room and one person would start the game by softly whispering a sentence in another's ear. Then that one would turn and again whisper what he heard, as he understood it, to his neighbor, and so the message would be relayed around the circle. Invariably it came back greatly changed, unrecognizable, usually with no connection whatever to the first whispered sentence! So it is with gossip and that is one reason the Bible condemns so sharply such talking about others. Hearsay, gossip, is usually perverted and twisted by ignorance and winged by malice, sped by hate. People *speak* evil of their neighbours because they *think* evil of their neighbours. Alas, too often "The wish is father to the thought" and we accuse people of doing what we hoped they did. So Christians are commanded not to suffer as 'busybodies in other men's matters' (I Pet. 4:15), and women particularly are warned about "wandering about from house to house; and not only idle, but tattlers also and busybodies, speaking things which they ought not" (I Tim. 5:13).

In the same seventh chapter of Matthew where Jesus tells us, "Judge not, that ye be not judged," is another statement often used as an excuse for judging. Verse 16 says, "Ye shall know them by their fruits. Do men gather grapes of thorns, or figs of thistles?" People admit that the Saviour commanded not to judge but in the same breath they say that He permitted us to judge men by their fruits. But a little care will show that verse 1 and verse 16 in the seventh chapter of Matthew do not contradict each other. In verse 16 Jesus was talking about false teachers. In verse 15 He says, "Beware of false prophets, which come to you in sheep's clothing, but inwardly they are ravening wolves." False teachers can be known as false teachers by their fruits. You cannot know the heart of a false teacher, cannot know his motives, cannot surely know whether he is saved or not. But you can compare his teaching with the Bible and learn whether or not he is a false prophet. For instance, one who denies the deity of Christ or the inspiration of the Bible or the blood atonement is a false prophet. You may know him by his fruits. But to know a man is wrong in doctrine does not give you the right to judge him personally. Jesus did not mean this as an excuse to speak evil of brethren or to pass judgment on their motives or hearts.

Criticism of Ministers Is Especially Forbidden

And the same chapter (I Tim. 5:19) warns particularly, "Against an elder receive not an accusation, but before two or three witnesses." An elder, in Bible language, means a minister. Of all those who suffer from slander and gossip, none are so sinned against as ministers of God. They are public men. All they do is of interest to the public. They are held to be examples, as they ought to be, and so people expect of them more than of other people. Preachers who preach against sin offend many people and so there are many who look for something to criticise. The gainsaying outside world which hated Jesus Christ naturally is not friendly toward His ministers who serve Him faithfully. Thus they are subject to criticism. So Christians are warned not to receive an accusation against a preacher except by the mouth of two or three witnesses. The Scripture evidently means eyewitnesses.

I fear that some preachers sometimes sin grievously in judging their brethren harshly. If a preacher does not have the same belief about methods we too often criticise harshly, too often go by hearsay. I have more than once been rebuked in my own mind for believing what people told me about preachers. One notorious preacher did what seems to me a very sad and wicked thing. At various times he accused six different preachers of immorality with women. All had been his intimate friends. If a certain preacher away from home

wired back for money, he doubtless had been in some un-
savory scrape, this critic hinted. If another's health was
broken down, you might be sure there was a woman in the
case. About another preacher it was, "I understand they have
bad trouble in his church—woman trouble they *tell* me!"
The implication was clear. Another preacher and his wife had
a misunderstanding and my friend said it was because she
learned about a certain red-headed woman. In another case
it was, "A friend tells me he had to leave a former pastorate
out West because of a woman." I felt then and feel now that
the suspicions cast on those six preachers were unjust. There
was no proof ever given, and all but one are still very useful,
earnest men of God. In most of the cases, if there was any
truth at all in the insinuations and accusations, it was probably greatly overdrawn. Even if it had all been true, which it
was not, it ought never to have been said. And let every
one who reads this search his own heart to see whether or not
he has been guilty of similar sins. The Bible commands,
"Speak not evil one of another, brethren."

A world-famous evangelist, a marvelous soul winner, whose
long life in the white light of public gaze had been spent without a reproach, lost his beloved wife. His hungry heart had
long been starved for the companionship which other men
have in their homes, but which he was denied by his world-
wide service for the Lord and his constant travels. So after
a year or two he married again. His sin was only that his
bride was a *young* woman, though most devout and blameless.

With critics it mattered not at all that his life was blameless, that his influence over millions was only for good. Many
Christian know-it-alls criticised, said, "It's too bad!" and
prophesied, "You'll see—it will be the end of his great ministry." The more "fundamental" the ministers sometimes the
more catty were their gossipy remarks. Meantime this magnificent man of God has gone on with his blessed ministry in
the marvelous power of the Spirit.

We are reminded of God, "Touch not mine anointed, and

do my prophets no harm" (Psa. 105:15). It is a special sin to speak evil of preachers.

"That Ye Be Not Judged"

Christians ought not to judge others; first, because it is wrong and our judgment is usually so far from correct. We are commanded not to judge. But then another very sensible and practical reason is given—"that ye be not judged." Jesus said, "Judge not, that ye be not judged. For with what judgment ye judge, ye shall be judged: and with what measure ye mete, it shall be measured to you again" (Matt. 7:1, 2).

If we want people to deal truly with us then let us be doubly sure that we deal truly with others. We do not want to be accused on hearsay evidence; then let us not accuse others about things concerning which we are not certain. And even when we do wrong, we want our frailty to be measured with kindness. "With the same measure that ye mete withal it shall be measured to you again" (Luke 6:38), the Saviour says. If we want kindness we should give kindness. If we want our faults to be covered with charity and brotherly love and forgiveness, then God help us to be as kind and as charitable to others. Forgive where you would be forgiven. Have mercy where you yourself so greatly need mercy.

You say the other man has a mote in his eye, and probably you are correct about that. All of us have motes in our eyes. The world we live in has plenty of motes, dust and trash, worldliness and sin floating about our moral natures just as the dust and trash is blown about in the air and may get in our physical eyes. All of us are sinners and there is plenty of room to criticise the best saint of God that ever walked this earth. I know I could do a grand job of criticising Moses or David or Peter. And Paul could not get along with Barnabas. Besides, he was headstrong and went to Jerusalem when God plainly commanded Him not to. So I could criticise Paul and tell the truth. In fact, I believe I could find room for criticism in any Christian. Only God Himself is perfect. But before you start out to pick the mote out of your neighbour's eye, first pull the beam (the timber or plank) out of your own eye. Most of us are not fit to criticise others.

The woman you criticise—are you sure you love God better than she? Are you sure that your record is as clean in God's sight? If you were burdened, as she may be, or tempted the same way, would you stand the test? That man who drinks—if you had his taste, his background and his environment and companions, are you certain you wouldn't be tempted to drink, too? And if you do not sin in just the same way, do you not sin in other ways? Who are you to condemn a servant of God, one for whom Christ died? Remember that the Bible says, "To his own master he standeth or falleth" (Rom. 14:4). Why not have the love and forgiveness of Christ, and remember that the Bible says, "Who is he that condemneth? It is Christ that died, yea rather, that is risen again . . ." (Rom. 8:34). Christ knew all about sinners and yet He died for them and you may do well to have the same attitude.

The woman taken in adultery (John 8:1–11), certainly deserved condemnation. Those who spoke against her were eye-witnesses of her shame—didn't they have a right to talk? Didn't they have a right to stone her as she really deserved according to the Mosaic law? No, not as long as they had been guilty of sin too. "He that is without sin among you, let him first cast a stone at her," Jesus said (John 8:7). If all of us waited until we were without sin before throwing stones, we would surely never speak evil of our neighbours, never harass and burn and bring tears or shame or broken hearts. We would never discourage a weak Christian nor give joy to the wicked unsaved who delight in the faults of God's people. Well does the Scripture say, "Brethren, if a man be overtaken in a fault, ye which are spiritual, restore such an one in the spirit of meekness; considering thyself, lest thou also be tempted" (Gal. 6:1). Criticism leads to further sin. Criticism is a proud and haughty sin that leads the critic away from prayer and so brings him out of touch with God into greater temptation and so finally down to a fall and shame. Criticism is part of the pride that goes before destruction, part of the haughty spirit that goes before a fall, so 'consider lest ye also be tempted.'

Christ's Example

We might well consider the example of our dear Saviour in this matter "Who, when he was reviled, reviled not again" (I Pet. 2:23). There were multitudes of people about whom Jesus could have said the bitterest things and said them truly, and yet He did not say them. Concerning those who crucified Him, He said, "Father, forgive them; for they know not what they do " (Luke 23:34). He went like a lamb to the slaughter, and as a sheep before her shearers is dumb, so He openeth not his mouth. He did not embitter the broken hearts of His followers by criticism of others at this time. He did not engender hatred in their hearts against their rulers when He could have so easily done it. When Judas kissed Him with the traitor's kiss, He called him "friend," and when His heart was broken at the Last Supper He dipped in the sop with Judas and said no evil word about the man who was even then preparing to bargain with the priests and sell his master for a few pieces of silver.

Consider the sermons of Jesus. When He spoke of some one personally and by name, it was usually only in kindness. In the true story of the rich man and Lazarus, He gives the name of Lazarus which would be joy to his loved ones and friends. Charitably He leaves unsaid the name of the poor rich man who died and went to Hell. Not a brother or sister or child could ever be grieved or shamed by his name being called, though certainly Jesus knew his name! To the Pharisees themselves He spoke boldly and plainly about their hypocrisy and sin, but we do not know that He ever spoke in the third person about any individual Pharisee in unkind terms. He knew many of them that were lost and wicked and hypocrites and could have called them by name, but as far as we know

He never did in speaking of them to others. When Mary anointed Him with ointment He praised her openly and said, "She hath done what she could." At the same table and involved in the same incident was wicked, godless, covetous, traitorous Judas, protesting that the ointment ought to be sold and the money given to the poor. Yet Jesus did not expose Judas. How easy it would have been! And how quickly many of us preachers would have done it! And Judas deserved it. But it would have done no good, would have brought division, hate and shame.

How kind was the Holy Spirit in His inspired statements about Joseph of Arimathea. In the Gospels written by Matthew, Mark and Luke, presumably while Joseph and his intimates were alive, we are told how Joseph was a rich man, a councilor (a member of the Sanhedrin), one who looked for the coming of Jesus, and are told how he gladly gave his new tomb and came boldly to Pilate to ask the body of Jesus. It is only in the Gospel of John, written many, many years later when Joseph himself and practically all that generation had died, that the Holy Spirit inspired John to say that Joseph was a disciple, ah, yes, "but secretly for fear of the Jews" (John 19:38). The shameful fact of his cowardice, his refusal to speak up for Jesus in the Sanhedrin, his fear for the loss of money and friends—they were not revealed until they could cause Joseph no bitterness of heart. And then this was written for our admonition. So if you know a Christian who is a coward, perhaps you had better say nothing about it until he is gone to Heaven!

Dear old abused Paul, the aged prisoner of Jesus Christ, spoke thus of one of his bitterest enemies, "Alexander the coppersmith did me much evil: the Lord reward him according to his works" (II Tim. 4:14). As far as I know that is the worst that Paul ever said about anybody. He did not give the details. Probably he only mentioned the matter because the sin was a public sin in the church turning the hearts of the people against Paul and for that reason it was proper to mention it publicly. One man in Corinth was living in such shameful sin that Paul counselled them to withdraw fellowship from him at once. But he went into no detailed discussion of the man's sins. In II Corinthians, after the man had repented, Paul urges that he be forgiven quickly and confirmed in the faith (II Cor. 2:5–8), and in neither account is the man's name called. In later years that man could never be reproached by strangers who had read in Paul's epistles of his sins!

If you know a man's wicked past but now he is sorry for it, then never mention it. Some one you know has a girl who has played the harlot or a boy who is in the penitentiary; in God's name help them hide that shame and pray with them for the restoration of the erring one! All of us have sins enough and sorrow enough. Christians should not add to sorrow but rather "Bear ye one another's burdens, and so fulfill the law of Christ" (Gal. 6:2). In my heart are burdens and sorrows of many others, confessed to me, which I will carry with me to my grave or to the rapture, wept over, prayed about, but never mentioned, many of them even to my wife.

Do you suppose that you have grieved the Spirit of God by criticism? In the letter to the Ephesians, the last part of chapter 4 and the first part of chapter 5 deal with sins that grieve the Holy Spirit. Ephesians 4:30 says: "Grieve not the Holy Spirit of God, whereby ye are sealed unto the day of redemption." When you read that list, nearly all of them are sins of the tongue: "bitterness," "wrath," "anger," "clamour," "evil speaking," "jesting," and such like. Maybe that is one reason you do not win souls. Perhaps because of your critical, sinful tongue your prayers are not answered. Perhaps your criticism of your brothers or sisters for whom Christ died has so grieved the tender Holy Spirit that you do not feel the joy of His presence any more! Then confess your sin today, I beg you, ask God to give you such a tender heart of love and forgiveness that you will obey the Scriptural command, "Speak not evil one of another, brethren."

The Harm of Criticism

Let us summarize some of the evils that result from this sin of criticism. When you speak evil one of another, terrible results follow.

1. *It often ruins the life of the one criticised.* Many a girl has thrown herself away after her reputation was ruined by foul-minded and wicked gossipers. Many young Christians fell into sin and then because of unkind and unchristian criticism, with never a helping hand, they became so discouraged that they never went back to the church. Some have admitted to me that they sinned in going to dances or in getting drunk or getting angry, but were so severely criticised by those who did nothing to help that they never had heart to try again to live a Christian life. Many pastors have quit the ministry, unable to face the hounding of unreasonable, unspiritual, worldly-minded critics. The most unselfish preacher who ever lived, I suppose, has been accused repeatedly of "preaching for money." The boldest and most uncompromising of preachers has been accused of catering to public favor if he would not preach what his critics wished to have him preach. Many a preacher who is sound in doctrine and believes the whole Bible, yet differs from a long-tongued and evil-minded critic and so is called a modernist! Every warmhearted, soul-winning, Spirit-filled preacher has been called a fanatic. Preachers' wives and children are subject to merciless criticism. Criticism has ruined the life of many a preacher.

Criticism causes suicides, broken health and ruined nerves. Gossip has broken countless homes, has estranged brothers, has divided churches. Evil speaking of other Christians is a heartless, cruel and terrible sin which often ruins lives.

2. *Young Christians are often caused to stumble by hearing criticism of other Christians.* In thousands of cases, children in a family lose interest in Sunday School and church because their parents criticised the Sunday School teachers or the

pastors or the members of the church. They quickly become disheartened and disgusted. When young Christians hear so much criticism they often feel that there is no one they can trust, that it does not pay to try to live for God. They become discouraged. Of such cases as these Jesus said, "Whoso shall offend one of these little ones which believe in me, it were better for him that a millstone were hanged about his neck, and that he were drowned in the depth of the sea." (Matt. 18:6). Colossians 3:21 says, "Fathers, provoke not your children to anger, lest they be discouraged." Parents, too critical, may sin here. Every young Christian needs someone to look up to and depend upon and pattern after. Do not ruin the lives of young Christians by heartless, profitless and thoughtless evil speaking of other Christians. Whatever faults you know of in a Christian, it always invariably does harm instead of good to discuss them before others.

3. *Evil speaking gives Christianity a bad name with the outside world.* Christians are supposed to love each other, and the most ignorant sinner knows instinctively that brotherly love is the mark of a Christian. Jesus said, "By this shall all men know that ye are my disciples, if ye have love one to another" (John 13:35). We are told in I Corinthians, thirteen, that love is the greatest thing in the world. Disagreements among Christians should be few and corrected as quickly as possible. Jesus said, "Agree with thine adversary quickly, whiles thou art in the way with him" (Matt. 5:25). And we are commanded to "Let not the sun go down upon your wrath" (Eph. 4:26). Critical, suspicious, quarrelling Christians are the poorest possible recommendation of the Lord Jesus Christ!

In a revival in west Texas, one night I preached on the sin of divorce. Unknown to me, two men active in the church work had been divorced and remarried. One of them had married a divorced woman. These two hotly resented my sermon; one threatened me with physical violence, and they talked bitterly in their homes about the preaching. But in

a few days the power of the gospel broke the hearts of these
men. In tears, humbly and ashamed, they came to beg my forgiveness and asked me to pray for their families. One man
was particularly concerned over his teen-aged daughter who
had shown some interest in her soul early in the revival.
However, as he had raved angrily concerning the preacher,
this girl's convictions had all seemed to leave her. Now she
could not be reached, it seemed. Her angry father had broken
down her confidence in the preacher. Later, when her father
and I together earnestly tried to win her to Christ, the child,
with set face and hardened heart, resisted every appeal. The
man went away convinced, as I was, that he had blocked the
salvation of his own daughter by his criticism of the preacher.
No doubt there are multitudes in Hell who went there because of critical tongues of Christians who spoke evil one of
another and particularly of preachers and Sunday School
teachers and Christian workers.

Before you ever accuse an evangelist of preaching for
money or a pastor of favoritism among the members or any
Christian worker of worldliness or sin, you had better consider whether you will thereby block the only influence God
has for the winning of your children or loved ones. When
we learn to earnestly respect Christians, particularly Christian
workers, and strive to maintain their good reputation, then
the outside world will respect them as we do and never
before.

4. *Evil speaking brings division and strife.* Years ago my
talented stepmother used to give a reading that ended in
these words,

> Words unexpressed may sometimes fall back dead,
> But God Himself can't kill them when they are said!

Critical tongues and evil speaking have more to do with
divisions in churches and among Christians than any other
factor in the world. Proverbs 26:20 tells us: "Where no wood
is, there the fire goeth out: so where there is no talebearer,

the strife ceaseth." Evil speaking leads to misjudging of one another, leads to exaggerations and misrepresentations of sin. It leads to hate and vengeance and a hundred other sins. Evil speaking and criticism are talebearing and the fuel for all the sins of dissension and division.

5. *Do not forget that, most important of all, the Holy Spirit of God is grieved by the sin of evil speaking and criticism.* Perhaps this sin, more than others, is responsible for the spiritual coldness and lack of the presence and power of the Spirit of God in our churches and in our homes.

What to Do When a Brother Sins

If you know of a brother or sister who has sinned, what should you do about it? There is always something you can do.

1. If it is a sin against you, then go to the offender directly and kindly. Jesus said:

"Moreover if thy brother shall trespass against thee, go and tell him his fault between thee and him alone: if he shall hear thee, thou hast gained thy brother. But if he will not hear thee, then take with thee one or two more, that in the mouth of two or three witnesses every word may be established. And if he shall neglect to hear them, tell it unto the church: but if he neglect to hear the church, let him be unto thee as an heathen man and a publican."   —Matt. 18:15–17.

That Scripture gives the course of action when one has wronged you. It does not mean that you are then to talk about him nor campaign against him nor to get even. In every case you are to forgive him. If possible, you are to help him to make it right.

2. If you know a Christian has sinned but he has not wronged you personally, there may be times when you can be a blessing. Do not criticise. If you can go in Christian love and if your life is such that you will have the respect and confidence of the man who has sinned, he will probably welcome you. If you are not filled with the Spirit then you

are not fit to reproach anybody about his sin. If your life is not better than the one you hope to help, then very likely you cannot do good.

3. You can always pray. Pray for those in trouble as you will want people to pray for you when you get into trouble. Be a partaker in the intercessory work of Jesus Christ, 'Who ever liveth to make intercession for us.' There are plenty to accuse. Why not resolve that, God helping you, you will always pray for. those who are attacked and talked about, whether they are guilty or not guilty? Moses interceded for the nation Israel when they made the golden calf, and through Moses' prayer the nation was spared. Abraham interceded for worldly Lot, and though Sodom and Gomorrah were destroyed, the angels said they could do nothing at all until Lot was taken from the city. Daniel, in captivity, confessed the sins of his people and interceded for them, opening his window three times daily to pray toward Jerusalem. Samuel prayed for the wicked, fickle-minded Israelites who demanded a king, and said, "God forbid that I should sin against the Lord in ceasing to pray for you" (I Sam. 12:23). One thing you can always do for people who do wrong and that is pray!

4. Restore those who are accused of sin. Get other Christians to receive them. Good old Barnabas interceded for Paul and he was received by the apostles at Jerusalem (Acts 9:26, 27). Jonathan loved and interceded for David when accused by Saul. Joab interceded for Absalom before David. If you are spiritual, then help restore the man overtaken in a fault, in the spirit of meekness as God has commanded His people. Do not sin by evil speaking.

Don't

If an impulse comes to say
Some unthoughted word today
That may drive a friend away,
    Don't say it.

If you've heard a word of blame
Cast upon your neighbor's name
That may injure his fair fame,
 Don't tell it.

If malicious gossip's tongue
Some vile slander may have flung
On the head of old or young,
 Don't repeat it.

Even if the story's true,
Think of all the harm 'twould do;
How much better, then, if you
 Don't rehearse it.

Thoughtful, kind, helpful speech,
'Tis a gift vouchsafed to each—
This the lesson we would teach:
 Don't abuse it.

"Speak not evil one of another, brethren."

Chapter 9.

```
JUDGE NOT!
```

*"Judge not, and ye shall not be judged: condemn
not, and ye shall not be condemned: forgive, and
ye shall be forgiven."*   —Luke 6:37.

$\mathcal{M}$Y HUSBAND says he is a Christian,
but he is not," said a lady the other
day. "That man is not a Christian; he claims to be, but I
know he is not by the way he lives," said a pastor.

How common that is! Yet what a wicked sin it is, clearly
and repeatedly forbidden in the Bible. God plainly commands us not to judge others. We are not to judge whether
one is saved or not; we are not to judge his motives, his sincerity, nor anything else about his heart.

Not a single Christian on the earth is to pass judgment on
the state of any person's heart or to judge whether others are
saved. Yet here is a widespread sin. The more fundamental
in doctrine Christians are the more they are tempted to become like Pharisees, feeling themselves perfectly capable to
pass judgment on others. Often the more Christians are
separated from the world, the more like Pharsaical hypocrites
they become, freely passing judgment on others who profess
to be children of God, but who do not live clean lives separated from worldliness. In literally hundreds of cases, Christians have told me that one who attended a picture show was
certainly not saved. I know the evils of the movies (see my
book, *What's Wrong With the Movies?*), but I know I have

177

no right on that basis to judge whether one is a child of God, whether he has ever been born again or not.

Since my articles on "Lodges Examined By the Bible" (now in book form) were printed in *The Sword of the Lord,* I have had a heavy mail on that subject. A number of people have written saying that one who was a lodge member could not possibly be a child of God. In the manuscript of the book on lodges, I gave the example of my godly father, a minister, who joined several lodges and the harm it did him, and said, "But my father was a saved man." The book came back from the publisher with the quotation changed by the judging editor to, *"I think* my father was a saved man," inferring a doubt.

This week, I have just answered a letter from a woman who insisted that if one fell into out-broken sin, he could not possibly have been born again.

In revivals I am constantly shocked by pastors telling me how sure they feel that certain of their members are not saved. They refer to members who can name a time and place when they definitely trusted Christ for salvation but have now grown backslidden and cold.

To all this the Lord Jesus gives a clear and definite command: "Judge not!" It is a wicked sin, a sin of pride, of self-righteousness, of arrogance. It grieves God and does unmeasured harm. I beg you, my readers, do not be guilty of this sin!

While Christians cannot judge people, they may judge certain things, certain facts. It will clear our minds if we discuss, before going further, the things that a Christian may and should judge.

First, a Christian can judge false doctrine. In Matthew 7:15–20 is a passage often misinterpreted. It is in the same chapter where Jesus said, "Judge not, that ye be not judged" (Matt. 7:1). Read this passage carefully:

"Beware of false prophets, which come to you in sheep's clothing, but inwardly they are ravening wolves. Ye shall know them by their fruits. Do mer. gather grapes of thorns, or

*figs of thistles? Even so every good tree bringeth forth good
fruit; but a corrupt tree bringeth forth evil fruit. A good
tree cannot bring forth evil fruit, neither can a corrupt tree
bring forth good fruit. Every tree that bringeth not forth
good fruit is hewn down, and cast into the fire. Wherefore by
their fruits ye shall know them."*   —Matt. 7:15–20.

Careless people seeking an excuse for their sin love to take
verse 20 of the above passage as contradicting the command
to judge not and therefore giving them a right to judge people by their fruits and thus determine whether they are saved.
But that is not the meaning of the passage as any honest and
prayerful student will see.

In these verses Jesus is talking about false prophets. The
fruit of a false prophet is false teaching, unscriptural doctrine.
Thus one may compare the preaching, teaching or writing
of a religious leader with the Bible and determine whether
or not his doctrine is true. One may read "Christian Science"
literature, for example, and see that it denies the fact of sin,
denies the blood atonement of Christ, denies the need for a
new birth, denies the fallen nature of man. One can see that
"Christian Science" makes Mary Baker Eddy about on an
equal with Christ and counts her writings inspired like the
Bible. Then any reader has a right to judge the doctrines of
Mary Baker Eddy as false doctrine. By such doctrine, then,
one knows that she was a false prophet. We cannot tell
whether or not she was saved. It looks doubtful, but no one
can know. Saved people have often fallen into false doctrine.
We cannot tell whether she was sincerely and earnestly trying
to do right. Her divorces, her taking material without giving
credit to other teachers, her boldness in placing her own writings equal to the Bible, indicate a sinful attitude of heart.
But we must leave it to God as to whether she was more
wicked than others in her heart. We certainly know her teaching is false and that she was a false teacher, a false prophet.
"Ye shall know them by their fruits."

Thus, every hearer has a right to weigh the teachings of

pastor, evangelist, Bible teacher, and author, and carefully, diligently, to compare them with the Bible. That is what the noble hearers did in Berea when they heard the preaching of Paul and Silas. "These were more noble than those in Thessalonica, in that they received the word with all readiness of mind, and searched the scriptures daily, whether those things were so" (Acts 17:11).

Christians have a right to judge doctrine but not to judge the hearts of men.

Second, Christians have a right to judge concerning right and wrong. Instead of having Christians carry differences to law to be tried in secular courts in any controversy of wages, wrongs, or damages, other Christians should be called in to arbitrate the matter prayerfully.

"Dare any of you, having a matter against another, go to law before the unjust, and not before the saints? Do ye not know that the saints shall judge the world? and if the world shall be judged by you, are ye unworthy to judge the smallest matters? Know ye not that we shall judge angels? how much more things that pertain to this life? If then ye have judgments of things pertaining to this life, set them to judge who are least esteemed in the church. I speak to your shame. Is it so, that there is not a wise man among you? no, not one that shall be able to judge between his brethren?"—I Cor. 6:1–5.

A child of God should have a right to help other Christians to come to an agreement about what would be right and just in their treatment one of another. But that is entirely different from judging persons, hearts and motives. If a Christian brother's cow got into a fellow Christian's corn, I might prayerfully judge how much damage was done to the corn and how much his neighbor, who left the gate open, should pay to make it right. But it would be foolish and wicked for me to judge on circumstantial evidence how much malice was in the heart of one neighbor against the other and that one man was unconverted because of the way he treated his neighbor.

In fact, the only way a Christian would be useful as a mediator in such a case would be by maintaining the spiritual attitude commanded by the Saviour in Luke 6:36, 37: "Be ye therefore merciful, as your Father also is merciful. Judge not, and ye shall not be judged: condemn not, and ye shall not be condemned: forgive, and ye shall be forgiven." Judging right and wrong in matters and things is not the same as judging people, their hearts and motives.

Third, Christians may even pass judgment on the lives of other Christians to the extent of publicly withdrawing fellowship from them in the church, excluding them from membership in the congregation. In I Corinthians, chapter 5, Paul calls the attention of the church at Corinth to a member who was living in open sin, committing fornication with his stepmother. The sin was well known and was causing great reproach on the church. Paul insisted: "That he that hath done this deed might be taken away from among you. For I verily, as absent in body, but present in spirit, have judged already, as though I were present, concerning him that hath so done this deed" (I Cor. 5:2, 3).

He commanded them that when they were gathered together they should with his spirit and with the power of Christ purge out the leaven, that is, publicly they should "deliver such an one unto Satan for the destruction of the flesh, that the spirit may be saved in the day of the Lord Jesus" (I Cor. 5:5). They were not to keep company with anyone who was called a brother but was known to be "a fornicator, or covetous, or an idolater, or a railer, or a drunkard, or an extortioner" (v. 11). They were not to eat with such a person nor have fellowship with him. And the chapter closes with this command, "Therefore put away from among yourselves that wicked person."

It is clear, then, that Christians have a right to judge concerning certain sins that should break Christian fellowship. Christians who commit such sins bring a great reproach on the church. Such people should first be visited to try to win them to the right way (Matt. 18:15–17). If such a wayward

Christian is penitent, he should be immediately forgiven. Paul said about such cases, "Brethren, if a man be overtaken in a fault, ye which are spiritual, restore such an one in the spirit of meekness; considering thyself, lest thou also be tempted" (Gal. 6:1).

But where there is a continual course of disgraceful sin, contaminating others, bringing shame on the cause of Christ, then Christians ought to withdraw from the fellowship of any such church member. To ignore or endorse such flagrant and publicly-known sin, unconfessed and unrepented, would grieve God and do great harm. Christians, then, have a right to judge about publicly known sin and to avoid fellowship and companionship with those who continue in such sin.

But what a wonderful lesson does the inspired Apostle Paul give us in I Corinthians, chapter 5, about judging one another! Though he knew the horrible nature of the sin of this man continuing in fornication with his stepmother, and though he insisted that the man be turned out of the church at the next meeting, yet Paul never once said that man was not saved! Rather he urged that the man be publicly delivered to Satan "for the destruction of the flesh, *that the spirit may be saved* in the day of the Lord Jesus" (I Cor. 5:5). Sin brings ruin to the body, and even the child of God cannot avoid the fearful reaping of the wages of sin in his flesh. But Paul confidently trusted that the spirit of even this wicked fornicator would be found saved in the day of the Lord Jesus! While Paul judged concerning the man's deed, he did not attempt to judge the man's heart or motives and did not say that the man was unsaved, nor did he encourage anyone else to say so.

And Paul's trust was vindicated. The people in Corinth turned out that brother and refused to associate with him because of his disgraceful life. When Paul wrote to them again, the brother had shown such penitence, such sorrow, such a change in life, that Paul urged them quickly to forgive him and receive him (II Cor. 2:5–11). He was evidently a truly saved man all along.

A Christian then may judge doctrine, comparing it with the Bible. He may judge sin, prayerfully, without judging the sinner. But no Christian ever has a right to pass judgment as to whether someone else is saved or lost. And no Christian has a right to presume that he knows the motives and intentions of any heart.

If one declares that he has trusted in Christ as his Saviour and has assurance that his sins are forgiven by faith in the shed blood of Christ, then I ought charitably to take his testimony the best I can. If he does not live as a Christian ought, then I must consider my own frail attempts, my own failures, my own sins, not so well known to the public, perhaps, but intimately known to God.

If one does not claim to have trusted in Christ and to have accepted Him as Saviour, then we do right to take his testimony that he is unsaved. We know that if one claims to be saved by his own goodness, or saved by church membership, he is mistaken because we have the plain statements of the Word of God that only those who trust in Christ are saved. We have the right to suppose that one who does not claim to have trusted Christ for salvation is lost. And, charitably, we can only hope that one who professes to know and love the Saviour and to have trusted Him wholly for salvation is really a child of God.

Doubtless, in many cases, our suppositions are not true. Some are saved who cannot give any clear testimony as to when and how it happened. Something very definite happens in the heart of one who is saved; but often not much happens in the head, not much of assurance, nor of clear testimony, until the Word of God brings light to the mind. Babies are born a good while before they know much. And babies would never know who their fathers or mothers were or anything about their birth unless they were taught by others. So some are saved who have no clear testimony, and some are saved who do not act like they are saved. But a percentage of others, we are taught in the Word, are not saved, though they claim to be. And many are unrighteous sinners who appear very moral and religious. We can only trust that those have trusted Christ and have been born again who say they have.

We are apt to be mistaken sometimes, being human after all. Seeing now only through a glass darkly, we cannot judge the heart. "Judge not that ye be not judged."

Bible Examples Prove That Many Are Saved Who Do Not Act Like It

If I had intimately known Lot, the rich man who moved his family down to Sodom and had fellowship with the wicked Sodomites calling them brethren; if I had heard him offer to send his virgin daughters out into the night for the lewd pleasure of a crowd of sex perverts; if I had known his life of covetousness, of worldliness, and drink, so that his religion was the joke of his sons-in-law, I would have assumed, no doubt, that he was an unsaved hypocrite. He never won a soul. He kept the company of wicked men and strove to please them. He took his wine with him out to the cave whither he fled and then got drunk and ruined both his remaining daughters! Did anyone ever have more marks of a Christless, wicked man? Certainly I would have judged him to be unsaved. But I certainly would have been mistaken. God calls him "just Lot," says he was "vexed with the filthy conversation of the wicked," and says that he was a righteous man who vexed his righteous soul from day to day with the unlawful deeds of the Sodomites (II Pet. 2:7, 8). Only God knew the heart of Lot, that he was really a just man, that he really was sincere, and that he had a changed heart, a "righteous soul." Reader, you dare not judge!

If one of our self-righteous critics had been in Jerusalem when King David loitered on his palace roof and saw Bathsheba at her bath, led her into adultery and then skilfully planned the death of her husband, Uriah, our critic would certainly have judged David to be an unregenerate sinner, a hypocrite who never knew salvation. That was simply one of the many cases in which a child of God was overtaken in a grievous sin, a sin that brought great reproach on the name of God. And the casual observer would never have known the real anguish of heart that the born-again David had about his sin. By divine revelation it is pictured in Psalm 51. David was a saved man, a man with a new heart, a man who hated sin and loved God, a man after God's own heart. But like all other Christians, he still had the old nature, too, and the temptations our human flesh is heir to until our bodies are changed and glorified at Christ's coming. Anyone who judged David a lost man would have been a presumptuous sinner passing judgment on the heart which only God can see.

Simon Peter did not act like a Christian when he sat down with the enemies of Christ and first denied and then cursed and swore that he did not know Jesus and that he was no friend of the Saviour. Surely that sin was as bad as adultery or murder. It was the combined sin of bad company, lack of faith, lying, blasphemy and denying the Saviour in the greatest hour of His trial. Peter did not act like a Christian but he was one. The presumptuous judge would have said that Peter was not saved, that he had no true love for the Saviour. I have no doubt that many did say that. There is a hint of that in the anguished cry of Peter to Jesus later by the sea of Galilee when Peter said, "Lord, thou knowest all things; thou knowest that I love thee" (John 21:17). Others did not know that Peter loved Christ, but Peter knew that Jesus knew. What a comparison to all of us when our sins have shaken the faith of others in us and when the critical and self-righteous pass judgment upon us! God knows our hearts and He knows whether we truly love Him, even though our lives shamefully fail to show it.

A Christian cannot commit the unpardonable sin nor any other sin that would involve the loss of his salvation. But aside from that unpardonable sin, a child of God may be guilty of any outward, gross sin, however vile, that a lost sinner might commit. If it is drunkenness, then Noah whom God picked out of the whole world as the best man and saved him and his family in the flood—Noah got drunk (Gen. 9:21). So did Lot (Gen. 19:33). So did some Christians in the church at Corinth. They got drunk at the Lord's Supper and died and were taken on to Heaven because of their sin (I Cor. 11:21, 30). So have thousands of other born-again Christians so that the most spiritual church mentioned in the Bible, the Ephesians, needed to be warned: "Be ye not drunk with wine."

Can a Christian commit the sin of fornication or adultery? Many Christians have committed it. David did (II Sam. 11:4). So did Lot (Gen. 19:32–36). So did the man whom Paul had the church at Corinth to exclude from membership and then receive again (I Cor. 5:1).

Can a lost sinner commit murder? So did more than one Christian in the Bible. David did (II Sam. 11:14–17). David was a man of blood and for that reason was not allowed to build the temple (I Chron. 22:8). Moses killed a man (Exod. 2:12). Peter certainly tried to kill the servant of the high priest, when he cut off his ear (John 18:10). And the sin was counted so disgraceful that neither Matthew, Mark, nor Luke was allowed to tell who did it, but only John whose gospel was written long after Peter was dead. We know that a certain kind of cold-blooded, murderous hate is not possible to a Christian (I John 3:15), because being saved involves a change of heart and a partaking of the divine nature. But it is certain that saved people must beware lest they fall into even the grossest sins, such as drunkenness, cursing, adultery or even killing. Surely these examples ought to show us that we are utterly incapable of seeing the human heart and judging it. There is no possible way by which we may know whether another is saved or lost.

"For man looketh on the outward appearance, but the Lord looketh on the heart" (I Sam. 16:7).

Lost People May Appear to Be Saved

Appearances are deceitful. Human judgment is unreliable. If one cannot certainly judge by another's life that he is lost, just so one cannot be sure that those who appear to be saved are saved.

Judas Iscariot evidently convinced everyone who knew him, save Jesus alone, that he was a Christian. Not a single time is a question raised about the sincerity of Judas as a Christian. He was made treasurer of the band and carried the bag. When Jesus plainly told the disciples that one of them was a devil who did not believe in Him (John 6:64, 70, 71), there is no indication that anyone suspected Judas. Later, when at the Last Supper, Jesus said, "One of you shall betray me," everyone of them began to say, "Lord, is it I?" (Matt. 26:21, 22). No one said, "Is it Judas?" The tenth chapter of Matthew indicates that Judas was sent on the missionary tour with the others to heal the sick and to cast out devils. And Matthew 7:22, 23 states that many like him that are lost sinners will be turned away from the gate of Heaven.

Doubtless, many a self-righteous hypocrite in the churches, unconverted, appears so pious, teaches the Bible so well, so prays in public, sings in the choir, tithes, and lives a moral and upright life as to convince everyone that he is a child of God. It is impossible for a frail human being to really judge, and to attempt to do so is wicked sin. Jesus commands, "Judge not, that ye be not judged."

The Warning of the Tares

In Matthew, chapter thirteen, the Saviour illustrates the Kingdom of Heaven by a field sowed with good seed into which an enemy came and sowed tares. The tares and wheat appeared so much alike that all were deceived for a time.

Then the servants wanted to pluck out the tares but the householder said, "Nay; lest while ye gather up the tares, ye root up also the wheat with them" (Matt. 13:29). Any self-righteous, arrogant judge who would take upon himself the duty and privilege of plucking out of the church all of the unsaved ones would root up the wheat with tares. Only the angels of God at the proper time will be wise enough to take the tares and burn them and gather the wheat into the barn. Some tares appear to be wheat and wheat appears to be tares. And if you really knew all the sins of every Christian in the world without knowing their hearts, then every one of them would look to you like a lost sinner.

Salvation Is by Grace Alone

We are all such sinners that it is only the grace of God that can save any of us. No one ever deserved salvation before he was saved, and it is equally true that not a one of us deserves salvation after we are saved. The best and purest Christian in the world is still an unprofitable servant. Of us all it is true, "There is no difference: For all have sinned, and come short of the glory of God" (Rom. 3:22, 23). Every one of us who are children of God deserved to go to Hell. We deserved it before we were saved and we deserve it now. We were sinners before we were saved and we are sinners now. We had a fallen nature with all the inward taint of sin before we were saved, and now, we have a new nature, we are born again, we are "partakers of the divine nature" (II Pet. 1:4). We are now the children of God, but, alas, we still have the old nature, too. Our bodies are the bodies of fallen men and women and if we are honest, we must say like Paul, "For I know that in me (that is, in my flesh,) dwelleth no good thing: for to will is present with me; but how to perform that which is good I find not" (Rom. 7:18). And again, "So then with the mind I myself serve the law of God; but with the flesh the law of sin" (Rom. 7:25).

Therefore, it is evident that the lost man has one nature

and it is bad; but the saved man has two natures, both the old which is bad and the new which is good. There are no Christians except sinning Christians. Therefore, if we knew all about any Christian in the world, there would be plenty of reason to be shocked and disgusted with his sin and plenty of reason for a presumptuous judge to decide that any Christian was not saved, judged by his life.

It is clear that those who feel so free to judge whether others are saved, need to learn more clearly the precious doctrine of salvation by Christ and the doctrine of all-pervading sin.

The Inexcusable Presumption of Those Who Judge Others When Equally Guilty

The wicked sin in judging others is that the one who judges deliberately excuses or ignores his own sin which is just as bad as that he so vigorously condemns in others. Romans 2:1 says: "Therefore thou art inexcusable, O man, whosoever thou art that judgest: for wherein thou judgest another, thou condemnest thyself; for thou that judgest doest the same things."

That Scripture is the plain warning that the wrath of God is waiting to fall on such an inexcusable sinner as one who judged others.

One who judges others is the same kind of sinner. That is the reason for the warning in Matthew 7:1: "JUDGE NOT, THAT YE BE NOT JUDGED." The following verse says, "For with what judgment ye judge, ye shall be judged: and with what measure ye mete, it shall be measured to you again." The sin of passing judgment on others, judging their hearts, their motives, judging their sincerity, their salvation, and condemning them, is so great that God has determined everyone guilty shall be measured in the same bushel and shall be judged in the same way. In Luke 6:37, God looks at it from the other side and promises, "Judge not, and ye shall not be judged: condemn not, and ye shall not be condemned:

forgive, and ye shall be forgiven." Those who are merciful
and charitable to others shall have others be merciful and
charitable to them. Those who refuse to condemn will not
be condemned. Those who are quick to forgive will be forgiven themselves. Oh, blessed are the merciful, for they shall
obtain mercy!

It is often true that those who judge others are guilty of
greater sins as Jesus Himself plainly taught. He said:

*"And why beholdest thou the mote that is in thy brother's
eye, but considerest not the beam that is in thine own eye?
Or how wilt thou say to thy brother, Let me pull out the
mote out of thine eye; and, behold, a beam is in thine own
eye? Thou hypocrite, first cast out the beam out of thine own
eye; and then shalt thou see clearly to cast out the mote out
of thy brother's eye."*   —Matt. 7:3–5.

How aptly the Saviour shows us the wickedness of our
hearts. Many of us with a two-by-four timber in our eyes,
figuratively speaking, go round about offering to get the saw-
dust out of other people's eyes! Jesus plainly calls such a
judge, "Thou hypocrite." And He shows that the sin of those
who judge others is that they consider not the beam that is in
their own eyes.

How often it is that our self-righteousness is only a cloak
for more wicked sins than those we condemn in others! A
woman called me across a certain city once to talk to her
husband who had the habit of drink. The husband prayed
with me with contrite confessions, with many, many tears,
pleaded with God to give him grace. But his wife with eyes
snapping and bitter words accused her husband, "I don't believe he even tries! He has promised me he would never drink
again. He has promised his children the same. But just as
soon as he gets his pay check, if some of his cronies want him
to go to the tavern he takes one drink and then he is off on a
big drunk again. I don't believe he loves us as he says he does.
I don't believe he loves God as he says he does. If he did, he
wouldn't get drunk."

I told the wife, "Your husband is sick. His will is broken

down. He needs your love, your pity, your help, and not your scolding. He has one temptation and you have another. He has a temptation to take a glass of beer with the boys, and you have a temptation to lose your temper and nag and scold until he has no peace, until life is a burden, until home is a hell on earth. Then to drown his sorrow he is tempted all the more to drink. Your sin is at least as great as his."

Not long afterwards it was discovered that he had an incurable brain tumor. On trying to operate, the surgeon found he was beyond help. How many scathing words had struck like arrows in the heart of this poor, sick man trying to hold on to his job, trying to walk straight, yet the victim of temptation he could not master, especially in view of his infirmity.

I tell you now, that many a self-righteous Christian, judging others, condemning their sin, is as guilty in God's sight as the drunkard and the harlot, the blasphemer and the thief! Oh, whoever thou art that judgest others, thou are inexcusable! The sin of judging is a presumptuous sin, a sin of the proud and haughty and self-righteous Pharisee. It is a sin that God hates and upon which He has vowed retribution!

We are all made of the same kind of dirt. We are all of one blood. We are all alike—sinners. Only the mercy of God could take any of us to Heaven. Those of you who have not fallen into disgraceful sin may yet do so. You who do not commit adultery may lust in your heart which is the same sin in God's sight (Matt. 5:28). You who do not kill, may hate. You who do not steal, may covet. But if God withdraws the hedges and barriers with which He has protected you more than others, you, too, may become a drunkard, an adulterer, or a thief. "Wherefore let him that thinketh he standeth take heed lest he fall" (I Cor. 10:12). And remember that sweet injunction of Galatians 6:1: "Brethren, if a man be overtaken in a fault, ye which are spiritual, restore such an one in the spirit of meekness; considering thyself, lest thou also be tempted."

Considering thyself lest thou also be tempted! If we con-

sidered our own frailties, our own sinfulness, we would not
so quickly judge others.

I think preachers have stronger temptations than other
people, and there are certain kinds of temptations to which
preachers are more prone than others. So it seems that preachers who preach against sin and who have high ideals and
strong standards of Christian living are themselves more often
the victim of the temptations to judge others.

Not long ago, I was grieved by the attack on the president
of a great Christian school. Mimeographed pages were handed
me with an assortment of charges. Even if I had known none
of the facts of the case I could see how unjust and unchristian
were the criticisms made. One woman was quoted as saying
that this man of God who had won so many souls and been
so greatly used of God should certainly not be in his present
position because previous to his conversion he was an actor
on the stage! Nothing was intimated against his character
now, no charge of sin even when he was an actor. Another
unknown correspondent was quoted, without giving either
the name or any reasons, prophesying that in ten years the
school would be given over to modernism. Intelligent and
godly people would surely not take seriously such judging.
It showed in the first place the utter ignorance of the deep
humility, the holy life, and the Spirit-filled ministry of the
man who was criticised. On the other hand it revealed the
self-righteous and haughty sin of the critics.

Nearly every clique and clan among fundamentally sound
Christians criticises and passes judgment on others who do
not affiliate with them, but who are just as true to the Word
and just as useful to God. Some preachers think it is a major
part of their calling to "expose," to "uncover," to criticise, to
lambast and to break down confidence in other earnest Christians. May God pity us preachers and help us to love one another and to be forbearing, forgiving, to minister to one
another in the spirit of Christ, particularly since we are so
often guilty of the sin or sins just as bad in God's sight.

To judge others is presumptuous. We draw conclusions out of inaccuracies and ignorance instead of from perfect knowledge.

To judge others involves lack of brotherly love. Love "thinketh no evil" (I Cor. 13:5). Love is blind. If we loved people as we ought, we should be as slow to judge them as a mother is to condemn her child.

To judge others is the sin of a Pharisee, a hypocrite; it ignores and hides and makes an alibi for one's own weakness and sin, while drawing the worst conclusions possible from the frailty of others.

To judge others is a sin of false doctrine, too. It exalts human righteousness and minimizes the power of God. It encourages people to reform instead of being reborn. It would exalt Judas above Peter, and the Christ-rejecting Pharisee above the repenting publican.

Judging others—how different from the spirit of Christ, His mercy, His humility, His love, His quick forgiveness!

Therefore, let us judge not and we shall not be judged; let us condemn not and we shall not be condemned; let us forgive and we shall be forgiven!

Chapter 10

"BE YE NOT UNEQUALLY YOKED TOGETHER WITH UN-BELIEVERS"

> *"Be ye not unequally yoked together with un-believers: for what fellowship hath righteousness with unrighteousness? and what communion hath light with darkness? And what concord hath Christ with Belial? or what part hath he that believeth with an infidel? And what agreement hath the temple of God with idols? for ye are the temple of the living God; as God hath said, I will dwell in them, and walk in them; and I will be their God, and they shall be my people. Wherefore come out from among them, and be ye separate, saith the Lord, and touch not the unclean thing, and I will receive you, And will be a Father unto you, and ye shall be my sons and daughters, saith the Lord Almighty."* —II Cor. 6:14–18.

*T*HE ABOVE Scripture, little used by modern preachers and little practiced by modern Christians, is nevertheless what the Bible says about Christians being joined with unbelievers in marriage, in lodges and in the churches.

Christians ought not to be yoked up with non-Christians. God's people ought to separate from the Devil's people. Twice-born people are entirely different from once-born people and should keep themselves separate. Certainly Christians

should love lost people. We should be good neighbors with
them, should love and seek them. We should have them in our
homes and visit them in their homes, always having in mind
to be a blessing. But Christians should not be bound up in
the same yoke with unsaved people. Between the saved and
the lost there is the same difference that there is between light
and darkness, between righteousness and unrighteousness, between an idol and the temple of God! That is what the Scripture teaches! Eventually, the separation between the saved
and the lost will be the difference between Heaven and Hell,
between God and Satan! On this is based the Bible doctrine
of separation, that Christians should not yoke up with unbelievers.

Christians Not to Be Yoked, Have Fellowship, Communion, Concord, Part, or Agreement With Unsaved

Examine the above Scripture carefully and take it at face
value. The word *unbeliever* means one who has not believed
on Christ as his own personal Saviour. That word speaks of
the same kind of person as John 3:18 and John 3:36, "he that
believeth not is condemned already" and "he that believeth
not the Son shall not see life; but the wrath of God abideth
on him." The Scripture means not to yoke up with one who
has not trusted Christ as Saviour.

This Scripture is very explicit concerning the association
of saved people and lost people. Christians are not to be
"yoked together" with unbelievers. Righteousness is not to
have "fellowship" with unrighteousness. Light is not to have
"communion" with darkness. Christians are not to be yoked
with unbelievers just as Christ has no "concord" with Belial.
Verse 15 plainly asks, "What part hath he that believeth with
an infidel?" The word *infidel* is the same as the word *unbeliever*. It does not mean a man who believes there is no God,
but one who does not trust Christ as His Saviour. Verse 16
even suggests that a Christian should not have "agreement"

with unsaved people since a saved person's body is the temple of God and the body of the unsaved is an idol, possessed of Satan.

Christians are urged, therefore, to "come out from among them, and be ye separate, saith the Lord," and on this basis God promises to receive us and be a Father to us while we are to be His sons and daughters.

Teaching of Separation Throughout The Bible

One of the plainest doctrines in the Bible is this doctrine of Christian separation. It was the one teaching that God pressed daily, repeatedly, eternally, upon Jews. Much of their ceremonial law pointed to this particular thing alone. Abraham was called to "Get thee out of thy country, and from thy kindred, and from thy father's house, unto a land that I will shew thee." Jews were to be circumcised as a brand or mark of their separation from other people. Jews were commanded not to eat pork, not to eat catfish, etc. (Lev. 11:7, 10), not because pork and catfish were unfit for food, but as a mark to separate them from Gentiles around about. God was teaching Israel the doctrine that His people should be separate from heathen or unsaved people. Later we are plainly commanded not to observe the Jewish dietary laws, and told that every creature of God is good for food (I Timothy 4:4), but the doctrine of separation still stands. A Jew was not allowed to plant two kinds of seed in one vineyard, not allowed to hitch an ox and a donkey together, not allowed to wear a garment of two different materials, for instance, part wool and part linen. In Deuteronomy 22:9–11, is given this remarkable Scripture:

"Thou shalt not sow thy vineyard with divers seeds: lest the fruit of thy seed which thou hast sown, and the fruit of thy vineyard, be defiled. Thou shalt not plow with an ox and an ass together. Thou shalt not wear a garment of divers sorts, as of woollen and linen together."

When a Jewish boy was eight days old, he was marked with circumcision to remind him all his life that he was of a separate people, set apart for the Lord.

When a Jew sat down at the table he was reminded, "I must watch what I eat; I am God's man."

When a Jew put on his shirt, he was reminded in his heart, "I cannot wear a garment of mixed cloth as linen and wool— that reminds me that I must not mix with idolators and unbelievers, those who do not serve my God."

When the Israelitish farmer hitched up his team, he said in his heart, "God commands me not to plow with a mixed team. I may plow with two oxen or two donkeys; but I cannot mix them, because God wants me to remember that I am not to mix with those who are not God's people."

When the Jew started to sow his vineyard, God's word rang in his heart and he said, "I must not mix the seed in the same vineyard, because God wants me to remember not to mix with unbelievers."

A prophet of God, sent to pronounce judgment on Jeroboam and his evil worship in the northern kingdom, Israel, was commanded not to eat bread nor drink water even in that nation where such wickedness was tolerated. Because he went back to eat dinner with a backslidden prophet who had not condemned idolatry, God sent a lion to kill him in the road! (I Kings 13:21–24). Throughout the Old Testament we find this clear and ringing teaching both by precept and example, that God's people must not intermingle, keep company, nor yoke up with unsaved people.

These Teachings for New Testament Christians

All the ceremonial laws of the Old Testament have a New Testament application. The Jew was circumcised in body, but that pictured a circumcision of heart which Jew and Gentile alike must have if they see God in peace. Christians are under no obligation to keep ceremonial laws concerning diet, the wearing of garments of mixed material or hitching ox and ass together or sowing the vineyard with divers seed. Those are the letter of the law. That part is not binding on us. But the spiritual lesson which Jews should have gotten from those ceremonial laws is a lesson for us today. New Testament Christians under grace need not observe the letter of the law but we ought to be more particular about the spirit than Jews were. God wants us to be separate. So here in II Corinthians 6:14–18 we are plainly commanded that a Christian is not to be yoked together with an unbeliever.

I. CHRISTIANS SHOULD NOT BE YOKED WITH UNBELIEVERS IN MARRIAGE

The command of God about being yoked with unbelievers certainly applies to marriage. Marriage is a yoke. The only one who would deny this is a man or woman who has never been married. When a Christian man or woman takes in marriage a husband or wife who has not been saved, then he disobeys this explicit command of God. He yokes a believer with an unbeliever; he puts righteousness in fellowship with unrighteousness; he puts light in communion with darkness; he puts Christ in concord with Belial. He, a believer, has part with one who is an unbeliever and he makes the temple of God in agreement with an idol. Children of God should never marry those who are not children of God, no matter how virtuous or high-minded or cultivated or pleasing they may be outwardly. Inwardly they are rebels against Christ, children of Hell. To do so is a sin against God and a sin against one's own best self. It is a sin certain to be reaped with sorrow in the future. Some one has well said that one who marries the Devil's child is sure to have trouble with his father-in-law. The Christian, married to one not a Christian, is certain to have trouble. Such a marriage should not be broken, and the Christian believer should not depart from his unbelieving mate (I Cor. 7:10–16). The time to do right about that is before marriage. After marriage is too late to avoid trouble. All one can do then is to pray that God will

save the unsaved ones and try one's best to atone for the sin
of yoking up in marriage with an enemy of your Saviour and
your God.

In I Corinthians 7:39 the Scripture says: "The wife is
bound by the law as long as her husband liveth; but if her
husband be dead, she is at liberty to be married to whom she
will; ONLY IN THE LORD." Widows have a right to re-
marry if their husbands are dead, but they have a right to
marry "only in the Lord." God mentioned specifically widows
here, but we have already had the general teaching that every
Christian should only be yoked up with believers, not with
unbelievers.

The Flood Caused by Intermarriage of Saved and Lost

The Bible is full of accounts of tragedies caused by the
mixture of God's people with the Devil's people. In Genesis
4:25, 26 we are told of the birth of Seth, evidently a godly
man, given to Eve as "another seed instead of Abel, whom
Cain slew." This good man, Seth, had a son, Enos, and "then
began men to call upon the name of the Lord."

But in the sixth chapter of Genesis we are given the account of how the godly line of Seth, saved people, "sons of
God," intermarried with the unsaved people, "daughters of
men."

*"And it came to pass, when men began to multiply on the
face of the earth, and daughters were born unto them, That
the sons of God saw the daughters of men that they were fair;
and they took them wives of all which they chose. And the
Lord said, My spirit shall not always strive with man, for that
he also is flesh: yet his days shall be an hundred and twenty
years. There were giants in the earth in those days; and also
after that, when the sons of God came in unto the daughters
of men, and they bare children to them, the same became
mighty men which were of old, men of renown. And God
saw that the wickedness of man was great in the earth, and
that every imagination of the thoughts of his heart was only*

evil continually. And it repented the Lord that he had made man on the earth, and it grieved him at his heart. And the Lord said, I will destroy man whom I have created from the face of the earth; both man, and beast, and the creeping things, and the fowls of the air; for it repenteth me that I have made them." —Genesis 6:1–7.

The descendants of these mixed marriages became so terribly wicked that God destroyed the earth with a flood. The influence of a saved man is lost when he compromises and sins against God by marrying an unsaved woman. The children of such marriages usually follow after the unsaved parent, not the saved one. As Peter lost his courage when he sat down to warm by the soldiers' fire, and as Samson found the Lord departed from him with his head in the lap of Delilah, with his hair cut off; so the average Christian who marries an unsaved person finds his joy gone, his testimony fading and a constant weight around his neck as he tries to live for God. The trouble that falls on the unsaved husband or wife is shared by the Christian companion yoking up with him or her. Remember that the family of Achan was stoned with him when that troubler of Israel died in the valley of Achor (Joshua 7:24–26).

Solomon, the wisest man that ever lived, married unsaved women and they turned away his heart. First Kings 11:4, 5 tells us about it as follows:

"For it came to pass, when Solomon was old, that his wives turned away his heart after other gods: and his heart was not perfect with the Lord his God, as was the heart of David his father. For Solomon went after Ashtoreth the goddess of the Zidonians, and after Milcom the abomination of the Ammonites."

For this cause God took away ten tribes of the kingdom from Solomon's son.

Nehemiah rebuked the sin of the Jewish remnant in his day in marrying unsaved women and used Solomon as an example. In Nehemiah 13:23–27 the account is given.

*"In those days also saw I Jews that had married wives of
Ashdod, of Ammon, and of Moab: And their children spake
half in the speech of Ashdod, and could not speak in the Jews'
language, but according to the language of each people. And
I contended with them, and cursed them, and smote certain
of them, and plucked off their hair, and made them swear by
God, saying, Ye shall not give your daughters unto their sons,
nor take their daughters unto your sons, or for yourselves.
Did not Solomon king of Israel sin by these things? yet among
many nations was there no king like him, who was beloved
of his God, and God made him king over all Israel: nevertheless even him did outlandish women cause to sin. Shall we
then hearken unto you to do all this great evil, to transgress
against our God in marrying strange wives?"*

If one reads this who is a Christian, a child of God, but who
plans to marry a child of the Devil and be yoked up with an
unbeliever, then I beg you now not to commit this sin against
God, not to bring this trouble upon yourself and upon your
children!

"Why Didn't Some Preacher Show Me That Fifteen Years Ago!"

I once held revival services in a small town in north Texas
and preached on "Be Ye Not Unequally Yoked Together
With Unbelievers." The next day a woman who was not
present at the preceding service chided me saying, "I know
what you preached last night and I don't believe it." From
hearsay she had been displeased with my sermon. However, I
told her that it was not my message but God's, and I turned in
the Bible to II Corinthians 6:14 and had her read the plain
command of God not to be yoked up with unbelievers. I knew
her case. She had married an unsaved man. A fourteen-year-
old son was already grieving his mother's heart and following
in the footsteps of his unsaved father. When she read the
Scripture she turned to me and her eyes filled with tears. This
is what she said—"Why didn't some preacher show me that

fifteen years ago!" I answered back that I could not say for other preachers but for my part I wanted no brokenhearted woman, because of ignorance of the Word of God, blaming me for her sin and unhappiness when it was fifteen years too late! Therefore I am warning people not to be yoked up with unbelievers.

In revival meetings again and again people make requests for prayers that their loved ones may be saved. If a father sincerely says, "Pray for my lost boy," I find that usually that prayer is answered and the lost boy is saved. Where Christians do right God is good to answer our prayers and requests; and when Christians join in prayer, many times their prayers are answered and unsaved loved ones are brought to God. But in every revival campaign I hold there is one kind of request made again and again—the request of wives that people pray for the salvation of their unsaved husbands. I am sorry to say that in a majority of cases the revival services come to a close and such husbands are not saved. Women ignore the plain command of God, go against the Bible and marry unsaved men, and then turn and ask God to put His blessing upon their sin. In many cases a good and merciful God does answer their prayers, but in hundreds of such cases, for some good reason, He does not.

Dear Christian girl, if you want some man saved, then get him saved before you marry him. To sin against God in this matter often means that you will so displease God and so compromise your own Christian influence that you will be unable to win to Christ the man who is to be the father of your children and your lifetime companion. After you marry then you ought not to leave your husband. But if you plan such a marriage, then heed the command of God and break up your plans, even though it be only one day before the wedding. You may think it will break your heart now, but a heart broken in doing right will soon be healed by the mercy of a loving heavenly Father. I warn you now that if you go headlong against the direct command of God in this matter your heart will be broken a thousand times. After all, only one thing brings real trouble, and that is to sin against God. "Be ye not unequally yoked together with unbelievers."

II. THE SIN OF CHRISTIANS' JOINING LODGES

I suppose that half the preachers in some areas are members of lodges and secret orders. They have the Masonic Order to lay their cornerstones, they preach special sermons for Odd Fellows, they act as chaplains for the Ku Klu Klan, and encourage their members, both men and women, to join such secret orders. Probably the average preacher has not studied the Bible prayerfully and seriously enough even to know that to be a member of the lodges violates the explicit command of the Bible!

All over the country an examination would often find the same names on the church roll and the lodge roll. The same faces show up at the deacon's or steward's meeting and the Shriner's dance; the same young men are on the B. Y. P. U. or the Epworth League program and at the revels of the De-Molay. The church and the world, saved and lost, are yoked together all over this country; and the shameful fact is that the world is going to Hell largely because one cannot tell the difference between God's man and the Devil's man, the saved and the unsaved, the redeemed and the condemned.

Once I was in a great revival in Greenville, Texas, and found that young men of the churches had been led into the DeMolay Lodge by older Masons, particularly by some preachers. When I preached plainly on this subject a young man came to me greatly troubled and explained that they always had prayer at every meeting of the DeMolay. I had just been told that the DeMolay Lodge regularly had dances, and so I said to him, "Do you have prayer at the dances?" "Oh, yes," he answered, "we begin every dance with prayer." Do you believe that God heard and was pleased? Lodges may have the outward form of righteousness, but they are a snare to any Christian who enters them. May God have pity on the preacher who leads the prayer asking God to bless the dances held by the lodges! It is a sin to be yoked up with unbelievers!

Saved people who yoke up with unbelievers lose their testimony, lose their influence until sinners can tell no difference and see no reason to be alarmed at their own wicked state.

Lodges Filled With Unbelievers

One who joins any of the principal secret orders violates this command of God not to yoke up with unbelievers. I will readily admit that there are many converted men in the secret orders. I know many good men who have done wrong about this matter. Many preachers have. My own father made this mistake. But it is certainly true that not all the men in the lodges are Christian men. They are not required to be, they are not expected to be. A man does not need to profess to have been born again to be a good Mason, Odd Fellow, Elk or Klansman. A man who becomes a Mason must profess to believe there is a Supreme Being in whom he puts his trust. But that God may be the god of Mohammedans, the god of Buddhists or the god of the American Indian or any heathen deity. The orthodox Jew who believes that Jesus Christ is the bastard son of a Jewish harlot, an impostor and deceiver, still makes a perfectly good Mason and is received without any request that he take the Lord Jesus Christ as his Saviour.

There are Masonic Lodges in India that use the sacred Hindu writings for the Greater Light on the altar, instead of the Holy Bible. The sacred writings of any group which believes in a "Supreme Being" are acceptable enough for Masonic ceremonies. This means that while Masonry is a religion, it is not the Christian religion. The god of Masonry need not be the God of the Bible, the true God, and the Bible of Masonry need not be the true Bible. I am simply saying that when one joins a Masonic Lodge, or any other major secret order, he is yoking together with unbelievers, and directly violating the command of God, by binding himself with those, many of whom do not profess to have trusted Christ as Saviour.

When as a young minister I followed the advice of preacher friends and asked to be made a Mason, I was shocked beyond measure to learn that the man who had the leading part in initiating me as an Entered Apprentice, was a man who did not believe in the miracles, the virgin birth, the bodily resurrection nor anything of the kind. He was an out-and-out rationalist and the most influential member of that lodge! A man of profane language and infidel belief, yet preachers in that lodge deferred to him and followed him! Young, inexperienced, and not knowing much about what the Bible taught on that subject, yet I felt then that I was out of place in the company of such men. I feel the same now. I asked God to forgive me, and I have never been back since. Since that time I have read all the authorized Masonic literature I could find, *Monitors, Burial Service, Masonic Encyclopedia, New Age Magazine, The Men's House* and much else besides. And the more I read the Bible, the more certain I become that the religion of Masonry is not the religion of the Bible. It is a religion of being saved by being good, not a religion of being saved by the blood of Christ. Masonry, like other lodges, teaches that God is the Father of all men alike, not requiring people to be born again. The burial service of an unsaved Pharisee, conducted by a Masonic or other lodge, would be the same as for a soul-winning preacher. Masonry does not teach that men need to be born again, does not show a man how to be born again, does not even require a personal faith in Christ, does not ask the applicant for membership to confess Christ as Saviour. The result is that saved and lost alike are in the lodge together. The unsaved have as much influence as the saved, usually more. The Christian man in the lodge is not the highest type of Christian, not the vigorous, aggressive, soul-winning Christian leader. The unsaved group dominates and sets the program for those compromising Christians who join with unbelievers in the lodges.

Other Orders as Bad as Masonry or Worse

I have used as an example the Masonic Order, for several reasons. It is the most ancient, probably the best known, and one of the best of the orders, but it is unchristian, contrary to the Bible, and largely filled with unbelievers. What is true of Masonry is true in like manner of every other secret order with which I am familiar. They all receive members who do not profess to have been born again on the same basis as children of God. All alike encourage lost men to believe that they can be saved without the blood of Christ, that all one needs is to live up to his vows. Remember that the one, plain, unmistakable command of God on this matter is that Christians should not yoke up with unbelievers. Whatever else good or bad you know about the lodges, you must admit, and all informed people do admit, that the lodges do not demand a change of heart as a requirement for membership.

Lodges Do Much Good

You may say that lodges do much good and I do not deny it. I am glad for all the orphan children cared for by Masonic and Odd Fellows orphan's homes and all crippled children treated by the Shriners. But if that is the reason for joining a lodge, there would be a far better reason for joining the Roman Catholic Church. While Masons take care of the children of Masons, or of elderly Masons and their wives, Catholics throughout the world have given a wonderful example in the care of orphans and the poor and the old. Honest men must admire the unselfish Catholic sisters who usually make no distinction between the Catholic and Protestant in their benevolent institutions. Yet I cannot agree that New Testament Christians ought to join in with the Roman Catholic Church. While I honor Catholics for all the good deeds they do, yet I do not believe that Roman Catholicism is Bible Christianity, nor that saved people should join them. No, good deeds done by some lodges, whether selfishly or unselfishly, are no reason for Christians joining with them and thus disobeying the plain command of God, "Be ye not unequally yoked together with unbelievers."

Good Men in the Lodges

My critics will say that the lodges have many good men, and I grant it freely. I believe that in most of the lodges, perhaps all, there are many good men, even converted men, men who love God and want to serve Him. I am sorry to say, there are thousands of preachers who are members of the lodges. But that does not make it right, and one should not join the lodges because somebody else did. Many preachers use tobacco though it defiles the body, grieves the Holy Spirit and sets a sorry and filthy example before the world. I cannot follow their example. Many preachers attend the lewd and vulgar modern picture show. They ought not to do it, and I cannot follow their example. If there are good men in the lodges, they are there contrary to the plain command of God who said, "Be ye not unequally yoked together with unbelievers." Even though they are good men, we should not follow them in their sin.

There are Christian people in lodges, but I remind you that they are not the happiest nor most useful Christians. Through these many years I have been carefully watching to see if I could find a man active and high up in the lodges and at the same time a successful and fervent soul winner. I find that soul winning and lodge membership do not go together. The man who disobeys God about yoking together with unbelievers, loses power, loses testimony, and usually loses his interest in soul winning. How many preachers have left the pulpit to become Masonic lecturers! My own dear father, one of the best men that I ever knew, an humble preacher of the gospel, became so absorbed in Masonic work that for two years' time he did not enter, for regular services, the building of the church where he was a member! What a joy it was to me in a great revival at Decatur, Texas, to enlist my father, preach to him the gospel, and see him again as in former years go out among men to put his arms around hardened sinners and lead them to Christ. God opened again for him the fountain of tears over sinners. God turned his feet again in soul-winning ways. But the lodges had dried up his soul until he had well-nigh lost faith in the doctrines he had once preached.

I have held revival campaigns in thirty-two states these last twenty years. Everywhere I have gone, I have found that those active in lodge work were not active in revivals. The chairman of the boards of deacons, the Methodist stewards, the Sunday School teachers who were active lodge members, remained away from the revival on lodge night. My experience proves that God's Word is right. But experience or no experience, I know that the only safe guide is the Word of God, and it commands, "Be ye not unequally yoked together with unbelievers."

What Should the Lodge Member Do?

The Scripture at the beginning of this message tells us what to do. "Wherefore come out from among them, and be ye separate, saith the Lord, and touch not the unclean thing; and I will receive you, And will be a Father unto you, and ye shall be my sons and daughters, saith the Lord Almighty" (II Cor. 6:17, 18). God tells you what to do and He said, "Come out from among them."

Leave the silly trappings of the lodges. You are not a child, to dress up in a cowboy suit and ride a stick horse nor to wear an Indian suit with feathers down the back. God does not mean His people to help unbelievers in such foolishness.

Come away from the secret things, the things taught behind closed doors, the things you are not free to share with other Christians, those secret things that God will one day bring to light.

Come away from those lodge oaths. They are blasphemy. The yoke is real; it is oath-bound. The oath you take upon you in the lodges binds you by oath to favor lodge members, even if they are unsaved, above Christians who are not lodge members. When Jesus commanded us to "swear not at all," then it is poor business for a Christian to take such blasphemies upon his lips and to bind himself in a yoke with unbelievers. Come out from among them, God says! And then we have the promise of God that He will receive us, He will be to us a Father and we shall be truly His sons and daughters. If you want the joy of the Spirit's presence, the joy of unbroken fellowship with God, then break your yoke with unbelievers today. Come out and be separate and God will bless you. (The author's eighty-eight-page book, *Lodges Examined By The Bible,* gives much fuller help on this important question.)

III. TO YOKE UP IN CHURCHES AND DENOMINATIONS WITH UNBELIEVERS IS A SIN

The Bible has much to say about God's people living a life of separation from sinners, but the greatest emphasis is always placed on the teaching that Christians should not mix with unbelievers in the matter of religion. If it is wrong for a Christian to yoke up with unbelievers in marriage and for God's people to join with unbelievers in oath-bound lodges, it is even more important that Christians should have no "yoke," no "fellowship," no "agreement," no "part," no "concord" with unbelievers in churches and religious programs.

Years ago it was taken for granted that every man in the church believed the Bible. It is not so now. Unsuspecting Christians sometimes think that all preachers and Christian leaders certainly believe the Bible. The shocking fact is that many preachers are practically infidels.

Infidelity Among Preachers

A few years ago the following account of a questionnaire sent out to preachers, concerning the fundamental doctrines of the Christian faith, was published in the public press.

"Existence of Real Hell and Devil Denied by Pastors in Questionnaire"

"Chicago, Feb. 8—Existence of hell as a real place was denied today by 69 of each 100 Protestant ministers in answer to a Northwestern university school of education questionnaire that disclosed many modifications in religious belief.

"That 'there is no devil' was the assertion of 54 per cent of the clergymen. A majority of the pastors were opposed to having children taught that so-called God-sent punishment such as earthquakes, fires and floods were punishment for sin.

"Eighty per cent voted against teachings that 'hell is a place of burning.'

"Of the 500 ministers who answered the questionnaire only 48 per cent said they would teach junior high school pupils that judgment day is really coming. Thirty-nine per cent said it would not come to pass.

"The existence of heaven was doubted by 41 per cent who recommended that it be eliminated from church instructions. Sixty per cent believed in angels.

"All were virtually unanimous in their belief that 'God still runs the world.' On the question of a future life 92 per cent recommended teaching that those who die go right on living.

"Nineteen per cent held that God keeps a record of the individual's bad deeds in a book, while 74 per cent disagreed. Seventy-two per cent supported the deity of Jesus Christ while 26 per cent were in opposition."

Sixty-nine out of every hundred of these preachers believed that there is no real Hell! More than half of them said, "There is no devil"! More than half did not believe in teaching that judgment day is really coming, and nearly half doubted the existence of Heaven! Eighty per cent did not believe Hell was a real place of burning. Of these 500 Protestant preachers, only one out of five believed what the Bible says about Hell, and others doubted the inspiration of the Bible, the deity of Christ, even the fact of immortality of the soul! It is a startling fact that many preachers, many professors in so-called Christian colleges and denominational leaders, are unbelievers. They do not believe the Bible, they do not believe Christ, many of them have not trusted Him as Saviour. What does the Bible say about yoking up with these unbelievers?

False Teachers and False Prophets Were Foretold

It is not surprising to one who knows the Bible, that some preachers should prove false to their sacred trust and preach their unbelief. The Bible has plainly forewarned us of the coming of such preachers. Paul, leaving the great church at Ephesus with tears, warned the elders or preachers of that church as follows:

"Take heed therefore unto yourselves, and to all the flock, over the which the Holy Ghost hath made you overseers, to feed the church of God, which he hath purchased with his own blood. For I know this, that after my departing shall grievous wolves enter in among you, not sparing the flock; Also of your own selves shall men arise, speaking perverse things, to draw away disciples after them. Therefore watch, and remember, that by the space of three years I ceased not to warn every one night and day with tears."—Acts 20:28–31.

Paul knew that men, even preachers, would turn away from the faith.

In I Timothy 4:1 the same warning is given again: "Now the Spirit speaketh expressly, that in the latter times some shall depart from the faith, giving heed to seducing spirits, and doctrines of devils." "In the latter times" this departing from the faith will be worse than before, we are told!

Again in Paul's second letter to Timothy, II Timothy 3:13, Paul warns the young preachers, "But evil men and seducers shall wax worse and worse, deceiving, and being deceived." In the next chapter this warning continues, that the time should come when people will "turn away their ears from the truth, and shall be turned unto fables."

"There Shall Be False Teachers Among You, Who Privily Shall Bring in Damnable Heresies"

Poor, blind weaklings that we Christians are, the Lord saw that we needed to be warned again and again concerning false teachers! In II Peter 2:1–3, is the following passage:

"But there were false prophets also among the people, even as there shall be false teachers among you, who privily shall bring in damnable heresies, even denying the Lord that bought them and bring upon themselves swift destruction. And many shall follow their pernicious ways; by reason of whom the way of truth shall be evil spoken of. And through covetousness shall they with feigned words make merchandise of you: whose judgment now of a long time lingereth not, and their damnation slumbereth not."

The Scripture does not use soft words in talking about false teachers. It says that they "shall bring in damnable heresies, even denying the Lord that bought them," and we are told that this false teaching will be brought in "privily" and "with feigned words." What an accurate picture that is of modernists! They pretend to believe the Bible, the miracles, salvation, Heaven, etc. But when they say the Bible is inspired, they mean as like other books are inspired. They say that Jesus is the Son of God, but they say that so are we all the sons of God! They may say they believe in miracles, but in the next breath they say that the radio and printing press are miracles. Actually their words are "feigned words," for secretly, that is privily, they are bringing in damnable doctrines that deny the Lord that bought them, deny the Bible, God's Word. When you read the news clipping above concerning the five hundred preachers, most of whom do not believe the Bible, and read this passage of Scripture, you will see that the Lord knew what He was talking about! What the Lord foretold in His Word has now come to pass.

Sad truth is told, in verse 2 above, that "many shall follow their pernicious ways"! In these wicked, modern days, many people follow unbelievers and modernists. Verse 3 tells us that such modernists and unbelievers still claim to be preachers, still claim to be Christians, though they do not believe the very fundamentals of the Christian faith and sometimes deny the Lord Himself and would take away from His head the crown of deity. But they hold on to the form of Christianity, while they preach their wicked unbelief "through covetousness." They want to deceive common Christian people so they can receive their nice salaries! How true the Bible proves itself to be! Before our eyes today we find these words fulfilled.

What Should Christians Do?

What should Christians do when they find such false teachers, preachers and Christian people untrue to the Bible, unbelievers in the Bible, the blood atonement, the deity of Christ, the miracles, and a literal Hell? That question is plainly answered in the Scriptures. Christians should not be yoked together with unbelievers. Particularly they should not be yoked with unbelievers in the churches and religious work. To be in a church with unbelievers, skeptics and doubters, is to disobey the plain command of Christ. To support such a preacher or teacher is a sin against God for which one will certainly have to give an account to God when he stands at the judgment seat of Christ.

"Earnestly Contend for the Faith"

Every Christian who wants to please Christ should be a campaigner, a sincere crusader for the true gospel. Jude, verses 3 and 4, gives us the instruction that we should "earnestly contend for the faith" and warns us again of evil men who will creep in unawares, denying the only Lord God. Read these verses.

"Beloved, when I gave all diligence to write unto you of the common salvation, it was needful for me to write unto you,

and exhort you that ye should earnestly contend for the faith which was once delivered unto the saints. For there are certain men crept in unawares, who were before of old ordained to this condemnation, ungodly men, turning the grace of our God into lasciviousness, and denying the only Lord God, and our Lord Jesus Christ."

There will be some Christians who will contend for "peace." But this Scripture does not tell us to have peace with modernists, rationalists, unbelievers, false teachers who deny the Lord Jesus Christ. Some people do not like "contentions," they say. But whether we like it or not, to contend for the faith is the plain duty commanded for every Christian. Any kind of Christianity that wants peace with unbelievers and agreement with doubters and fellowship with modernists, goes against the plain command of II Corinthians 6:14–16. Read again what God says about having "peace" or "fellowship" or "communion" or "concord" or "part" or "agreement" with such unbelievers.

"Be ye not unequally yoked together with unbelievers: for what fellowship hath righteousness with unrighteousness? and what communion hath light with darkness? And what concord hath Christ with Belial? Or what part hath he that believeth with an infidel? And what agreement hath the temple of God with idols?"

According to this Scripture it is sin to seek peace with such company. They are the enemies of Christ and the Bible. Honest Christians may differ as to some details of Bible interpretation, but honest Christians cannot differ about the deity of Christ nor whether the Bible is all God's Word, infallibly true, nor about the blood atonement nor about the miracles such as the virgin birth and the bodily resurrection of Christ, the creation of the world by the direct act of God, etc., nor about a literal Hell. When a man dissents from what the Bible says on such great fundamentals of the faith, then that man has no right to call himself a Christian, much less a preacher of the gospel or a teacher of the Bible. Such a man is an impostor, a deceiver, a false prophet. An honest infidel one might somewhat respect even though the Bible calls him a fool. But an infidel in the garb of a preacher, with language of deceit because of covetousness, is a wolf in sheep's clothing, a base hypocrite. He forfeits the respect of decent people and should have open scorn and public exposure at the hands of true Christians everywhere. The Bible commands us to contend earnestly for the faith.

Do Not Receive False Teachers Into Your House Nor Bid Them God Speed

The attitude of an honest Bible-believing Christian toward unbelievers and those who do not abide in the doctrine of Christ is plainly told in the second epistle of John, verses 9 to 11.

"Whosoever transgresseth, and abideth not in the doctrine of Christ, hath not God. He that abideth in the doctrine of Christ, he hath both the Father and the Son. If there come any unto you, and bring not this doctrine, receive him not into your house, neither bid him God speed; For he that biddeth him God speed is partaker of his evil deeds."

You can see from the above Scriptures that the Lord here means not simply an unsaved man but one who brings the wrong doctrine about Christ, one who does not believe what the Bible teaches about Him. Here is the proper attitude for a Christian toward an unbelieving preacher, one who does not hold to the great fundamentals of the faith: "RECEIVE HIM NOT INTO YOUR HOUSE, NEITHER BID HIM GOD SPEED"! Do not let a modernist preacher eat at your table. Do not let him sleep on your bed. Do not pay his railroad fare. Do not wish him prosperity. Do not do anything to endorse or support a modernist. If you do the Bible says that you are a partaker of his evil deeds and will certainly suffer part of his punishment. This is another way of saying, "Be ye not unequally yoked together with unbelievers." Any yoke that binds a believer in the Bible with one who does not believe the Bible is an unequal yoke, and it is wicked for a Christian to be bound by such ties.

If Your Pastor Is a Modernist, What Then?

Suppose you are a member of a church whose pastor is a modernist. I do not mean the pastor who may be wrong on some interpretation of Scripture. That is not modernism. I do not mean a pastor who is worldly. Worldliness is wrong, but that is not modernism. A modernist does not believe that the Bible is what it claims to be, the very Word of God. A modernist does not believe in the virgin birth of Christ, does not believe in His bodily resurrection. A modernist does not believe in the substitutionary death of Christ; that Christ actually died in the sinner's stead and paid for our sins on the cross. The modernist does not believe in a personal regeneration, salvation through faith in the shed blood of Christ. The modernist does not believe in a literal Hell for Christ-rejecting sinners. Now supposing that your pastor is a modernist, an unbeliever in the Bible sense, and therefore is Satan's man instead of God's man, and brings Satan's doctrine instead of Christ's doctrine. What should a Christian do in such a case?

The answer is plainly given in the Bible. Have no part or lot or agreement or concord or fellowship with such a man. Give not a penny to his salary for in so doing you would bid him God speed and be a partaker of his evil deeds. That is the first thing. The second is to openly expose his modernism and "earnestly contend for the faith." Christians ought not to be quiet and cowardly when it is plain duty to be like Paul, "set for the defense of the gospel" (Phil. 1:17). The third duty, I think, is obvious. If you cannot put out such a leader from the pastorate of the church where your fellowship is, then only one thing remains to be done and that is to leave it immediately. You cannot please God and remain yoked up with such unbelievers.

To listen to a modernist without protest is a sin. To pay his

218 The Ruin of a Christian

salary is wickedness. To associate with him is to put righteousness with unrighteousness, light with darkness, Christ with Belial, and the temple of God with idols. "Be ye not unequally yoked together with unbelievers." Modernists often cry, "Peace, peace," but there is no peace.

It is important that we use terms correctly. A man is not a modernist because he differs with you on baptism, though he may be wrong. To be untaught or to be mistaught on the second coming of Christ is not modernism. It is true that modernists are postmillenial in their belief, but not all postmillenialists are modernists. It is wrong, unbrotherly, and misleading to call people modernists because you believe them to be wrong on some matter of Scriptural interpretation. But on some major matters there is no room for essential disagreement among real Christians. On the fact of the inspiration of the Bible, on the deity of Christ, on the blood atonement, on salvation by faith, real Christians agree. They may differ in the way they express those doctrines, and may differ on some corollaries of those doctrines, but real Christians must believe that the Bible is what it claims to be, the inspired Word of God, and that Christ is what He claims to be, the virgin-born Son of God, who died for our sins. Christians must believe that salvation is by the blood of Christ. One who does not so believe is a modernist, and Christians should not be yoked with modernists.

There can be no peace on religious grounds between believers and unbelievers, children of God and children of Satan.

Should a Christian Support Modernistic Denominational Programs?

Here is a most serious question which many Christians have to face. Suppose your church is in the main true to Christ. Your pastor believes the Bible and preaches it. He preaches salvation by the blood of Christ. He warns sinners that they must repent and be born again, or be lost forever. Your pastor is a man of God and the church members are, generally, real Christians; but your church is affiliated with a denomination which supports modernistic schools, perhaps, or which sends out modernists, unbelievers, as 'missionaries.' What is the duty of a Christian in such a sound, Bible-believing church, affiliated with the denomination whose leadership is modernistic?

Some would say that it is a sin for any Christian to remain in a church connected with one of the main denominations. I do not say so. I do not believe the matter is that simple. Certainly it is not right for a Christian to compromise. Certainly it is not right for a Christian to support modernism. Prayerfully, I make some suggestions.

1. No Christian should give a single penny of money to the support of modernism. If a denominational secretary denies the essentials of the Christian faith, then you should make sure that you do not participate in his support in any wise. If your denomination supports a school where professors break down the faith of students, where they teach that the Bible is not the infallible Word of God, and that Christ Jesus is not the virgin-born Son of God, God incarnate, then make sure that none of your gifts ever go to support such a school. If the foreign mission board or society of your denomination sends out some 'missionaries' who are modernists, then make sure that none of your money supports such missionaries. Make sure that the money God has put in your hands does not go to strengthen any such modernistic mission board. Do not yoke up with such a modernistic mission board in the Lord's business. To do so is a sin. To yoke up with a modernistic foreign board violates the command, "Be ye not unequally yoked together with unbelievers."

If your pastor believes the Bible, then likely provision is made in your church so that those who give to the support of the local church give to a separate fund which is not used for the denominational budget. Likely members of the church are invited to designate their gifts to sound missionary objects. If there is one general church budget, and if a definite percentage of that budget goes regularly to a modernistic denominational church program, so that by giving to the church budget one would be supporting modernism, then in my humble judgment, it would be wrong to give your money to such a church budget. Christian money should go to support work that is true to Jesus Christ and true to the gospel. Even at the risk of misunderstanding and persecution, a Christian should not support modernism with his money. Surely, on this, Christians can agree.

2. A Christian should not help in the support of modernistic literature and propaganda. In some churches where the Bible is believed and preached, Sunday School literature is tainted with modernism. Mark it carefully, that I speak not of shallowness nor worldliness, and not of mistakes in lesser doctrines, but of real modernism on the essential doctrines. If your Sunday School literature denies the inspiration of the Bible and its accuracy, denies salvation by the blood of Christ, denies the deity of Christ, His virgin birth, His miracles or His bodily resurrection, then no Christian should have his children taught from such literature, and no Christian should cooperate in the spread of such literature and propaganda.

Once I planned to join a certain church which had a good pastor, true to the Word of God. But denominational promotional literature was regularly given out in the church. This literature minimized the importance of the Bible, insisted on cooperation with modernistic denominational leaders, the support of schools which deny the faith, and the support of a foreign missionary society which is principally controlled by modernists and their friends. I could not in good conscience put my family under the influence of such literature. I was not willing to be a member of a church which regularly spread such propaganda, written by enemies of Christ and the Bible.

What can an earnest Christian do in such a matter? If your

pastor believes the Bible and your church is a Bible-believing church, and yet if hurtful and dangerous and wicked propaganda, denying the essential doctrines of the Christian faith, are circulated in your church, either in the Sunday School literature or denominational promotional literature, what should you do? First, be a real Christian. Your pastor is probably just as anxious as you are to do right. Prayerfully and with humility, talk to your pastor. Your judgment might be wrong about what is modernism and what is not. Or your pastor very probably would gladly take his stand against any outright modernism. Take time, be prayerful, do not accuse others, and usually God's people, as they are informed and properly led, will get rid of the offending literature and stay true to Christ and the Bible.

There will be some sad cases when Christians must suffer for Christ. Sometimes Christians must leave the church where they have worshipped since childhood, the church where there are many lovely Christians and where the fellowship has been sweet. If that is clearly one's Christian duty, then do it for Christ in love and faith, knowing that He will reward.

But let each Christian make sure that he does not break fellowship over his own opinions and whims. Sometimes those who make the loudest cry about "modernism" are simply those who lost a place of leadership in the church and then accused others. Be sure that you act only for Jesus' sake. To accuse people of modernism is a most serious thing, and a Christian should not do so except on definite proof. To bring division or dissension in a church, to arouse contention, is a grievous sin, except where it is really necessary for one to "earnestly contend for the faith," as Jude clearly commands us.

If a Christian cannot stay in a church without supporting modernism, then he should leave the church and put his influence and labor and offerings where they will honor Christ and support work that is true to the Bible.

Open Rebuke for Sin Is Necessary

In Galatians 2:11–14 Paul tells us how he found even the Apostle Peter dissembling, and that he "walked not uprightly according to the truth of the gospel." Paul withstood him to the face "because he was to be blamed." Paul says, "I said unto Peter before them all, If thou, being a Jew, livest after the manner of Gentiles, and not as do the Jews, why compellest thou the Gentiles to live as do the Jews?"

Paul was right about it. There is only one course for Christians and that is to earnestly contend for the faith and have no fellowship with the evil things that surround us.

Jehoshaphat, the good king of Judah, pleased God in many ways, but he sinned in having fellowship with the wicked king of Israel (the Northern kingdom). In II Chronicles 19:2 we find the words of God's displeasure carried to him by a faithful prophet, Jehu: "And Jehu the son of Hanani the seer went out to meet him, and said to king Jehoshaphat, Shouldst thou help the ungodly, and love them that hate the Lord? therefore is wrath upon thee from before the Lord." Should Christians help the ungodly? Should we who are bought with the precious blood of Christ love them that hate the Lord? Surely that matter ought not to be hard for us to decide. James 4:4 gives us plain words about compromising Christians who yoke up with unbelievers. Hear what God's Word says: "Ye adulterers and adulteresses, know ye not that the friendship of the world is enmity with God? whosoever therefore will be a friend of the world is the enemy of God." Those who are married to this wicked world are spiritual adulterers. Even the friendship of this world is the enmity of God. To be a friend of this world is to be the enemy of God!

IV. CONCLUSION

As a closing thought let me remind you that the Lord Jesus Christ, our great High Priest, is praised by Holy Writ as one "who is holy, harmless, undefiled, SEPARATE FROM

SINNERS" (Heb. 7:26). Jesus is fitted to be a High Priest because He is separate from sinners. This world was no friend to the Lord Jesus Christ; why should it be a friend to me? Jesus said, "If the world hate you, ye know that it hated me before it hated you" (John 15:18). Surely the servant is no better than his Master nor the disciple than his Lord. Why should I seek the friendship and keep fellowship with a wicked world that crucified the Lord Jesus Christ? Why should I be yoked with men who hate Him today and will not take Him into their hearts? Whether it be in business or society or lodge or church, or anywhere else, the man who is the enemy of Christ would be my enemy if I were enough like Jesus. All that will live godly in Christ Jesus shall suffer persecution" (II Tim. 3:12). No wonder the Bible says, "Woe unto you, when all men shall speak well of you!" (Luke 6:26). No wonder we are commanded to rejoice and be exceedingly glad when men revile us and hate us for Jesus' sake!

I May Witness to Sinners But Not Be Yoked With Them

Jesus died to save sinners and yet the Scripture says that He was "separate from sinners." Jesus was called "the friend of publicans and sinners" and yet his denunciation of their sin was so great that the jeering crowd mocked Him while He died on the cross.

I may preach to sinners as Peter did at Pentecost, boldly denounce their sin, but if I would please God and keep my testimony, I must not sit down as he did with the soldiers who would crucify Jesus!

I may oppose the Philistines as Samson did, but I must not lie, as he did, with my head in the lap of Delilah if I would retain my God-given strength!

I may go like the man of God out of Judah unto Jeroboam with his false altar at Bethel and then cry against the idolatry of that idolatrous king and that unconsecrated place. If I am true to the Word of God then God will protect me from the wrath of Jeroboam and make my prophecy come true. But I dare not stop to eat or drink in that place lest I should meet a lion in the road to destroy me, as did that man of God in I Kings, chapter 13.

If you let this clear teaching of separation keep you from loving sinners, keep you from seeking them, weeping over them, yearning, pleading, winning them, you will have utterly misunderstood this Bible teaching. Oh, we must love sinners as Jesus loves them, and must run after them for Him and compel them to come in and be saved. But we must not bind ourselves to their ways nor yoke up with them.

No Distinction Between Saint and Sinner, Between Saved and Lost

Surely the reason for our troubles is this, that Christians have sold out to the world, have compromised with sin, have yoked up with unbelievers, so that God cannot bless us and sinners will not hear us. I find the average church member lives the same kind of life as a self-confessed, Hell-bound sinner. The deacon and the bootlegger often have much in common. The one is as mad for money as the other. They lie, they steal, they work on Sunday, they sell beer, they rent their property for immoral purposes, very much alike. Money is the god of both. What is the difference?

The church member and the worldling go to the same rotten picture show, see the same scenes of lust and gangland and murder. What is the difference?

Both saint and sinner tell the same dirty yarns. Both smoke the same brand of cigarettes, both smell just the same. The Christian is yoked up with the world.

The bootlegger does not have family prayer, but neither does the average Christian! What is the difference? The harlot woman does not teach her children the Bible, but neither does the woman church member. The unsaved woman bobs her hair in defiance of the plain command of I Corinthians chapter 11, but so does the president of the Women's Mis-

sionary Union or Ladies' Aid of the church and the solo
singers in the choir. What is the difference?

The Devil's crowd dances and so do the church members.

The children of darkness go to the night clubs and there
they drink their beer, but there they meet at the same tables
with members of the church from the town where they live!
And why should they not? Wasn't the beer voted in largely by
church members? God have mercy!

The saved marry the unsaved. They join with them in
lodges, take the same blasphemous oaths, take part in the
same unholy amusements. False prophets arise to lead away
our young people from the Bible, and church members support them with their money.

God's Invitation: "Come Out From Among Them"

Christian, have you missed the joy of the Holy Spirit's
presence in your life? Have you lost the joy you had in early
years? Are you hungry for more fellowship with God, more
power? Would you like to win souls? Then God's answer is,
do not be yoked up with unbelievers. *"Wherefore come out
from among them, and be ye separate, saith the Lord, and
touch not the unclean thing, and I will receive you, And will
be a Father unto you, and ye shall be my sons and daughters,
saith the Lord Almighty."*—II Cor. 6:17, 18.

Chapter 11.

WASHING DIRTY FEET

*T*HE PLACE was the upper room where Jesus and the disciples ate the preliminary meal of the passover season. The time was the very night before He was crucified. When the conversation around that very table was finished, Jesus was to say, "Arise, let us go hence" (John 14:31). Then Jesus and the eleven were to talk on the way to the garden of Gethsemane, Jesus would give them the teaching of chapters 15 and 16 of John, would utter the prayer in John 17. That night as He prayed and sweated blood in the garden of Gethsemane, Judas was to come and betray Him. He was to be taken before the secret meeting of the Sanhedrin, then before Pilate in the early morning, and by nine o'clock of that next day Jesus was to be hanging on the cross! And that night before Jesus was crucified He washed His disciples' feet. Let us prayerfully study the Scriptures given and find rich blessing for ourselves.

"Now before the feast of the passover, when Jesus knew that his hour was come that he should depart out of this world unto the Father, having loved his own which were in the world, he loved them unto the end. And supper being ended, the devil having now put into the heart of Judas Iscariot, Simon's son, to betray him; Jesus knowing that the Father had given all things into his hands, and that he was come from God, and went to God; He riseth from supper, and laid aside his garments; and took a towel, and girded himself. After that he poureth water into a bason, and began to wash the disciples' feet, and to wipe them with the towel wherewith he was girded. Then cometh he to Simon Peter: and Peter saith unto

227

*him, Lord, dost thou wash my feet? Jesus answered and said
unto him, What I do thou knowest not now; but thou shalt
know hereafter. Peter saith unto him, Thou shalt never wash
my feet. Jesus answered him, If I wash thee not, thou hast
no part with me. Simon Peter saith unto him, Lord, not my
feet only, but also my hands and my head. Jesus saith to him,
He that is washed needeth not save to wash his feet, but is
clean every whit: and ye are clean, but not all. For he knew
who should betray him; therefore said he, Ye are not all clean.
So after he had washed their feet, and had taken his garments,
and was set down again, he said unto them, Know ye what I
have done to you? Ye call me Master and Lord; and ye say
well, for so I am. If I then, your Lord and Master, have
washed your feet; ye also ought to wash one another's feet."—*
John 13:1–14.

I. JESUS WASHING THE DISCIPLES' FEET.
1. Here Is an Example of Love Under Pressure!

We are told that "Jesus knew that his hour was come that
he should depart out of this world." But though He faced the
crucifixion, though in an hour or two He would be at the
point of death from grief and sweating the bloody sweat in
Gethsemane, still "having loved his own which were in the
world, he loved them unto the end." And He took time for
the tenderest expression of devotion and washed the dusty
feet of His sandal-shod disciples.

Here is a strange fact; Jesus made no allowances for Himself. His love was not changed by His own dire extremity, by
His own sadness. He had loved the disciples before. Now He
loved them still, loved them unto the end.

We excuse ourselves for sharp words to those we love the
best, if we are not well, if we are fretted by the cares of business or home, if tempers are strained to the breaking point.
It is a shameful fact that we speak the sharpest to those we
love the best. And we excuse ourselves with the thought that
they will understand, that they know we love them, that the

circumstances are unusual and stressful. And so hearts are wounded, a barrier comes between husband and wife, between brother and sister, between parent and child, that is never entirely removed. It is a barrier of thoughtless words, of sharp accusations, of bitter selfishness.

Or perhaps when you are burdened, when you have a headache, when you have problems too heavy, perhaps when you are under great burdens, when you are troubled and perplexed you do not speak sharp words of reproof as others. No, instead you are disconsolate, and those who love you cannot be happy for your sorrow. How they would brighten under your smile, your pleasant greeting! How they long for some strength, some comfort, some encouragement from you they love so well! But you do not give it. You are absorbed in your own burdens, your own problems. You have no light to shine in the darkness around you. You have no salt to save others, no words to bless them, no smile, no expression of love nor of comfort to cheer them. How different, how shamefully different we are from the Saviour. When He was under pressure He loved His disciples just the same. He was unselfish in thinking of them just the same. He was to die in a few hours in the most horrible agony, and He knew it, and still He loved His disciples, still He comforted them and taught them. Under pressure His love never failed.

The kind of Christian character that does not stand up under temptation is not the right kind of character. The kind of faith that will not make us happy Christians even in war time, happy Christians when food is rationed, when boys are in the armies, when we do without our coffee, or sugar, or meat, or cars, is not enough faith. Love that falters in its expression in time of trouble and temptation is not perfect love.

How many of us are fair-weather Christians! How many of us can be happy when we are well but not when we are sick; can be gentle and unselfish and kind until we suffer, until we lose friends, until we face disaster! How many of us are good Christians until we are tired, are good Christians until someone speaks sharply, are good Christians as long as everything is easy! Bless God for the example of the dear Saviour who "the same night He was betrayed," knowing the torment that faced Him, still loved His disciples, still gently washed their feet and taught them to love one another! Does Jesus shine in you when you are sick or tired or disappointed or in trouble? Do you still love people when under pressure?

2. The Creator of the World at Slave Labor!

Christ made the worlds when He was in the beginning with God. "All things were made by him; and without him was not any thing made that was made" (John 1:3). He was the Father's Agent in creation; "For by him were all things created, that are in heaven, and that are in earth, visible and invisible, . . . all things were created by him, and for him" (Col. 1:16). And this mighty Creator, the night before He died for the sins of the world, took off His outer garments, tied a towel about His waist, and like a house slave, He washed the dirty feet of the disciples! The feet were soiled, the feet of men who walked the unpaved, dirty roads in sandals, without socks. The washing of the feet was customary when people came inside the house. Servants would bring water and towel, remove the sandals and wash the soiled feet. But the Lord Jesus, who made the world, took the place of a servant. He who had the right to sit down with the Father in His throne in Heaven, became the lowliest Servant and waited upon His disciples without shame and embarrassment, and in the tenderest love!

He "laid aside his garments," says the Scripture (John 13:4), as, before this He had laid aside His garments, too. For when the disciples saw Him for a moment, on the mount of transfiguration, His face had shown like the sun, and His garments were as white as the light! If He had not, before coming unto the world, laid aside His garments, His heavenly glory, His august presence He now wears in the heavenlies, all should have been stricken blind or dead who looked upon Him! The flames and smoke and earthquake, like that at Mount Sinai when the law was given, would have attended Him! Those He touched would have died like Nadab and Abihu, false priests who brought strange fire into the tabernacle (Lev. 10:1, 2), or like Uzza who died because he put his hand to the ark of God (I Chron. 13:9, 19). Uzza only touched the sacred box wherein rested the tables of stone and the pot of manna and Aaron's rod that budded; how could any live who touched the very Son of God, the express image of God's glory, the Creator of the heavens and the earth, if He had not laid aside His heavenly garments before He came to men! Jesus laid aside His garments!

I know good men who love to tell to the glory of God how God saved them in direst sin and made them preachers. They tell their life stories under such titles as "From Prison to Pulpit." And Abraham Lincoln's life story was expressed in the phrase, "From Rail Splitter to President." We are impressed with the rise of some poor lad from ignorance and poverty to greatness and wealth, but all this was reversed with the Lord Jesus. He emptied Himself of His glory, He laid aside His right to crown and sceptre. He surrendered His command of the unnumbered legions of angels. God became a man! He who made all the wealth in the universe was born in poverty, was laid in a borrowed manger, was wrapped in coarse swaddling clothes. The birds had nests, the foxes had holes, but the Son of man had not where to lay His head. He took a coin which Peter found in the mouth of a fish with which to pay His taxes. When He died He left an estate of one seamless garment. He was buried in a borrowed grave! Oh, He laid aside His garments!

I can hardly wonder that Simon Peter, astonished, said, "Lord, dost thou wash my feet?" "Jesus answered and said unto him, What I do thou knowest not now; but thou shalt know hereafter." But that was not enough for Peter. Who can understand such love, such condescension! I think nobody

who saw it that night *before* the crucifixion could understand it. But this side of the cross we have a measure of the
compassion, of the humble, unselfish love of Christ, that
makes us understand the washing of feet. The astonished
Peter said, "Thou shalt never wash my feet"! (John 13:8).
He meant no rebellion; he relented if it must take this to be
counted one of the Saviour's own. Peter felt here much as he
did when he saw the miracle of the net filled with fish, the
boat nearly sinking, and fell on his knees, saying, "Depart
from me; for I am a sinful man, O Lord" (Luke 5:8). It is
not remarkable that Peter was astonished and awed by the
Son of God on His knees, with a towel about Him, washing
dirty feet. It is only remarkable that the rest of us are not
astonished, too, that Jesus laid aside His garments and washed
the feet of men.

3. All Christians Have Dirty Feet

Jesus said to Peter, "What I do thou knowest not now; but
thou shalt know hereafter" (John 13:7). They thought that
He was simply washing dirt from tired feet that needed washing. He did that, yes—but that was only incidental. He did
much more than that. Some people have thought that He was
showing His humility, and surely it did reveal His humility,
but He did much more than that. Some people have thought
that Jesus meant to establish a ceremony, an ordinance in all
the churches so people could practice the public show of
humility, as if humility were ever humility when it is put on
display! No, no, the Saviour meant much more than this. He
meant that all Christians have dirty feet, that Christians walking in a sinful world need day-by-day cleansing.

The disciples had had their baths, no doubt, because in
verse 10 Jesus said to Peter, "He that is washed needeth not
save to wash his feet." And as their bodies had been washed
in water, so, before this, their souls had been saved, and they
had been born into the kingdom of God, cleansed by the
washing of regeneration, saved by the renewing of the Holy

Ghost. The washing of their bodies symbolized the cleansing of our natures by regeneration when we are born again. But the washing of their feet by the Saviour afterwards, symbolized that Christians, though we are truly born again, though we have already escaped condemnation and Hell, yet need to come to Christ for daily cleansing.

Every Christian should learn the distinction between forgiveness in the sense of salvation, and forgiveness in the sense of daily cleansing, when God removes the sin that is confessed and lamented, so it does not interrupt our sweet communion with Him, does not hinder our prayer, does not demand His chastisement.

Oh, who has not grieved at the defilement of the world around us! What real Christian is there who is not grieved to hear the sound of profanity? What separated and clean Christian does not grieve when he comes from the office or train where his clothes are steeped in tobacco smoke? What Christian does not grieve over the unbelief all about us, the worldliness, the lust, the covetousness! It is a dirty world we walk in. And the old nature we have is still, in some sense, a part of this world. And our daily contacts, our temptations, the steady pull of the old nature that is still within us, although we also have a new nature, defile us. And so every Christian needs to face this solemn fact that, walking in a dirty world, he needs his feet washed every day.

That is what the Saviour had in mind when He taught His disciples to pray in the Lord's prayer or model prayer, "And forgive us our sins" (Luke 11:4), or "Forgive us our debts, as we forgive our debtors" (Matt. 6:12). That model prayer is a daily prayer. It asks for daily bread. So it asks for daily forgiveness.

It is this same fact about Christians having dirty feet that the Holy Spirit had in mind in I John 1:8, 9 which says: "If we say that we have no sin, we deceive ourselves, and the truth is not in us. If we confess our sins, he is faithful and just to forgive us our sins, and to cleanse us from all unrighteousness." The sins mentioned there are sins of Christians. The forgiveness and cleansing there is the forgiveness and cleansing of Christians. In the same chapter John says he is writing Christians, "that your joy may be full" (v. 4). *"Fellowship"* is mentioned twice in verse 3, once in verse 6 and once in verse 7. Christians who want to maintain happy fellowship with the Father and with the Son are daily to confess their sins and daily have cleansing and forgiveness. Christians have dirty feet. But thank God we can daily have our feet washed, can daily have cleansing and daily have forgiveness. Every day, therefore, a Christian can walk in fellowship, can look up into the face of the Lord Jesus and say, "Nothing between my soul and the Saviour" if he day by day confesses and forsakes known sins and gets daily washing for his spiritual feet.

4. Christians Are All Clean but the Feet

I know how it was, when I once thought I needed to get saved again every time I sinned. It was, first, frustration. Then it was confusion, uncertainty. Then it was blank despair. Dr. Ironside in his remarkable and helpful book, *HOLINESS, The False and the True,* tells his own experience and how he claimed sinless perfection and tried honestly to live what he professed. But he found, he says, that he was "holy only in spots." How sweet was the lesson he learned, that salvation is *wholly* of grace, that God saves people who do not deserve it, and that salvation cannot be earned by our daily walk or daily life. And then how sweet it was to him, as to me, to learn that we can day by day be cleansed in our walk and fellowship, after our hearts have been already cleansed by the blood of Christ once for all.

When a Christian sins, does he become a *lost* sinner? Is he condemned to Hell? No, for Jesus said in John 5:24 that one who trusted in the Father who sent Jesus into the world to save sinners, "hath everlasting life and shall not come into condemnation." And Jesus said about His sheep, "And I give unto them eternal life; and they shall never perish, neither shall any pluck them out of my hand" [leave out *man* since it is not in the original] (John 10:28). And Romans 8:1 says that "there is therefore now no condemnation to them which are in Christ Jesus," while the same blessed chapter ends with the triumphant, glorious claim that there is no separation from the love of Christ for one of God's own children.

When Jesus insisted to Peter, "If I wash thee not, thou hast no part with me," He meant that God *must* deal, and *does* deal with the sins of His own born-again children. He forgives and cleanses them when they are confessed, He judges them and chastises His children when they are not confessed. But God must deal with the Christian's sin, either in cleansing and forgiveness or in chastising.

Peter, appalled at the thought that if Christ did not cleanse one he was not one of God's own, immediately pleaded with Jesus, "Lord, not my feet only, but also my hands and my head"! Oh, whatever it took, Peter thought, he wanted it. But Jesus reassured him, "He that is washed needeth not save to wash his feet, but is clean every whit" (John 13:10). Then Jesus said, "And ye are clean, but not all," that is, that all the twelve were clean but one, Judas, who had never been saved. Eleven were saved and so were clean and needed only the daily washing to maintain fellowship and avoid chastising which God gives to His own born-again children who need it.

I remember the time when I thought I had lost my salvation. I prayed and begged God to save me again. I was like Peter saying, "Lord, not my feet only, but also my hands and my head."

I can imagine that Peter remembered this incident in his own life, when he was inspired of the Spirit to write that the Christian who does not grow in Christian grace, but is barren and unfruitful, "hath forgotten that he was purged from his old sins" (II Pet. 1:9). So many Christians forget that when they trusted Christ they were really born again. They actually became children of God. They became partakers of the divine nature. Their names were written down in Heaven. All their sins were charged against Christ and marked paid. And Romans 4:7, 8 tells us, "Blessed are they whose iniquities are forgiven, and whose sins are covered. Blessed is the man to whom the Lord will not impute sin." Sin, in the sense that it damns souls to Hell and makes people aliens and strangers forever from God, cannot be charged against a Christian! Oh, dear stumbling Christians, though you need day by day to confess that you have dirty feet which need washing; though you need day by day to confess and turn your heart away from the things which grieve your heavenly Father and break fellowship and communion with Him and hinder your usefulness and joy, yet it is good to remember that "He that is washed needeth not save to wash his feet, but is clean every whit."

Let us all learn the lesson that born-again Christians who have dirty feet are not lost sinners. We must not judge that a man has never had a bath because his feet are dirty. We must not suppose that Christians whose walk is unworthy have never been born again. Those who have once really been washed need only to wash their feet and are clean every whit, Jesus said!

5. Jesus Is Always Ready to Cleanse His Own

If God has spoken to your heart through the Scriptures, then you already know what I am trying to say—that if you are a child of God, the way is open and clear for you to come with confession about your sins, and that every day! The Lord Jesus is in the foot-washing business. To ignore your sins, your mistakes, your failures is wrong; you should confess them. To deny them is wicked; that will make you a Pharisee and liable to the grossest breakdown in character. Those who claim sinless perfection strangely enough furnish more than their share of adulterers, for example. The reason is that if a man never washes his feet they get dirtier. And if a man has dirty feet then he does not so much mind walking in filth. The way to happiness and fellowship for a Christian is not to ignore his sin, not to deny it, but day by day to confess it to the Lord Jesus who is always ready to cleanse and forgive.

Dear Christian who falls into sin, do you think that Jesus despises you? Do you think He does not know about your weakness? Do you think He has no sympathy with your temptation? Ah, let us then remember that Jesus is our High Priest and His regular business is interceding for us before the Father in Heaven. Hebrews 4:14–16 says:

"Seeing then that we have a great high priest, that is passed into the heavens, Jesus the Son of God, let us hold fast our profession. For we have not an high priest which cannot be touched with the feeling of our infirmities; but was in all points tempted like as we are, yet without sin. Let us therefore come boldly unto the throne of grace, that we may obtain mercy, and find grace to help in time of need."

The Lord Jesus who knelt that night on the floor and lifted the dirty feet of the disciples, one by one, into His basin and washed them, and then gently dried them on a towel, knows all about human frailty. "He knoweth our frame; he remembereth that we are dust" (Psa. 103:14). Jesus was tempted in all points like as we are. So Christian, when you sin, confess your sin, coming boldly to the throne of grace to obtain mercy and to find grace to help in time of need! Jesus is always ready to cleanse His own. You confess; He forgives and cleanses! That is His plain promise in I John 1:9. So when your heart has honestly lamented your sin and forsaken it as best you know, admitting your sin to Jesus, then fret no more about it. Do not dwell upon it. Let your tears be, not the bitter tears of despair, but the glad tears of a penitent forgiven, a prodigal son received home with the kiss of forgiveness, of a beloved child at one with his father.

II. CHRISTIANS ARE TO WASH ONE ANOTHER'S FEET

After Jesus had washed the disciples' feet, He drew lessons from it and gave commands for us. In John 13:12–17 are His instructions:

"So after he had washed their feet, and had taken his garments, and was set down again, he said unto them, Know

*ye what I have done to you? Ye call me Master and Lord: and
ye say well; for so I am. If I then, your Lord and Master, have
washed your feet; ye also ought to wash one another's feet.
For I have given you an example, that ye should do as I have
done to you. Verily, verily, I say unto you, The servant is not
greater than his lord; neither he that is sent greater than he
that sent him. If ye know these things, happy are ye if ye do
them."*

Jesus has now "taken his garments" again. He has returned to the Father. He has been glorified with the glory
which He had with the Father before the world was (John
17:5). He who created all the worlds, now sustains them;
"by him all things consist" (Col. 1:17). He is now set down
with the Father in the Father's throne in Heaven (Rev. 3:21).
Hebrews 1:3 tells us that Christ is now "the brightness of
[God's] glory, and the express image of his person, and up-
holding all things by the word of his power," that He has
now "sat down on the right hand of the Majesty on high."
And after Jesus, that fateful night, had put on again His garments and was set down, He applied His lesson to the disciples. And now that, in symbol, He has put on His heavenly
garments of glory, His lesson is still for us. We are to wash
one another's feet.

1. This Does Not Mean That Foot-washing Should Be a Church Ceremony, a Religious Rite

Some good people have believed that Jesus meant to establish here a church 'ordinance,' to give an official ceremony
to be regularly repeated in the church services. Such people
have sometimes come to church after carefully bathing their
feet and putting on clean hose at home, and then to show
their humility (!) Christians, with carefully chosen partners,
have publicly washed feet that did not need washing, as a
symbol of their brotherly love and humility. But such humility has often turned to pride. And poor people who may
have needed physical care did not get it, and faulty Christians
who needed their spiritual feet washed, needed to be restored

to fellowship with God and men, were neglected. That is not what Jesus is teaching here. Jesus clearly did not intend to set up a ceremonial rite to be observed officially in the churches.

Several evidences might be given to show that this was not the Saviour's intentions. However, three conclusive ones are mentioned here.

First, Jesus plainly said here that "Ye also ought to wash one another's feet." That is far different from a public show of the whole church. Here we are instructed that one Christian ought to be perfectly willing to wash the feet of another if they are dirty and need it. And this command ought to cover other personal attentions and services such as the servant might do for his master. This means holding our brother's coat for him, or it means waiting on him when he is sick, or it means shining his shoes, or pushing his car, or serving him with meals. Jesus taught here personal service, in humility, one Christian for another Christian.

Second, the principal meaning is certainly spiritual. Jesus did not primarily wash the disciples' feet to remove physical dirt. Rather, He was teaching them the blessed lesson that all Christians need their spiritual feet washed; that we need to come to Christ in daily confession of our sins, to have cleansing and forgiveness. So it was not a formal rite, but a deeply spiritual lesson He intended to teach.

Third, and unanswerable, is the well-known fact that these disciples themselves did not understand Jesus to mean that they should have foot-washing as a church ceremony. There is not a record, not a hint of any New Testament church having such a ceremony. These apostles understood Jesus perfectly; they knew He was not setting up a church ceremony, a religious rite.

2. Christians Need the Humility That Serves

Jesus taught us here, not a professional humility, but the genuine humility of a servant who, out of love and duty, takes on the menial tasks. How well good mothers sometimes learn this lesson toward their children! How many millions of mothers have taken it as a commonplace duty, even a privilege, to wash the filthy clothes of their babies, to pick up after their children, to wash and cook and clean house and be the unpaid servants of their own children! Oh, may Christians learn this secret, one toward another, "Submitting yourselves one to another in the fear of God" (Eph. 5:21).

D. L. Moody, in the Chicago World's Fair near the close of the nineteenth century, brought to Chicago a number of great English preachers for his city-wide campaign. One English minister, accustomed to having the servant shine his shoes after they were put outside his bedroom door, in England, set his shoes in the hall at Moody Bible Institute where he was quartered. The great D. L. Moody, the most famous preacher in the world at the time, with all the enormous weight of vast enterprises resting upon him, took the English minister's shoes and shined them and returned them to their place outside his door!

Elisha as a servant poured water on the hands of Elijah. Timothy, Epaphroditus and Philemon acted as secretaries for Paul, and wrote his letters, tradition tells us. And the saintly Paul himself, meantime, was servant to all, that by all means he might win some. May God give us the humility to be servants. Often real humility and Christ-likeness is shown better by carrying a fellow man's packages, by helping do a sick woman's washing, or sitting up with a sick neighbor who cannot pay a hospital bill, than it is shown by testifying in prayer meeting or singing in the choir!

3. But, Primarily, Christians Are to Wash One Another's Spiritual Feet

We are to forgive erring Christians, we are to count them still our beloved brothers and sisters, we are to help restore them to the fellowship of men and to fellowship with God.

We had as well acknowledge the fact that all Christians walk in a dirty world and need day by day to confess their sins and failures and be cleansed anew. What shall be the atti-

tude of a Christian toward Christians who fail, who do not
live as Christians ought, who bring reproach on the cause of
Christ? Certainly, the first aim and effort of a Christian in
such cases is to seek to wash the dirty feet, that is, seek to help
the erring one to see and forsake the way that is wrong, or
the sin into which he may have, unawares, fallen, tempted
and trapped by Satan. Oh, how wicked it is to hurt an imma-
ture Christian, to discourage him, to disfellowship him!

Jesus said about little children and young Christians, "But
whoso shall offend one of these little ones which believe in
me, it were better for him that a millstone were hanged about
his neck, and that he were drowned in the depth of the sea"
(Matt. 18:6). And in the same eighteenth chapter of Matthew
Jesus tells us that one who receives one such child Christian
in His name, receives the Lord Jesus; tells us how the shep-
herd seeks a lost sheep, and tells us that if our brother shall
trespass against us, there is a sweet plan to gain the brother.
First, "Go and tell him his fault between thee and him
alone" (v. 15). Tell no one else, bring no charges, hold no
grudges. Go see your brother and try to gain him. Second, if
he will not hear you, take two or three others with you and
try to win him, before the matter is taken to the church.

And remember that the object all the time is not to vindicate yourself, but to 'gain thy brother.' That plan will not
work if it is to "get even." That plan will not work if it is to
vindicate ourselves. That plan will not work if it is to shame
those who do wrong. But oh, if it is love's kindly method to
restore the broken fellowship and help one you love, God
will bless it!

Galatians 6:1, 2 commands us: "Brethren, if a man be overtaken in a fault, ye which are spiritual, restore such an one
in the spirit of meekness; considering thyself, lest thou also
be tempted. Bear ye one another's burdens, and so fulfil the
law of Christ." There it is again, Christians washing Christians' dirty feet! Christians restoring poor, stumbling, weak
Christians to sweet fellowship one with another, and with
God!

We "ought to bear the infirmities of the weak" (Rom. 15:1). Even those weak in the faith, that is, unsound and untaught in doctrine, we are to receive in our churches, just so they do not cause disputes and doubts (Rom. 14:1). And I Corinthians, chapter 5, makes it clear that even Christians who have committed the grosser sins are not to be dismissed from Christian fellowship except when they are impenitent and do not take rebuke. And that poor man mentioned in I Corinthians, chapter 5, guilty of fornication with his stepmother and excluded from church fellowship, was not left outside. In II Corinthians 2:5–11 Paul commands that his sins be forgiven since he had repented, and the Corinthian Christians were besought, "that ye would confirm your love toward him." They washed his spiritual feet. That is, they forgave him, they helped him to be restored to the fellowship of Christians and the intimate communion and joy with his heavenly Father, as a wayward child come home. O Christian, let us wash the feet of those about us, with humility, with tears, with compassion, with forgiveness. Let us love and restore them as we would have others do to us in our many failures and sins.

4. How the Apostles Carried out the Teaching and Example of Jesus

The timing of this beautiful lesson in humility, forgiveness and restoration of erring Christians was exactly right. Jesus knew that that night Judas would betray Him. He knew that early the next morning Simon Peter would curse and swear and deny that he even knew his Master. He knew that within the three ensuing days all the disciples would be in the blackest despair, utterly abandoning their hope for the resurrection of their Lord. He knew that doubting Thomas would not believe the stories of His resurrection, and that even after Jesus was risen from the dead, Simon Peter would lead a good number of the apostles to forsake their ministry and return to the fishing business. With all that in mind, no doubt, the Saviour washed the disciples' feet and taught them to wash one another's feet.

And they must have taken the lesson to heart! It is one of the marvels of the New Testament that not a single one of the apostles, nor any New Testament Christians ever railed at Judas, ever accused him; not when Judas dipped the sop with Jesus the same night, not when he planted the traitor's kiss on the cheek of our Lord in the garden, not later when Judas hanged himself and went to Hell! Poor, weak, frail Christians, these apostles in humility withheld their hot words, and I cannot but believe they wept over Judas and loved him yet when they learned that he had never been saved, and when they knew his awful perfidy! If they had compassion on Judas, surely they were ever forgiving and kind in restoring one another.

Whoever rebuked Peter for denying the Lord and for his cursing and swearing? What Christian said, "I will never hear such a preacher as that preach!" knowing of Peter's sin?

Who was there that scorned Thomas the doubter?

Who was there to remind James and John of their ambition, their quarrelsome efforts to be first with the Lord Jesus?

It is the work of the Holy Spirit who inspired the Gospels, and yet it must be an evidence too of the way these apostles received the teaching of Jesus, that only John, of all the Gospel writers, and he long after the death of Joseph of Arimathaea, tells us that Joseph was a coward! (Compare John 19:38; Luke 23:50–53; Matt. 27:57–60).

Christians, we are no better than our Master and Lord. If Jesus washed His disciples' feet, we ought to wash one another's feet. That does not mean foot-washing as a public church ceremony, but it does mean humble service one to the other and especially helping erring Christians to have their spiritual feet washed. We should restore them to fellowship with God and His people. If Christ is so willing to forgive us, let us gladly forgive frail Christians, as we ourselves need daily to be forgiven.

Chapter 12.

A NEW START

*"And God said unto Jacob, Arise, go up to
Bethel, and dwell there: and make there an altar
unto God, that appeared unto thee when thou
fleddest from the face of Esau thy brother."*
—Gen. 35:1.

*"And the word of the Lord came unto Jonah
the second time, saying, Arise, go unto Nineveh,
that great city, and preach unto it the preaching
that I bid thee. So Jonah arose, and went unto
Nineveh, according to the word of the Lord."*
—Jonah 3:1-3.

*"I will arise and go to my father, and will say
unto him, Father, I have sinned."* —Luke 15:18.

ALL CHRISTIANS need, periodically, to make a new start. I have no patience with the shallow argument that because we have made good resolutions before and have failed to keep them, therefore we should not make new resolutions. No man living ever did all he planned to do. No woman ever kept all her vows. But everyone who ever tried to do better was helped by it. People who try do more than those who do not try. People who resolve do more than those who do not resolve. And however much you have failed in the past, the coming of the new year or of some special time of refreshing or conviction from God is an ideal time to start over again to live for God and to be what God wants you to be.

245

The gospel of a second chance appears throughout the Bible.

Jacob Went Back to Bethel

Jacob, fleeing from his brother Esau, met God at Bethel. Asleep with his head on a pillow of stone, Jacob in a dream saw a ladder reaching to Heaven and angels of God ascending and descending. He arose and said, "Surely the Lord is in this place; and I knew it not" (Gen. 28:16). So he vowed that if God would be with him and feed him and clothe him, and bring him to his father's house in peace, then the Lord should be his God, and that he would surely give God a tenth of all his income (Gen. 28:20–22).

In the next score of years, Jacob had his ups and downs; he gained property and grew a great family; but one of his wives, at least, worshipped idols, and his daughter Dinah was ruined by young prince Shechem, and two of his sons in murderous rage assassinated the entire male population of a city. People all about turned against Jacob.

Then to backslidden Jacob came the command of God—he was to go back to Bethel! *"And God said unto Jacob, Arise, go up to Bethel, and dwell there: and make there an altar unto God that appeared unto thee when thou fleddest from the face of Esau thy brother. Then Jacob said unto his household, and to all that were with him, Put away the strange gods that are among you, and be clean, and change your garments: And let us arise, and go up to Bethel; and I will make there an altar unto God, who answered me in the day of my distress, and was with me in the way which I went."*—Gen. 35:1–3. So the family did away with their idols, and with chastened hearts and clean garments they went back to Bethel and made a new start!

Jonah Got a Second Chance to Preach

Jonah was a terrible "flop" as a Christian. When God commanded him to go and preach to the great city of Nineveh,

Jonah rebelled and ran away from God. At Joppa he paid his fare on a ship and embarked on a voyage to a far country. But God prepared a storm; the troubled sailors seeking to appease God woke up sleeping Jonah and asked him to call upon His God. Jonah confessed his rebellion and had the sailors cast him into the sea to stop the storm. God had prepared a great fish which swallowed Jonah, and oh, what penitent praying Jonah did in the belly of that fish!

Then at last the whale disgorged Jonah at the coast. The Lord Jesus believed this story and authenticated it when he said, "For as Jonas was three days and three nights in the whale's belly; so shall the Son of man be three days and three nights in the heart of the earth" (Matt: 12:40). Therefore I have no trouble in believing it (nor anything else that God has said).

But to Jonah, far from home, whipped and ashamed, the word of the Lord came saying, "Arise, go unto Nineveh, that great city, and preach unto it the preaching that I bid thee." And this time "Jonah arose, and went unto Nineveh, according to the word of the Lord" (Jonah 3:2, 3). That greatest city of antiquity repented! The king and his nobles put on sackcloth and sat in ashes. The people repented of their sins and God spared the wicked city He had planned to destroy! Jonah got his second chance to preach. Nineveh repented, got its second chance at life itself.

Moses, After Forty Years in the Desert, Made a New Start to Deliver Israel

Moses knew what it was to make a new beginning in the service of the Lord. As a hot-headed man of forty, Moses, reared as the son of Pharaoh's daughter, decided to cast his lot with his people, the Hebrews. He killed one Egyptian oppressor and thought to deliver his people (Exod. 2:12). But the time was not ripe; the Jews themselves turned against him and Moses fled to the desert of Midian where he spent forty long, disconsolate years. And then, wonder of wonders,

God spoke to him through the burning bush and sent the seasoned and ripened Moses to deliver his people. Moses made a new start and this time succeeded.

Thank God for the doctrine of a second chance!

Samson, the Profligate, Blinded, Imprisoned Giant, Had God's Spirit Upon Him Again

Samson, too, knew what it meant to make a new start for God. Samson's birth was foretold by an angel. (Read Judges, chapter 13 through 16.) He became wonderfully filled with the Spirit of God to judge Israel. With his hands he rent a lion and killed him as if he had been a kid, and at one time killed thirty men of the Philistines, and at another time a thousand fell under the flailing jawbone of an ass in his hand. He carried off the city gate of Gaza in his strength and nothing could withstand him when the Spirit of God came upon him.

But Samson did not always honor God. He visited a harlot in Gaza. Later he loved Delilah and finally told her of the secret of his strength, of his Nazarite vow and his long hair. Delilah cut off his hair as he slept with his head in her lap, the Spirit of God departed from him, and his power was gone. The Philistines put out his eyes and bound him to turn a mill like a donkey, walking round and round.

There poor sightless, captive Samson turned his heart back to God. His hair began to grow again. And when Samson was brought to the house of idols to make sport for the Philistine people, he called on God and said, "O Lord God, remember me, I pray thee, and strengthen me, I pray thee, only this once, O God, that I may be at once avenged of the Philistines for my two eyes" (Judg. 16:28). God was with him, the heathen temple fell down when the two center columns were pulled down, "So the dead which he slew at his death were more than they which he slew in his life" (Judg. 16:30). Samson died gloriously with the power of God upon him, after he had made a new start for God.

Peter, After Cursing, Denying Christ and Quitting the Ministry, Made a New Start

Simon Peter came to the most disastrous fall of any man mentioned in the New Testament. After being the chief of the apostles, when Jesus was arrested, Peter's courage failed him. He cursed and swore and denied Jesus publicly and then went away and wept bitterly. His heart was broken over his cowardice, his shameful surrender to temptation and over the ruin of his testimony. Grief filled his heart over the way he had treated the beloved Lord Jesus. He seemed to lose all his faith. He planned to quit the ministry. He went back to fishing for a living.

But at the Sea of Galilee Jesus met him again. Jesus caused the empty nets to be filled with fish, cooked breakfast for the disciples, and then sent the humbled apostle again to "feed my sheep" and "feed my lambs." In a few days more Simon Peter was ready to preach at Pentecost—yea, ready to live and ready to die for the Lord Jesus. How blessed that Peter made a new start! How wonderful that the Lord Jesus had been praying for him all the time, never did give him up, did not let Satan have him! How wonderful that God gives us poor Christians another chance when we fail Him.

Prodigal Son Proves Anybody Can Start Over

The story of the prodigal son is the story of a man who started over again. That wild lad who went away from home proudly, who wasted his substance with riotous living and came to rags and hunger and a hogpen, at last "came to himself." He recalled:

"How many hired servants of my father's have bread enough and to spare, and I perish with hunger!" He resolved, *"I will arise and go to my father, and will say unto him, Father, I have sinned against heaven, and before thee, And am no more worthy to be called thy son: make me as one of thy hired servants."*

And then and there, "He arose, and came to his father" (Luke 15:17–20). That story has the happiest ending of all the "really truly" stories in the world. The father ran to meet him, met him with the kiss of forgiveness, brought for him a new robe, a ring, and shoes for the bruised feet, and killed the fatted calf and made a feast of rejoicing. The boy who was lost was now found. He who was dead was now alive! The poor prodigal boy was now at home and loved and happy again. Here again is the doctrine of a second chance.

How a Sinning Christian Is to Make a New Start

The war years have been sad and miserable years for many. They have been years of war and trouble, outwardly; to many a Christian they have been years of defeat, of surrender to temptation; years of powerlessness, of self-will, of backsliding. Oh, now that God has spoken to you anew, make a new start! Come back to the Father and start over again!

In I John 1:9 is a blessed promise so good for failing, sinning Christians: "If we confess our sins, he is faithful and just to forgive us our sins, and to cleanse us from all unrighteousness." Any backslidden Christian, any wayward child of God, any converted person who has lost his joy and assurance and the sweet consciousness of God's favor, can simply confess his sins to God and have them all wiped out in a moment! This is part of the contract we entered into with God at Calvary. God is now, to saved people, our Father, and is faithful and just to forgive us our sins, and to cleanse every erring one who confesses his sin.

In Proverbs 28:13 we are told, "He that covereth his sins shall not prosper: but whoso confesseth and forsaketh them shall have mercy." Oh, reader, admit your failures! Uncover your backsliding! Confess how far you have missed God's way, God's best. And with that honest confessing, that penitent uncovering of your sins, there will come sweet forgiveness and mercy, a new cleansing and blessing.

The fifty-first Psalm is the prayer of David confessing his

sin with Bathsheba, asking for a new pouring-out of the Holy
Spirit on him, promising that he would win souls if God
would renew a right spirit within him and forgive his sins.
Many of us need to pray the same prayer today.

Oh, well I know that many readers at this time do not look
back on a past of drunkenness and adultery and thievery.
Your sins, perhaps, are not as coarse and obvious as that.
Thousands of us, rather, have found our love grown cold. We
have had too little of the Spirit's power. The fruit we have
borne has been too little. How we preachers and Christian
workers do need to make a new start!

The Psalmist exults, "I shall be anointed with fresh oil"
(Psa. 92:10). Surely that is what all of us need for the coming
days. I know I need it, and by God's grace I intend to have it.
"I shall be anointed with fresh oil"! At Pentecost there was
a mighty pouring-out of the Spirit. "And they were all filled
with the Holy Ghost" (Acts 2:4). A few days later trouble
came and there was a new need, a new problem, a new burden. So the disciples gathered together in prayer again; "And
when they had prayed, the place was shaken where they were
assembled together; and they were all filled with the Holy
Ghost, and they spake the word of God with boldness" (Acts
4:31).

Notice these nine words from Acts 2:4 describing Pentecost: *"And they were all filled with the Holy Ghost."*

Notice the same nine words in Acts 4:31 describing a later
experience of the same people: *"And they were all filled with
the Holy Ghost."*

Oh, we can have again all the fullness and blessing we ever
had. Yea, we can have more, if we need more. Let us resolve
this holy resolve; let us make this holy vow; let us take upon
us this holy obligation—"I will not go into the responsibilities
of the future and through them without the manifest power
of the Holy Spirit upon me!" Let us make a new start, have
a new dedication, a new surrender and a new empowering
and anointing of the Spirit of God.

Lost Sinner, Start Now by Trusting Christ for Salvation

Perhaps you are an unconverted, lost sinner. Perhaps you never received Christ as your personal Saviour, never were born again. Then the only way you can make a new start that will please God is to repent of your sins and once and for all take Christ as your own Saviour. Let Him come into your heart, forgive your sins and save your soul. Let Him make you God's own dear child. Will you do it today?

You see, quitting your drink is not enough. Possibly you cannot quit it alone; possibly you can. But what God wants is a start *in the heart* and not merely *in the habit.* Instead of just quitting your cursing or quitting your smoking, God wants you to *quit your rebellion against Christ!* He wants you to change from Satan's side to God's side in your heart. He wants you to be not a Christ-rejector but a Christ-acceptor. Oh, lost sinner, all you need to do is to turn in your heart to trust in Jesus Christ as your own Saviour. He will do everything you need if you only surrender to Him and trust Him for forgiveness.

Probably every reader ought to take some definite stand in your heart, make some definite new start for God before you lay this book down. I suggest that you look over the following three statements to see which of them you can honestly sign. Check that square now. Then sign it. Then write me in your own words, or copy the decision which you have signed today; and I will send you some free literature that will help you follow through on your decision.

Date _____

Dr. Curtis Hutson
P. O. Box 1099
Murfreesboro, Tennessee 37130

Dear Dr. Hutson:

Today I honestly make the decision which is checked below:

☐ 1. I am a backslider. I have been previously converted but have drifted into sin and worldliness and lost my joy and assurance. Today I confess my backsliding to God and renew my vows. I trust Christ to forgive me and help me live for Him, out-and-out, beginning this very day. I will take my place as a child of God.

☐ 2. I am a Christian, but I confess that I am not filled with the Holy Spirit. I have not been the fruitful soul winner I ought to be. I have not had the warm-hearted love for God and His Word I should have had. I am saved, but I have not paid the price for power that I ought to pay. Here and now I confess my lack of power and come to God for a new anointing. I set out to seek His face daily, to confess every known sin, to surrender to every known will of His, confidently expecting that He will anoint me with the power of the Holy Spirit for a happier, more fruitful life.

☐ 3. I am a poor lost sinner who has never before been converted. Here and now I confess my sin to God. With penitent heart I ask His forgiveness and mercy. Today I trust Jesus Christ to forgive all my sins and save my soul, and I claim Him now as my Saviour. By His grace I will try to be known as a child of God from this day and to live for Him.

Signed _____

Address _____

_____

I will anxiously wait to hear from all who make a new start. Will you copy the decision above which you ought to make and do make and mail it to me at once? And may Christ Jesus have all your heart and all your service from this day forth!

Dr. Curtis Hutson
P. O. Box 1099
Murfreesboro, Tennessee 37130

Dr. Rice Teaches. . .

On Sound Doctrine

The Charismatic Movement

By Dr. John R. Rice. The most thorough coverage of the current popular movement sweeping through churches of practically all denominations in print today. Considering its twofold characteristic teachings—speaking in tongues and divine healing—Dr. Rice kindly and yet devastatingly demolishes the false and anti-scriptural foundation upon which this movement is built. The book is convincingly documented both with ample Scripture references and with illustrative quotations. 12 chapters on the tongues movement; 8 chapters on divine healing. 288 pages.

"In the Beginning. . ." (Commentary on Genesis)

By Dr. John R. Rice. A verse-by-verse commentary, with particular emphasis on the earlier chapters of the first book of the Bible. A scholarly and scriptural treatment of Creation versus Evolution, the "Gap" Theory, the Universal Flood versus Local Flood Theory, etc. Contains practical biographical sketches on the lives of the old patriarchs and prophets, with pertinent, timely applications and lessons for us today. A volume not just for the scientist or the theologian, but for every born-again child of God. 57 chapters, 559 pages. **Clothbound only.**

The Son of God (Commentary on John)

Another verse-by-verse commentary from the pen of Dr. John R. Rice. Great has been the demand for this commentary, and in spite of the fact that this book of the Bible has been commented on possibly more than any other, here you will find "things new and old" refreshingly presented and most practically applied. Here is expository preaching that will save sinners and instruct believers, emphasizing simple salvation truths as well as doctrine, such as the deity of Christ, His virgin birth, the inspiration of Scripture, etc. 21 chapters, 416 pages. **Clothbound only.**

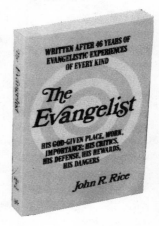